SCOTTISH WOMEN'S WRITING IN THE LONG NINETEENTH CENTURY

Walter Scott's tales of chivalry and adventure inaugurated a masculinized Scottish romance tradition that celebrated a sublime and heroic version of Scotland. Nineteenth-century Scotswomen responded to Scott's influence by establishing a countertradition of unromantic or even antiromantic representations of Scotland. Their novels challenge the long-standing claim that Scotland lacked any equivalent to the English realist novel. In turning from the past to the present and from the sublimity of Scott's Highland landscapes to farmhouses, factories, and suburban villas, Scottish women writers brought romance to everyday life, illuminating the magnificence of the mundane. Drawing on the evangelical discourses emerging from the splintering of the Presbyterian Church in 1843, they represented fiction as a form of spiritual comfort, an antidote to the dreary monotony and petty frustrations of daily existence. This volume introduces the previously overlooked tradition of nineteenth-century Scottish women's writing, and corrects previously male-dominated histories of the Scottish novel.

JULIET SHIELDS is a Professor of English at the University of Washington. She is also the author of *Sentimental Literature and Anglo-Scottish Identity* (2010) and *Nation and Migration: The Making of British Atlantic Literature* (2016).

CAMBRIDGE STUDIES IN NINETEENTH-CENTURY LITERATURE AND CULTURE

Founding Editors
Gillian Beer, *University of Cambridge*
Catherine Gallagher, *University of California, Berkeley*

General Editors
Kate Flint, *University of Southern California*
Clare Pettitt, *King's College London*

Editorial Board
Isobel Armstrong, *Birkbeck, University of London*
Ali Behdad *University of California, Los Angeles*
Alison Chapman, *University of Victoria*
Hilary Fraser, *Birkbeck, University of London*
Josephine McDonagh, *University of Chicago*
Elizabeth Miller, *University of California, Davis*
Hillis Miller, *University of California, Irvine*
Cannon Schmitt, *University of Toronto*
Sujit Sivasundaram *University of Cambridge*
Herbert Tucker, *University of Virginia*
Mark Turner, *King's College London*

Nineteenth-century literature and culture have proved a rich field for interdisciplinary studies. Since 1994, books in this series have tracked the intersections and tensions between Victorian literature and the visual arts, politics, gender and sexuality, race, social organisation, economic life, technical innovations, scientific thought – in short, culture in its broadest sense. Many of our books are now classics in a field which since the series' inception has seen powerful engagements with Marxism, feminism, visual studies, post-colonialism, critical race studies, new historicism, new formalism, transnationalism, queer studies, human rights and liberalism, disability studies and global studies. Theoretical challenges and historiographical shifts continue to unsettle scholarship on the nineteenth century in productive ways. New work on the body and the senses, the environment and climate, race and the decolonisation of literary studies, biopolitics and materiality, the animal and the human, the local and the global, politics and form, queerness and gender identities, and intersectional theory is re-animating the field. This series aims to accommodate and promote the most interesting work being undertaken on the frontiers of nineteenth-century literary studies, connecting the field with the urgent critical questions that are being asked today. We seek to publish work from a diverse range of authors, and stand for anti-racism, anti-colonialism and against discrimination in all forms.

A complete list of titles published will be found at the end of the book.

SCOTTISH WOMEN'S WRITING IN THE LONG NINETEENTH CENTURY

The Romance of Everyday Life

JULIET SHIELDS

University of Washington

CAMBRIDGE
UNIVERSITY PRESS

CAMBRIDGE
UNIVERSITY PRESS

Shaftesbury Road, Cambridge CB2 8EA, United Kingdom

One Liberty Plaza, 20th Floor, New York, NY 10006, USA

477 Williamstown Road, Port Melbourne, VIC 3207, Australia

314–321, 3rd Floor, Plot 3, Splendor Forum, Jasola District Centre, New Delhi – 110025, India

103 Penang Road, #05–06/07, Visioncrest Commercial, Singapore 238467

Cambridge University Press is part of Cambridge University Press & Assessment, a department of the University of Cambridge.

We share the University's mission to contribute to society through the pursuit of education, learning and research at the highest international levels of excellence.

www.cambridge.org
Information on this title: www.cambridge.org/9781108999816

DOI: 10.1017/9781009000048

First published 2021
First paperback edition 2024

A catalogue record for this publication is available from the British Library

ISBN   978-1-316-51826-7   Hardback
ISBN   978-1-108-99981-6   Paperback

Contents

Acknowledgments

I could not have written this book without a Fulbright Scholar Award, which allowed me to spend six blissful months at the National Library of Scotland. I deeply appreciate the warm welcome and knowledgeable assistance of all the staff at the NLS, especially Sally Harrower, Graham Hogg, Andrew Martin, Ralph McLean, Dora Petheridge, Kenny Redpath, Chris Taylor, and Helen Vincent. The Institute for Advanced Study in the Humanities at Edinburgh University provided a congenial community during my time in Edinburgh. Angela Gilchrist and David Stewart at D. C. Thomson in Dundee generously provided access to the company's archival material relating to Annie S. Swan and introduced me to the rich history of the *People's Friend*.

I'm immensely grateful to colleagues who supported the project in its early stages and offered suggestions as it grew: Kirstie Blair, Cairns Craig, Leith Davis, JoEllen DeLucia, Ian Duncan, Erin Farley, Penny Fielding, David Goldie, Peggy Hughes, Charlotte Lauder, Caroline McCracken-Flesher, Kirsteen McCue, the late Marjery Palmer McCulloch, Glenda Norquay, and Karina Williamson. The readers for Cambridge University Press provided the most thoughtful and thorough reports I have ever received. This book has been immeasurably improved by their insights. Warm thanks go to them, and to Bethany Thomas for seeing it through the review process.

A section of Chapter 4 appeared in *Studies in Scottish Literature* and a portion of Chapter 5 in *Scottish Literary Review*. An earlier version of Chapter 2 was published in *Victorian Periodicals Review*. I'm grateful for permission to republish the work here.

Finally, thanks go to my family: to Tom Lockwood for cheerfully rearranging his life to accommodate my trips to Scotland; to Rosemary Chadwick and Deborah King for enthusiastically seeking out books by Oliphant and the Findlater sisters; and to my mother Miranda Shields, who discovered Sarah MacNaughtan and Ethel F. Heddle before I did. This book is dedicated to her.

Introduction
The Scottish Novel after Scott

In August of 1871, on the centenary of Walter Scott's birth, *Blackwood's Edinburgh Magazine* featured an essay celebrating his achievements. It declared that only

> a hundred years ago there was no Scott known in Scotland. No Scott! No genius of the mountains, shedding colour and light upon their mighty slopes; no herald of past glory, sounding his clarion out of the heart of the ancient ages; no kindly, soft-beaming light of affectionate insight brightening the Lowland cottages.... No Highland emigration could depopulate those dearest hills and glens as they are depopulated by this mere imagination. A hundred years ago they were bare and naked – nay, they were not, except to here and there a wandering, hasty passenger.[1]

Without Scott's works, the essay asserts hyperbolically, Scotland would be unimaginable – a void – to most Britons. Its author, Margaret Oliphant, recognized a good century before Benedict Anderson the role that novels play in imagining national identity and in representing a nation to itself.[2] For, not only was there "no Scott known in Scotland" a century earlier, but

> There were no novels; and a hundred years ago, the past history of Scotland was a ground for polemics only – for the contentions of a few historical fanatics, and the investigations of antiquarians – not a glowing and picturesque past in which all the world might rejoice, a region sounding with music and brilliant with colour, as living as our own, and far more captivating in the sheen and brightness of romance than the sober-tinted present.[3]

---

[1] Margaret Oliphant, "A Century of Great Poets, from 1750 Downwards. No. II – Walter Scott," *Blackwood's Edinburgh Magazine* 110.670 (August 1871): 230–1.
[2] On the nation as imagined community, see Benedict Anderson, *Imagined Communities: Reflections on the Origins and Spread of Nationalism*, revised ed. (London: Verso, 1991).
[3] Oliphant, "Great Poets," 230.

If Walter Scott invented Scotland, as Margaret Oliphant and many after her have contended, he did so largely by inventing the Scottish novel.[4]

Before Scott, there were a few Scottish novelists – Tobias Smollett, Henry Mackenzie, and Jean Marischal, for instance – but no body of works or characteristic form that we could refer to as the Scottish novel. Scott's vastly popular Waverley novels changed that, defining the Scottish novel indelibly as historical romance. At a time when the average print run of a new novel was 750 copies, each of the Waverley novels commanded an initial print run of between 6,000 and 10,000 copies, and libraries in London reported ordering between 50 and 70 copies of each novel as it appeared in order to meet readers' demands.[5] The Waverley novels were a commercial success in large part because, as William St. Clair has shown, Scott "achieved an ownership of the whole literary production and distribution process from author to reader, controlling ... the editing, the publishing, and the printing of the books, the reviewing in the local literary press, [and] the adaptations for the theatre."[6] The Magician of the North, as Scott was known, was also an entrepreneur, a curator, and a manufacturer, shaping Scotland's cultural identity through his involvement in every aspect of the Waverley novels' production and marketing. The Waverley novels cultivated a vogue for Scottish fiction that brought attention and more limited success to Scott's contemporaries, James Hogg, John Galt, Susan Ferrier, and a rash of lesser-known novelists parodied in Sarah Green's *Scotch Novel Reading* (1820). Green's protagonist Alice, a Londoner, is addicted to reading "Scotch novels," which inspire her to dress in tartan and speak in Scots until she meets some real Highlanders – dirty, uncouth, and incomprehensible – who put an end to her obsession. With Scott's death in 1832, the Scottish novel's brief efflorescence would seem to have ended, at least until Robert Louis Stevenson took up Scott's literary mantle, trying his hand at historical romance with *Kidnapped* (1886) and *The Master of Ballantrae* (1889), among other works.

Over the past 150 or so years, scholars have debated the literary value of Scott's achievements, but the seminal position that Oliphant accorded him in Scottish literary history remains unchallenged. Nor do I intend to contest it here. Rather, I am interested in Oliphant's investment as a

[4] See, for instance, Stuart Kelly, *Scott-Land: The Man Who Invented a Nation* (Edinburgh: Polygon, 2010), and Tom Nairn, *The Break-Up of Britain: Crisis of Neo-Nationalism*, 2nd ed. (London: Verso 1981), 114–51.

[5] William St. Clair, *The Reading Nation in the Romantic Period* (Cambridge: Cambridge University Press, 2004), 418, 245.

[6] St. Clair, *Reading Nation*, 170.

Scotswoman and a novelist in this narrative, and in its implications for the other nineteenth-century Scottish women novelists who wrote, to borrow Ian Duncan's phrase, in "Scott's shadow."[7] The very moment of Scott's domination of the British literary marketplace was the moment that Scotswomen, for the first time, constituted a noticeable presence as novelists in that marketplace. The novels of Elizabeth Hamilton, Mary Brunton, Susan Ferrier, and Christian Isobel Johnstone, to name only the most prominent Scottish women novelists of the Romantic period, were all available to Oliphant and her Victorian successors as models. Sandra Gilbert and Susan Gubar, in their classic revision of Harold Bloom's theory of the anxiety of influence, argue that nineteenth-century women writers struggled to rewrite patriarchal literary traditions "by actively seeking a *female* precursor who . . . proves by example that a revolt against patriarchal literary authority is possible" and who consequently "legitimize[s] her own rebellious endeavors."[8] Yet despite the ready availability of female precursors, Oliphant and those who came after her looked to Scott. Instead of rebelling against patriarchal literary authority, as Gilbert and Gubar's theory suggests, Oliphant feminized it, transforming Scott, as Chapter 1 argues, into a prototype of the professional woman writer.

Nonetheless, as a literary predecessor and precedent-setter for Scottish women novelists, Scott posed problems. In *The Achievement of Literary Authority*, Ina Ferris argues persuasively that Scott's Waverley novels rendered the feminized and degraded genre of romance a respectably masculine form of writing.[9] They did so by reverting to an earlier understanding of romance, one that preceded its corruption by women who

---

7 Ian Duncan uses this phrase to refer to Scott's contemporaries, including James Hogg, John Galt, and Christian Isobel Johnstone, whose literary achievements were overshadowed by those of their more famous contemporaries. But Scott cast a long shadow over nineteenth-century Scotland, and his successors, male and female, also wrote in its shade. See *Scott's Shadow: The Novel in Romantic Edinburgh* (Princeton, NJ: Princeton University Press, 2007).

8 Sandra Gilbert and Susan Gubar, *The Madwoman in the Attic: The Woman Writer and the Nineteenth-Century Literary Imagination*, new ed. (New Haven, CT: Yale University Press, 2000), 49–50.

9 Ina Ferris, *The Achievement of Literary Authority: Gender, History, and the Waverley Novels* (Ithaca, NY: Cornell University Press, 1992). A great deal has been written on the Waverley novels and romance. See, for instance, Martha F. Bowden, *Descendants of Waverley: Romancing History in Contemporary Historical Fiction* (Lewisburg, PA: Bucknell University Press, 2016); Ayşe Çelikkol, *Romances of Free Trade: British Literature, Laissez-Faire, and the Global Nineteenth Century* (Oxford: Oxford University Press, 2011); Fiona Robertson, "Romance and the Romantic Novel: Sir Walter Scott," in *A Companion to Romance: From Classical to Contemporary*, ed. Corinne Saunders (Malden, MA: Blackwell, 2004), 287–304; Ian Duncan, *Modern Romance and Transformations of the Novel: The Gothic, Scott, Dickens* (Cambridge: Cambridge University Press, 1992); David Oberhelman, "Waverley, Genealogy, History: Scott's Romance of Fathers and Sons," *Nineteenth-Century Contexts* 15.1 (1991): 29–47; and Jerome Mitchell, *Scott, Chaucer, and Medieval Romance: A Study in Sir Walter Scott's Indebtedness to the Middle Ages* (Lexington: University Press of Kentucky, 1987).

wrote sentimental novels for the Minerva press. Scott's romances dwelt on
the past rather than the present, and on what he described as the "marvellous and uncommon" rather than the familiar and mundane.[10] Yet, as
Ferris shows, Scott at the same time brought to his novels a new precision
of detail that distinguished them from "highly conventionalized" sentimental fiction.[11] Reviewers repeatedly praised *Waverley* for "its 'variety' of
mode, scene, and characterization; and the 'fact' and 'accuracy' of its
historical and cultural representations."[12]

It is perhaps not surprising, then, that literary scholars from Georg
Lukács to Harry Shaw have found in *Waverley* and its successors the
origins of the realist novel. Like Scott's contemporaries, these more recent
readers have celebrated the Waverley novels' "human and historical par-
ticularity," whether as an end in itself or as a vehicle for exploring abstract
ideological processes.[13] But they have also recognized the limits of Scott's
realism, which might be described as material or formal rather than
psychological. For, as Shaw observes, in the Waverley novels "the focus
rests almost entirely on the social and historical aspects of human life, with
the inner life being relegated to the realm of the ineffable."[14] Scott's status
as an originator of the realist novel depends on his representation of
things – his re-creation of the texture of real life – rather than on his
representation of characterological interiority. His narrators do report
characters' thoughts and feelings, but readers rarely gain the less mediated
access to their "inner life" that free indirect discourse would provide.
Shaw's qualification of Scott's realist credentials echoes nineteenth-century
readers' reservations. In 1858 Walter Bagehot suggested that readers must
endure the Waverley novels' "peculiar interest . . . as if for their own sake"
in "antiquarian details" in order to enjoy their "sentimental element." In
1864 Henry James valued these details more positively, acknowledging
that although many of the Waverley characters "may seem little better than
lay-figures," readers might nonetheless take pleasure in "the sight of
unmistakeable velvet and brocade and tartan."[15] If early nineteenth-
century readers appreciated Scott's novels as romances that incorporated
history, late nineteenth-century readers, accustomed to greater depth and

[10] Walter Scott, "Essay on Romance," in *The Miscellaneous Prose Works of Sir Walter Scott, Bart.*, vol. 6
(Edinburgh: Cadell, 1827), 155.
[11] Ferris, *Achievement*, 81.   [12] Ferris, *Achievement*, 83.
[13] Harry E. Shaw, *Narrating Reality: Austen, Scott, Eliot* (Ithaca, NY: Cornell University Press, 1999), 14.
[14] Shaw, *Narrating*, 36.
[15] Walter Bagehot, "The Waverley Novels," *National Review* 6 (April 1858): 446; Henry James,
Review of *Essays on Fiction* by Nassau Senior, *North American Review* 99 (Oct. 1864): 585.

complexity of character, judged them as realist novels manqué, eventually relegating them to the status of children's literature.[16]

Scott himself regarded the "marvellous and uncommon" as entirely compatible with accuracy of detail, explaining in his *Essay on Romance* (1827) that romance and history were originally one and the same. As narratives of a tribe's or nation's origins were passed down over generations, they were enhanced by "tributes from the Imagination" of storytellers, thus becoming increasingly "mythological and fabulous" over time.[17] Scott's novels embody the definition of romance he offers in this essay, recounting a series of conflicts that were central to the centuries-long consolidation of the modern British nation-state. For instance, *Ivanhoe* (1820) tells of Anglo-Saxon resistance to Norman rule, *Old Mortality* (1819) of the Scottish Covenanters' opposition to the Stuart monarchy's Erastianism, *Rob Roy* (1817) of the unsuccessful Jacobite uprising of 1715, and *Waverley* (1814) of its similarly futile successor in 1745. Scott's tales of chivalry and adventure, superstition and enchantment, inaugurated a masculinized Scottish romance tradition that Robert Louis Stevenson, George MacDonald, James Barrie, and John Buchan, among others, would perpetuate in their own fiction. Twentieth-century critics from Edwin Muir and Hugh MacDiarmid to Tom Nairn and Stuart Kelly have charged Scott with inventing a Scotland of romantic illusions that displaced and discounted the material realities of Scottish life – including the effects of industrialization, migration, and agricultural modernization – and filled the void with tales of days gone by.[18] In 1932, MacDiarmid, disgusted by national events marking the centenary of Scott's death, dismissed Scott as a writer "full of false Romanticism," and with "no profound and progressive sense of his country."[19] But in 1871, when Oliphant celebrated the centenary of his birth, Scott's sway was still strong. He was, as William St. Clair has shown, "by several orders of magnitude, the author whose works had sold the largest number of copies in the English-speaking world."[20]

---

[16] John O. Hayden dates this transition in public perceptions of Scott to around 1885. Introduction, *Scott: The Critical Heritage*, ed. Hayden (London: Routledge & Kegan Paul, 1970), 2.

[17] Scott, "Essay on Romance," 181, 162.

[18] Edwin Muir, *Scott and Scotland: The Predicament of the Scottish Writer*, introduction by Allan Massie (Edinburgh: Polygon, 1982); Hugh MacDiarmid, "The Scott Centenary," in *Modernism and Nationalism: Literature and Society in Scotland 1918–1939*, ed. Margery Palmer McCulloch (Glasgow: Association for Scottish Literary Studies, 2004), 125–6; Nairn, *The Break-Up of Britain*, 114–51; and Kelly, *Scott-land*.

[19] MacDiarmid, "The Scott Centenary," 125–6. That MacDiarmid was responding to public events marking the centenary of Scott's death suggests that many people did not share his views.

[20] St. Clair, *The Reading Nation*, 419.

Romancing the Real

If romance was masculine literary territory in nineteenth-century Scotland, how did Scotswomen who aspired to authorship navigate this terrain? This is the question that this book seeks to answer. These women could not escape Scott's influence, but neither could they adopt or imitate his masculine mode of fiction wholesale. Each of the women discussed in this book responded differently to Scott and to the romance tradition he epitomized, but together their novels form an overlooked countertradition of unromantic or even antiromantic representations of Scotland – from stories of mundane domestic life in villages where nothing ever happens to accounts of grinding poverty in Glasgow's slums. Although claiming to reject romance, many of these women instead domesticated it, finding the "marvellous and uncommon" in the mundane. In doing so, they revised Scott's materialist realism. Instead of using descriptive detail to evoke the pastness of the past, they used it to evoke the beauty of the commonplace, or to reveal the romance in everyday life. This neglected body of writing challenges the claim that Scotland lacked any equivalent to the English Victorian realist tradition, with its novels of political debate and social reform.

Who were these women and why has their work been so neglected? Between Scott's death in 1832 and the beginning of World War II, when Scottish women writers came to recognize themselves as belonging to a distinct and gendered literary tradition, Scotswomen produced literally hundreds of novels, most of which are now forgotten. With the exceptions of Margaret Oliphant and Catherine Carswell, Scottish women writers of the long nineteenth century have received little critical attention individually, let alone as a group that includes Sarah Tytler [Henrietta Keddie], Lucy Bethia Walford, Flora Annie Steel, Annie S. Swan, Isabella Fyvie Mayo, Mary and Jane Findlater, Mona Caird, Robina Hardy, Sarah MacNaughtan, and O. Douglas [Anna Buchan], among others. While writing this book I have been asked repeatedly whether these women's novels are really worth revisiting, or whether they shouldn't simply be relegated to the dustbin of literary history.

In response I have argued, as I will argue here, that Scottish women's fiction constitutes a distinct and coherent chapter in the development of the British novel that demands scholarly attention for both its literary value and its historical significance. Moreover, I suggest that these women's novels are highly pleasurable reading. They will appeal not only to readers of Scott and Stevenson but also to admirers of Jane Austen, Charles

Dickens, and George Eliot. That these women and their works have disappeared so completely from our purview does not meant that they deserved to disappear. Rather, their current invisibility derives from a range of factors including the relatively recent rediscovery of Scottish Victorianism, the tacit Anglo-centrism of studies of nineteenth-century realism, the ephemerality of the media in which these women tended to publish their writing, and, it must be acknowledged, their own efforts at concealment. Above all, though, their disappearance reflects the masculinist bent of Scottish literary history, which has celebrated the male romancers who followed Scott over their female counterparts.

A quick glance at the third volume of *The History of Scottish Literature* (1988) will reveal the extent to which masculinist attitudes toward nineteenth-century Scottish literature have changed over the past thirty years. Douglas Gifford, the editor of the volume, laments that nineteenth-century Scottish literature, dominated by a backward-looking aristocratic romance tradition, "failed to respond imaginatively to society's changes, and failed to interpret and empathise with the mass of ordinary people."[21] Paul H. Scott, in his contribution to the volume, argues that the fifty years after Walter Scott's death saw "a loss of cohesion and self-confidence" in Scottish literary culture; Christopher Harvie echoes the indictment, describing the 1830s through the 1880s as a "great 'black hole' in Scottish creative literature and social thought."[22] Whereas Paul Scott traces the problem to the "disastrous" Disruption of 1843, when the splitting of the Presbyterian church destroyed the "bulwark of national identity," Harvie suggests that Victorian Scottish writers willfully neglected the problems accompanying Scotland's industrial growth: poverty, poor sanitation, and alcoholism.[23] In turning to romance, these writers failed to develop a Scottish version of the English Victorian "novel of political practice and public doctrine."[24]

Gifford's introduction to volume 3 of *The History of Scottish Literature* did affirm that Victorian Scotland was "an exceptionally male-dominated society,"[25] and in an essay published in *Scotland and the 19th-Century World* (2012) Gifford acknowledged that *The History of Scottish Literature's*

[21] Douglas Gifford, "Introduction," in *The History of Scottish Literature*, vol. 3: *The Nineteenth Century*, ed. Douglas Gifford (Aberdeen: Aberdeen University Press, 1988), 5.
[22] Paul H. Scott, "'The Last Purely Scotch Age,'" in Gifford, ed., *The History of Scottish Literature*, vol. 3: *The Nineteenth Century*, 13; Christopher Harvie, "Industry, Religion and the State of Scotland," in ibid., 24.
[23] Scott, "The Last Purely Scotch Age," 19.
[24] Harvie, "Industry, Religion, and the State of Scotland," 28.   [25] Gifford, "Introduction," 9.

third volume was similarly "male-dominated," neglecting "to recognize sufficiently the achievement of women like Susan Ferrier and Margaret Oliphant."[26] If we take women's writing into account, Gifford argues, Scottish literature in the latter half of the nineteenth century was in fact quite vibrant, with "the twenty years between 1835 and 1855 (with the Disruption of the Church of Scotland at its heart)" forming "the real nadir" of Victorian Scottish literature.[27] Perhaps it was editing, with Dorothy McMillan, the compendious *History of Scottish Women's Writing* (1997) that revealed to Gifford the wealth of nineteenth-century literature by women. This collection of essays on individual authors and trends in Scottish women's writing remains among the most substantial contributions to the topic even twenty years later. But its impact has been limited. Ironically, *Scotland and the 19th-Century World* makes even fewer references to women writers than *The History of Scottish Literature*. Significantly, it also has very little to say about the Scottish novel, focusing instead on periodicals, travel writing, balladry, and history. *Scotland and the 19th-Century World* takes the value of nineteenth-century Scottish literature to lie, as its title suggests, in its interactions with the "world" – a term encompassing British imperial expansion and the industrial-ization that enabled and was enabled by it. The editors assert that nineteenth-century Scotland was as "complex and contradictory as might be expected of any culture involved in negotiating ... cultural anglification, rampant indus-trialization, and willing partnership in British imperial enterprise."[28] The world in which they situate nineteenth-century Scotland seems very much a man's world, one that would necessarily exclude women's writing.

Yet Scotswomen did write about industrialization, imperialism, and Anglicization. Take, for instance, *Saint Mungo's City* (1884), by Henrietta Keddie, who wrote under the name Sarah Tytler. Set in Glasgow during the 1850s, this novel depicts the effects of industrialization and imperialism on the city. The three elderly Mackinnon sisters live in one of the great houses built in the eighteenth century by Tobacco Lords before the "tide of trade" had turned and "sugar had got the better of tobacco, and cotton had rivalled sugar, and iron distanced cotton."[29]

---

[26] Douglas Gifford, "Preparing for the Renaissance: Revaluing Nineteenth-Century Scottish Literature," in *Scotland and the 19th-Century World*, ed. Gerard Carruthers, David Goldie, and Alastair Renfrew (Amsterdam: Rodopi, 2012), 21.
[27] Gifford, "Preparing for the Renaissance," 23.
[28] Gerard Carruthers, David Goldie, and Alastair Renfrew, "Introduction," in Carruthers et al., eds., *Scotland and the 19th-Century World*, 19.
[29] Sarah Tytler, [Henrietta Keddie], *Saint Mungo's City: A Novel*, 3 vols. (London: Chatto and Windus), 1: 2.

These genteel but impoverished women avoid "silly pretence at polished instead of plain manners," and scorn "any attempt in Scotch people to speak 'high English.'"[30] By contrast, Mrs. Drysdale, whose husband owns a textile mill, has "somehow managed, with misdirected ambition, to give an undesirable varnish to the native Doric of her tongue, which, in robbing it of its simple rusticity, lent it a false lustre that by no means improved its quality."[31] The Miss Mackinnons represent the old ways of life that are rapidly disappearing as the newly monied Drysdales import the manners and values of the English middle class. Among the younger generation, however, Tam Drysdale sides with the workers in his father's mill, and Lieutenant Eneas Mackinnon eats "the sparse meal of enforced self-denial and petty economy" so that his aunts might remain in their grand but echoingly empty mansion.[32] Tytler addresses another effect of industrialization and imperial expansion in Scotland when Tam boards a steamer boat to Rothesay in the hopes of experiencing "for himself what the people's holiday was like," and encounters Rory, a man from North Uist who has recently arrived in Glasgow and is seeking work.[33] From the peasantry's difficulties in sustaining life in the Highlands and Islands, to the upward and downward mobility generated by industrialization, and the benefits and hardships of participating in British imperial endeavors, *Saint Mungo's City* is very much a novel about Scotland's engagement with the world and the world's impact on Scotland.

Saint Mungo's City is far from the only work that might be designated a Scottish equivalent to what is known as the "Condition of England" novel – a genre that, as in Elizabeth Gaskell's *North and South* or Charles Dickens's *Hard Times*, examined the effects of industrialization on traditional social structures. Annie S. Swan's *Mary Garth: A Clydeside Romance* (1902), like *Saint Mungo's City*, explores class conflict through generational conflict as Anne Garth supports the miners in her father's pits in their effort to unionize. *Mary Garth* is set in mining country in the southwest of Scotland, where Craigs village sits near the pitheads, a "square of depressed, ugly little brick houses" that forms "an unpicturesque blot on a landscape naturally fair."[34] Other novels by Swan explore the causes of economic inequality and represent the vulnerability of the working class, especially women, in Dundee's jute mills and in Glasgow's slums. Margaret Oliphant's *Harry Muir: A Scottish Story* (1852) explores another

---

[30] Tytler, *Saint Mungo's City*, 1: 13.   [31] Tytler, *Saint Mungo's City*, 1: 91.
[32] Tytler, *Saint Mungo's City*, 1: 227.   [33] Tytler, *Saint Mungo's City*, 1: 254.
[34] Annie S. Swan, *Mary Garth: A Clydeside Romance* (London: Hodder and Stoughton, 1904), 7.

of the evils of poverty: the eponymous protagonist's alcoholism and his sisters' struggles to compensate for its economic and social impact on the family. *Harry Muir* is set in Port Dundas, an area of Glasgow that in the nineteenth century was home to textile mills, chemical works, glassworks, and iron foundries. In Oliphant's novel, Port Dundas is primarily the realm of women, who labor in these mills, factories, and foundries – a fate that the Muir women seek to avoid. If Walter Scott left nineteenth-century Scotland "a wasteland," as the editors of *Scotland and the 19th-Century World* contend, his female successors transformed it into a flourishing landscape of cities, villages, and seaports, peopled with diverse individuals who reflected the changing composition of Scottish society during the nineteenth century.[35]

The critical neglect of Scottish women writers has given false validation to the claim that Scotland failed to develop a realist novel – the genre that we have come to regard as the acme of Victorian Britain's literary achievements. The successes of Scott, Stevenson, Barrie, and other romancers have been something of an embarrassment to scholars of Scottish literature because they imply that nineteenth-century Scottish prose fiction remained "stuck" in the romance mode, an earlier stage on the trajectory of literary evolution than realism. While I contend that Scotswomen did in fact develop a realist novel, it is worth pausing for a moment to recognize that even a concept as seemingly self-evident or universal as "realism" emerges from the study of what John Kerrigan calls "Anglo Eng. Lit.," a comparatively narrow canon of works dominated by authors situated in metropolitan England.[36] Thus, as Chapter 1 argues, Oliphant's Chronicles of Carlingford remain the best known of her ninety-odd novels because they mimic from an outsider's position the tradition of the provincial English novel as developed by Austen, Trollope, or Eliot. The familiarity of their technique accounts for their comparative longevity. By contrast, her Scottish romances, in which she revises the masculine tropes of Scott's novels, have been largely neglected. Rather than seeking a Scottish realist novel that looks like an English realist novel, and thereby imposing implicitly Anglo-centric definitions of realism onto Scotland, it might be more productive to see how Scottish literature troubles the categories that organize the study of Anglo-English literature – categories that

---

[35] Carruthers et al., "Introduction," 15.
[36] John Kerrigan, *Archipelagic English: Literature, History, and Politics 1603–1707* (Oxford: Oxford University Press, 2008), 12.

critics have been inclined to consider as, if not universal, then at least universally British.

Prevailing versions of literary history recount the emergence in nineteenth-century Britain of a realist novel that privileged interiority or depth as an indication of artistic sophistication, as exemplified in the works of Jane Austen, Charlotte Brontë, and George Eliot.[37] This depth model of interiority, or psychological realism, is rarely to be found in the nineteenth-century Scottish novel, whether by Scott or Stevenson, or by Tytler, Oliphant, or Swan. In its place, Scottish women writers developed a realist mode that eschewed the grand scale, sweeping vistas, and chivalric adventure of Scott's romances while embracing Scott's tendency to privilege plot development over character development, surface detail over psychological depth, and characters' interactions over characters' introspections. They brought these stylistic conventions of romance to the substance of mundane domestic life, a realm that Scott tended to eschew. He acknowledged as much when, after rereading *Pride and Prejudice,* he compared Jane Austen's style with his own: "The big bow-wow strain I can do myself like any now going; but the exquisite touch, which renders ordinary commonplace things and characters interesting, from the truth of the description and the sentiment, is denied to me."[38] Francis Jeffrey, writing for the *Edinburgh Review* in 1817, echoed this self-assessment when he found fault with Scott's "representations of the ordinary business of . . . conversation in polished life."[39] Setting his novels at moments of political crisis allowed Scott to indulge his talent for "big bow-wow" moments, and setting them in the past enabled him to avoid the "ordinary commonplace." Descriptive detail in the Waverley novels tends to foreground what might be unfamiliar and peculiar to readers by virtue of its very pastness: customs fallen out of use, legends scarcely recalled, objects without owners.

---

[37] Perhaps the most influential version of this account of the realist novel's development remains Nancy Armstrong's *Desire and Domestic Fiction: A Political History of the Novel* (New York: Oxford University Press, 1987); however, it persists in recent studies of nineteenth-century realism including George Levine, *Realism, Ethics and Secularism: Essays on Victorian Literature and Science* (Cambridge: Cambridge University Press, 2008); Rae Greiner, *Sympathetic Realism in Nineteenth-Century British Fiction* (Baltimore, MD: Johns Hopkins University Press, 2012); Fredric Jameson, *The Antinomies of Realism* (London: Verso, 2013); Jesse Rosenthal, *Good Form: The Ethical Experience of the Victorian Novel* (Princeton, NJ: Princeton University Press, 2017); and Elaine Auyoung, *When Fiction Feels Real: Representation and the Reading Mind* (New York: Oxford University Press, 2018).

[38] *The Journal of Sir Walter Scott,* ed. W. E. K. Anderson (Oxford: Clarendon, 1972), 114.

[39] Francis Jeffrey, Review of *Tales of My Landlord, Edinburgh Review* 28 (1817): 197.

In turning from the past into the present and from the sublimity of Scott's Highland landscapes to farmhouses, factories, and suburban villas, women writers brought romance to everyday life – to the "ordinary commonplace things and characters" that have long been considered women's proper objects of attention. Although these writers often declared, sometimes emphatically, to reject the extraordinary, their declarations served only to reinvest the everyday with immanent meaning. For, as Leisl Olson astutely explains, the representation of the ordinary is marked by paradox: "To say *this is ordinary* is to give significance to what is insignificant."[40] Once remarked on, the commonplace is no longer commonplace. Henri Lefebvre and Gayatri Spivak explore this paradox from different perspectives. For Lefebvre, the everyday is a lived experience that cannot be rendered in language or narrated. We recognize it as such only when, in attempting to describe or narrate it, we transform into something other than the everyday. Spivak, by contrast, posits that the everyday unravels the totalizing narratives that overwrite differences of perspective.[41] These seemingly opposing theories both emphasize the unutterability of the everyday as something that is lived rather than described. William Galperin suggests that this sense of ineffability emerges through retrospection, which reveals the everyday as "a missed or unappreciated stratum of experience" that is lost to us as a possibility as soon we become aware of its existence.[42] The everyday, as what Galperin terms a "counter-actual history," emerges in nineteenth-century Scotswomen's novels as the lived experiences that were marginalized or overwritten by Scott's romanticized version of Scotland.[43]

For Galperin, Jane Austen is the writer who most successfully captures these "missed opportunities." Austen was undoubtedly an influence on the women I discuss in this study, although not one that they acknowledged as frequently as they did Scott. In her *Literary History of England in the End of the Eighteenth and the Beginning of the Nineteenth Century* (1882), Oliphant looked back to Maria Edgeworth, Susan Ferrier, and Jane Austen as the first novelists to make everyday life their study, observing

[40] Leisl Olson, *Modernism and the Ordinary* (Oxford: Oxford University Press, 2009), 7.
[41] Henri Lefebvre, *Everyday Life in the Modern World*, trans. Sacha Rabinovitch, introduction by Philip Wander (New Brunswick, NJ: Transaction Publishers, 1990); and Gayatri Spivak, "The Making of Americans," *New Literary History* 21 (1990): 781–98. My understanding of the everyday is also indebted to Laurie Langbauer's *Novels of Everyday Life: The Series in English Fiction, 1850–1930* (Ithaca, NY: Cornell University Press, 1999).
[42] William Galperin, *The History of Missed Opportunities: British Romanticism and the Emergence of the Everyday* (Stanford, CA: Stanford University Press, 2017), 32.
[43] Galperin, *Missed Opportunities*, 6.

that "the life of average human nature swept by no violence of passion, disturbed by no volcanic events, came suddenly uppermost in the works of these women as it had never done before."[44] Among the three, though, Austen's power to invest the everyday with new interest was most striking:

> Without ever stepping from the shelter of home, or calling to her help a single incident that might not have happened next door, she held the reader, if not breathless, yet in that pleased and happy suspension of personal cares and absorption of amused interest, which is the very triumph of fiction. She had not even a new country to reveal like Miss Edgeworth, or a quaint and obscure region of odd manners and customs like Miss Ferrier. She had nothing to say that England did not know, and no exhibition of highly-wrought feeling, or extraordinary story to tell. The effect she produced was entirely novel, without any warrant or reason, except the ineffable and never-to-be-defined reason of genius which made it possible to turn all those commonplace events into things more interesting than passion. It would be difficult to find anything nearer witchcraft and magic.[45]

Importantly, Oliphant looks to the *effects* of fiction as a means of measuring its success – a measure that subsequent Scottish women writers would also employ. Good fiction, Oliphant implies, is all-engrossing, and Austen's achievement was to hold her readers' attention without resorting to sensational happenings, exotic settings, or anything other than the already familiar. In her assessment of Austen, Oliphant does not mention the psychological depth of her characters or her masterful use of free indirect discourse to create that depth – the accomplishments that later critics would celebrate. Rather, she focuses on Austen's ability to depict in arresting terms what was already recognizable to her readers: drawing-room conversations, muddy walks in country lanes, garrulous elderly women like Miss Bates, silly young ladies like Lydia Bennett. It was to similarly mundane material that nineteenth-century Scottish women writers would turn their attention.

Presbyterianism and the Proscription of Imagination

Nineteenth-century Scotswomen's exploration of the romance of everyday life cannot be attributed solely to Walter Scott's influence, far-reaching though it was. The broader cultural and economic conditions in which

[44] Margaret Oliphant, *The Literary History of England in the End of the Eighteenth and the Beginning of the Nineteenth Century*, 3 vols. (London: Macmillan, 1897), 3: 171.
[45] Oliphant, *Literary History*, 3: 171.

Scotswomen wrote also shaped their stories. All of the women I discuss in this study shared two important factors in common: they were raised in the Presbyterian Free Church or other evangelical varieties of Presbyterianism that emerged from the Disruption, and they belonged to the middle class. The latter capacious category includes those such as Margaret Oliphant, Henrietta Keddie, the Findlater sisters, and Isabella Fyvie Mayo, who wrote to support themselves and their dependents; and those who lived comfortably, often supported by a husband's income, but who wrote because they enjoyed it, such as Lucy Walford, Flora Annie Steel, Violet Jacob, Annie S. Swan, and Anna Buchan. In both cases their literary pursuits were not without problems at a time when middle-class women's identity depended very much on not working, or at least not working for money or outside the home.

Of course, middle-class ideals of domestic womanhood impinged on English as much as Scottish women writers. But nineteenth-century Scotland's evangelical Presbyterian culture exacerbated the restrictiveness of these ideals by conflating social propriety with religious piety. This conflation was largely enforced by the Free Presbyterian Church, which emerged from the Disruption of 1843.[46] The evangelical clergymen who broke away from the established Church of Scotland claimed to reject worldly interests – their livings in the Church – for the right to religious self-determination, but, ironically, the Free Church and the other varieties of reformed Presbyterianism that emerged from the Disruption soon became "dominated by the ethos and style of the bourgeoisie."[47] The newly invigorated evangelical sensibility that grew out of the Disruption fostered a spirit of industrious independence in the Scottish middle classes, but it also denounced the pleasures of the imagination and censored those who pursued them.

In *Mrs. Grundy in Scotland* (1936), published seven years after the breach between the established Church of Scotland and the Free Church was healed, Willa Muir offered an incisive analysis of the implications of the Great Disruption for nineteenth- and early twentieth-century Scotswomen. Muir's essay examines the impact on Scottish society of Mrs. MacGrundy, a Scottish Presbyterian version of Mrs. Grundy, a

---

[46] On the cultural impact of the Disruption, see Callum G. Brown, *Religion and Society in Scotland since 1707* (Edinburgh: Edinburgh University Press, 1997). The initial conflict between the Moderate and Evangelical parties occurred over the issue of patronage and was therefore drawn along socioeconomic lines. Moderates supported the right of landowners to choose a clergyman for their parish, while Evangelicals supported the right of the congregation.

[47] Brown, *Religion and Society*, 27.

fictional figure of performative middle-class respectability whose history dates to Thomas Morton's *Speed the Plough* (1798). "There was no native Mrs Grundy" in Scotland, Muir explains, because Scots had long been more concerned with the "drama of Heaven and Hell" than with the performance of social proprieties.[48] But the evangelical forms of Presbyterianism that emerged from the Disruption, along with Scots' "sense of inferiority" compared with their southern neighbors, proved particularly hospitable to Mrs. Grundy's concern with "proprieties in conduct."[49] As Scotland's growing middle class embraced religious piety as a marker of social respectability, the performance of "sanctimonious-ness" became more important than genuine religious feeling.[50] Muir recognized that women suffered more from MacGrundyism than did men, for the duties of performing religious piety and social propriety fell primarily on them. Mrs. MacGrundy embodied Victorian Scotland's provincial insecurities, compensating for its perceived cultural inferiority to metropolitan England with holier-than-thou "attitudinarianism."[51] Muir's play on "latitudinarian" tolerance of doctrinal differences empha-sizes the narrowness of middle-class Presbyterian mores, and their concern with the superficial signs of piety, such as closed blinds and no golf on Sundays.

Muir lamented Mrs. MacGrundy's tendency to quell the "ancient fervour" of the Presbyterian Church, which, she believed, constituted a "genuine creative force,"[52] but she also identified a potential source of imaginative inspiration in Presbyterianism's concern with the spiritual significance of the everyday. In Scotland, imagination had long been channeled into religion rather than literature, so that Scots looked to sermons for "the kind of excitement which in other countries has usually given birth to dramatic art."[53] Mrs. MacGrundy, by rendering this kind of "excitement" unacceptable, particularly when manifest by women, repressed an important source of creativity. "The worst that can be said of Mrs MacGrundy," Muir concludes, "is that she discouraged the free play of the mind, the free play of the emotions, from which all living creative achievement springs."[54] Perhaps the best that could be said was that Mrs. MacGrundy encouraged scrutiny of the mundane. Muir points out that Scots "could never have identified social respectability with

---

[48] Willa Muir, "Mrs. Grundy in Scotland," in *Imagined Selves*, ed. Kirsty Allen (Edinburgh: Canongate, 1996), 11.
[49] Muir, "Mrs. Grundy," 7.   [50] Muir, "Mrs. Grundy," 30.   [51] Muir, "Mrs. Grundy," 32.
[52] Muir, "Mrs. Grundy," 33, 44.   [53] Muir, "Mrs. Grundy," 22.
[54] Muir, "Mrs. Grundy," 75.

religion had they not inherited . . . a tradition which told them that every action of daily life had a religious significance."[55] Evangelical Presbyterianism asserted the importance of the everyday in both positive and negative ways. For while constant analysis of seeming trivia might encourage the superficial performance of pieties and proprieties, it also affirmed the transcendent significance of "every action of daily life" within a divine schema. Scottish women writers' explorations of the romance of everyday life, or the transcendent significance of the utterly ordinary, thus may have constituted a response both to the masculine romance tradition originating with Scott and to a Presbyterian worldview. Indeed, their rejection of romance was arguably indivisible from their religiously inflected scrutiny of the everyday, for Scott's romances embraced aristocratic and high church ideals.

Evangelical Presbyterianism's suspicion of artistic and literary creativity, on the one hand, and its valorization of sober industriousness, on the other, also proved a surprising source of inspiration for Scottish women writers. Together, these tendencies compelled the writers I discuss in this book to reflect almost obsessively on the value of their writing in aesthetic and economic terms. The aspersion cast by the Church on the reading, let alone writing, of novels as a form of diversion seems to have encouraged Scotswomen to make a case for the value of fiction as a restorative and consolatory form of escape from the monotony of the mundane. Most of these women disclaimed, sometimes vehemently, any aspirations to literary genius, declaring themselves competent craftswomen or skilled trade workers rather than inspired artists. Construing the writing of fiction as a form of remunerative and useful labor may have helped them to legitimate their artistic endeavors. Yet their fictional representations of women writers, musicians, painters, and needleworkers suggest that their work was hardly mechanical or uncreative. Through these figures, Scottish women writers metafictionally expounded their aesthetic philosophy, suggesting that, looked at the right way, the mundane was not so monotonous after all.

The Presbyterian Church's censoriousness toward artistic and literary creation was not merely a product of the Disruption but had a longer history. Scottish Presbyterianism fostered what Cairns Craig describes as a "distrust of the imagination, building on a powerful interpretive tradition in Judaeo-Christian theology" that since the Reformation had "become part of the very fabric of the traditions of Scottish writing and Scottish

---

[55] Muir, "Mrs. Grundy," 73.

thought."[56] The weight of these traditions is particularly evident in the novels of Mary Brunton, wife of a clergyman in the Church of Scotland, who declared her aim in writing to be "promoting virtue, if it be but in one heart."[57] Brunton shared this investment in fiction's didactic potential with many other early nineteenth-century women writers, but her skepticism concerning the value of artistic creation stands out. This skepticism is present in her first novel, *Self-Control* (1811), whose naïve protagonist hopes, fruitlessly, to support herself and her father by selling her paintings. It is even more marked in *Discipline* (1815), thanks to the novel's first-person retrospective narration through which the reformed protagonist Ellen Percy reflects disparagingly on her earlier artistic achievements and love of ornamentation. The beautiful, wealthy, and initially self-centered Ellen is a talented pianist whose "musical powers were pronounced equal to any which the public may command for hire."[58] But, as she recognizes in retrospect, she pays a price in cultivating her talent:

> This acquisition (I blush whilst I write it) cost me the labour of seven hours a day! – full half the time which, after deducting the seasons of rest and refreshment, remained for all the duties of a rational, a social, and immortal being! Wise Providence! Was it to be squandered thus, that leisure was bestowed upon a happy few! – leisure, the most precious distinction of wealth.[59]

Ellen regrets the time and energy she devoted to studying music, dismissing it along with more frivolous pastimes such as shopping and gossiping as a misuse of her gifts. Although it is not positively pernicious, music is without value as a pursuit because it impinges on, or at the very least does nothing to promote, the individual's fulfillment of her duties to God and her fellow beings.

Not only is art without spiritual value in Brunton's novels, but it also has little economic or social value, as Ellen finds when she attempts to turn her artistic talents to practical use in earning a living. Sharon Alker has shown that Brunton's novels contest the idea that genteel women should not involve themselves in the dirty world of commerce.[60] Nonetheless,

[56] Cairns Craig, *The Modern Scottish Novel: Narrative and the National Imagination* (Edinburgh: Edinburgh University Press, 1999), 201.
[57] Mary Brunton, *Emmeline, with some other pieces by Mary Brunton, to which is prefixed a memoir of her life including some extracts from her correspondence* (Edinburgh: Manners and Miller, 1819), xxxviii.
[58] Mary Brunton, *Discipline* (London: Pandora, 1986), 18.   [59] Brunton, *Discipline*, 18.
[60] Sharon Alker, "The Business of Romance: Mary Brunton and the Virtue of Commerce," *European Romantic Review* 13 (2002): 199–205.

there is no place for art in the commercial marketplace as Brunton understands it. When her father's death leaves Ellen impoverished, she decides to seek a post as a governess, believing that her "thorough knowledge of music, and . . . acquaintance with other arts of idleness" will prove an asset.[61] This phrasing reveals Ellen's subsequent religious conversion, as she has learned to see her musical skills not as a worthy accomplishment but as the legacy of a wasted youth. From her reformed perspective, music seems to register with Ellen – and implicitly with Brunton – as no higher than "the art of wearing . . . clothes fashionably, and arranging . . . decorations with grace and effect" in that it is neither spiritually useful nor economically practical.[62]

In contrast to art, religion is of the utmost use, even though it too has no discernible economic value. Ellen learns that religious faith makes the "petty miseries" of daily life endurable in a way that, for Brunton, art cannot.[63] If her newfound faith in God proves useful to Ellen on a daily basis as she endures petty slights and poverty in Edinburgh, it is even more so when, in a melodramatic turn of events, she falls ill and, because she has no friends to care for her, is committed to a madhouse. Ellen regards her confinement as a time to atone for her former sins, and an opportunity to practice her faith, declaring that "it should even be my choice to dwell for a time amidst scenes of humiliation, if here I can find the weapons of my warfare against the stubborn pride of nature and of habit. And whatever be my choice, this place has been selected for me by Him whose will is my improvement."[64] Ellen has developed the spiritual resources that she previously lacked, and can now take solace in small things, like the nest of young swallows outside her window, as signs of God's presence. She relates, "I had experienced that there are pleasures which no walls can exclude, and hopes which no disappointments can destroy; pleasures which flourish in solitude and adversity; hopes, which fear no wreck but from the storms of passion. I had believed that religion could bring comfort to the dreariest dwelling. I now experienced that comfort."[65] The use-value of religious faith for Brunton is similar to the "use" that later Scottish women writers would assign to fiction: it brings us comfort and pleasure and provides a temporary escape from suffering, even of the mundane sort. For Brunton, though, the pleasures of art are superficial and transient compared with those of religion.

---

[61] Brunton, *Discipline*, 211.   [62] Brunton, *Discipline*, 17.   [63] Brunton, *Discipline*, 221.
[64] Brunton, *Discipline*, 289.   [65] Brunton, *Discipline*, 297.

Brunton went to some lengths to suggest that her own novel writing had little in common with the pretty but useless "baubles" that Ellen sells to support herself.[66] The confessional narrative structure of *Discipline* creates a somber tone that Ellen's eventual marriage to Mr. Maitland, friend of her father and model of Christian virtue, does nothing to disperse. "The great purpose" of *Discipline*, as Brunton described it in a letter to her friend Mrs. Balfour, was "to procure admission for the religion of a sound mind and of the Bible where it cannot find access in any other form" or, in other words, to convert unsuspecting readers to the reformed Ellen's views.[67] Without this purpose, novel writing might be merely one of the "arts of idleness" that Ellen learns to despise. Hence, perhaps, the fierce warning Ellen issues to readers early in her story as she envisions their disdain for her youthful frivolity: "Detest me reader. I was worthy of your detestation! Throw aside if you will my story in disgust. Yet remember that indignation against vice is not in itself virtue. Your abhorrence of pride and ingratitude is no farther genuine, than as it operates against your own pride, your own ingratitude."[68] If readers who see no reason to detest Ellen's self-absorption are in for a rude awakening, even those who do recognize and repudiate her errors will remain unregenerate unless their virtuous sentiments inform their actions.

Although later nineteenth-century Scotswomen would adopt the use of artist figures to explore the aesthetic, social, and economic value of their work, there is no evidence that they read or were even aware of Brunton's novels. They were, however, inevitably exposed to the ambivalence toward, and even distrust of, imaginative creativity that Brunton's fiction exhibits. Rather than internalizing this ambivalence, as Brunton seems to have done, later Scotswomen challenged it – albeit in a quiet and understated way – by suggesting that art and literature constituted a legitimate form of spiritual consolation. They found novel writing a satisfying and justifiable pursuit precisely because it created something that they deemed useful – something that would give pleasure to others. They represented their novels as an escape from the spiritually depleting effects of modern life: industrialization, urbanization, and the "economic individualism" that, according to Callum Brown, dominated Scotland in the wake of the Great Disruption.[69] Following the lead of Edwin Muir, literary critics have tended to see the legacies of Calvinism as repressing or negating

---

[66] Brunton, *Discipline*, 252.   [67] Brunton, *Emmeline*, lxviii.   [68] Brunton, *Discipline*, 50.
[69] Brown, *Religion and Society*, 180.

artistic and literary creativity in Scotland.[70] Yet the novels of Victorian Scotswomen provide an overabundance of evidence to support Cairns Craig's suggestion that we might see evangelical Presbyterianism instead as a source of imaginative energy.[71] Indeed, the Disruption seems to have catalyzed Scotswomen's literary creativity: in its wake, they turned to novel writing in noticeably larger numbers than ever before.

The Making of a Tradition

Despite their increasing numbers, all of the Scotswomen I discuss in this book chose to spend at least part of their adult lives in southern England, generally in London. This was a practical professional decision as much as it might have been an attempt to escape Mrs. MacGrundy's oversight. While Edinburgh's literary scene flourished during the first few decades of the nineteenth century, the financial crash of the late 1820s "depressed the market for new novels" well into the 1830s. And when the market recovered in the 1840s, Ian Duncan explains, "literary production was decisively London based."[72] Scotswomen went to London, as Henrietta Keddie explained in her autobiography, "for the better furtherment of [their] literary career" – to mix with literary celebrities and meet publishers.[73] Keddie, who ran a school for girls in Cupar, published her first novel in 1852 but did not move to London until 1870, after the deaths of her mother and two of her sisters permitted her greater freedom of movement. Margaret Oliphant and Annie S. Swan moved to London much earlier in their careers but made frequent visits to Scotland, with Swan, like Mary and Jane Findlater, eventually returning permanently. Access to London's literary resources ensured a degree of longevity to Scotswomen's careers, and a degree of permanence to their works. Quite possibly there are works by Scottish women writers that still await discovery or that may never be recovered because they worked with regional Scottish publishers and printers, whose small print runs may not have survived.

Given that many Scottish women writers actively sought to participate in the literary life of metropolitan England, the decision to write about them in relative isolation from their English counterparts may seem

---

[70] Edwin Muir blames Calvinism for Scotland's failure to develop a national literature. See Muir, *Scott and Scotland*, 44–51.

[71] Craig, *Scottish Novel*, 35.   [72] Duncan, *Scott's Shadow*, 23.

[73] Henrietta Keddie, *Three Generations: The Story of a Middle-Class Scottish Family* (London: John Murray, 1911), 292.

questionable. They undeniably participated in broadly British literary trends: Oliphant wrote chronicles of provincial life similar to Anthony Trollope's; Mary and Jane Findlater experimented with fin-de-siècle aestheticism; Annie S. Swan developed a version of the social problem novel; and Flora Annie Steel's adventure stories were mistaken for Rudyard Kipling's. Toward the end of the nineteenth century many Scotswomen joined English authors in seeking answers to "the woman question": the question of what types of work women's natural inclinations and abilities might suit them for. As feminist scholars have long recognized, the question of whether to discuss women's writing separately from that of their male contemporaries or in relation to it is a vexed one. Similar problems exist when it comes to studying Scottish literature written after the 1707 formation of Great Britain. Should we treat Scottish literature as a tradition in itself, or as part of a broader British tradition? In the case of Scottish women writers, then, the questions of separation and integration multiply. But because the writers and works I discuss in this study are little known, I want to emphasize the shared characteristics that distinguish them as a group and that have also contributed to their neglect.

Moreover, by the final decades of the nineteenth century, Scottish women writers were beginning to see themselves as belonging to a distinct literary tradition. Even – or perhaps especially – while living in England, they continued to represent, and presumably to consider, themselves as Scottish, and affiliated themselves with other Scottish writers. While Margaret Oliphant looked to Walter Scott to legitimate her pragmatic approach to literary creation, later Scotswomen saw Oliphant as opening doors for them. She became for these later writers the female literary precedent that Oliphant herself could not find. Henrietta Keddie placed Oliphant in the "first rank of women novelists for intellectual merit, culture, and a high moral standard," adding somewhat censoriously that "it will not be to the credit of English literature and English readers if her sound and varied work is slighted and forgotten."[74] Annie S. Swan claimed to feel "passionate admiration, amounting to worship" for Oliphant, and Anna Buchan began an unpublished lecture on Oliphant with the assertion that "Mrs. Oliphant was without doubt the greatest Scotswoman of the century."[75] Buchan saw in Oliphant "a brave and beautiful soul, burdened with many sorrows, & heavy laden, but always steadfast, always

---

[74] Keddie, *Three Generations*, 291.
[75] Annie S. Swan, *My Life: An Autobiography* (London: Ivor Nicholson, 1934), 40.

struggling, often amid tears, not for fame, not for herself, but for others."[76] Although Oliphant was not Scotland's first woman novelist by a long shot, her immense productivity, comparative fame, and highly self-conscious reflections on authorship made her a model for her contemporaries and a literary matriarch of sorts for subsequent generations of Scotswomen.

Indeed, for Scotswomen who wrote in the latter half of the nineteenth century, Oliphant served as a real-life analog to the figure of the foster-mother, which appears repeatedly in their novels and is arguably another indication of their sense of belonging to a shared literary tradition. The foster-mother, or to borrow the title of one of Swan's novels, the "sister-mother," is generally an unmarried woman who retains her economic independence while assuming the task of nurturing children to whom she did not give birth, but who often are her kin.[77] As Alexander Welsh has shown, Scott's romances use the trope of patrilineal inheritance to represent the literal and symbolic consolidation of the modern British nation.[78] Some of Scott's heroes are alienated from their familial origins and their rightful inheritance; others are burdened by material and ideological inheritances that they do not want, or that prove ruinous. Yet the patrilinear transmission of property ensures the protagonist's place in the social hierarchy that, during his adventures, he has helped to protect.

Novels by nineteenth-century Scotswomen also feature instances of interrupted succession and disputed inheritances, but the foster-mother is more concerned with the passing down of manners and mores than of property. If Scott's novels feature a surfeit of father-figures, Scotswomen's novels – Oliphant's *Margaret Maitland* (1849), Swan's *Aldersyde* (1883), Mary and Jane Findlater's *Crossriggs* (1908), and O. Douglas's *The Setons* (1917), to name just a few – include an equally notable number of foster-mothers. Whereas Scott's protagonists prove their fitness to protect the property they will inherit and the nation they will help to govern, the foster-mother foregrounds the less tangible contributions that women make to the preservation, or more often the reformation, of the social order. Foster-mother characters do not stand to inherit property and rarely participate in striking adventures. Indeed, their power to reform the aristocracy, gentry, or even in some cases the middle class lies in their position outside the institutions – marriage and inheritance – that sustain

---

[76] Anna Buchan, "Mrs. Oliphant," Acc. 11627 #117, National Library of Scotland.

[77] Swan's *Ursula Vivian; or, The Sister-Mother* (1894) features a protagonist who must care for her younger siblings after their parents' sudden deaths.

[78] Alexander Welsh, *The Hero of the Waverley Novels*, revised ed. (Princeton, NJ: Princeton University Press, 2014), 77–83.

socioeconomic hierarchies. The foster-mother is related to the figure of the nurse, whose importance in Romantic-era novels, including those by Scott, Edgeworth, and Ferrier, Katie Trumpener has analyzed. Trumpener describes the nurse as "the bearer of cultural inheritance, able to rouse her grown-up charges from their disaffection with national life into a more committed engagement with its past and present."[79] Whereas the nurse participates in creating or preserving national identities based in shared cultural traditions, the foster-mother establishes class identities rooted in shared values and manners. The nurse, whom Trumpener describes as a "figure" and an "emblem," is notable primarily for what she represents to the protagonist – the nation's past and the protagonist's childhood.[80] The nurse is usually a relatively minor character, although her role in driving the plot may be significant. The foster-mother, by contrast, is often the protagonist. She is not merely an "emblem" but a character whose experiences give focus to the novel. Scottish women writers' foregrounding of the foster-mother's constant, unrequited self-sacrifices suggests that they may have identified more strongly with the foster-mother herself than with her charges.

   Oliphant's *Passages in the Life of Mrs. Margaret Maitland of Sunnyside* and Swan's *Aldersyde: A Border Story of Seventy Years Ago* take foster-mothers as their central characters and, through Swan's rewriting of her predecessor's work, illustrate Oliphant's role as foster-mother to later Scottish women writers. Both novels tell the story of a spinster disappointed in love who finds fulfillment in raising orphaned children who, when they are eventually restored to their rightful estates, know how to use their newfound wealth and privilege wisely. Oliphant's Margaret Maitland finds herself burdened with "more charge of bairns than many a mother of a family is trysted with," including her niece and nephew, and her wealthy ward Grace.[81] She brings up these children "to the knowledge of His name" through "daily reading of the Word," and in doing so helps to unite the gentry's money with the moral values of the newly established and predominantly middle-class Free Church.[82] Grace marries Margaret's nephew Claud, a clergyman who joins the Free Church in the Disruption of 1843, and the two set out to "make another Sunnyside" of Grace's estate, Oakenshaw.[83] And Margaret's niece Mary marries Mr.

---

[79] Katie Trumpener, *Bardic Nationalism: The Romantic Novel and the British Empire* (Princeton, NJ: Princeton University Press, 1997), 202.

[80] Trumpener, *Bardic Nationalism*, 198.

[81] Margaret Oliphant, *Passages in the Life of Mrs. Margaret Maitland of Sunnyside* (London: Henry Colburn, 1851), 164.

[82] Oliphant, *Passages*, 31.   [83] Oliphant, *Passages*, 44.

Allan, Laird of Elphinstone, whom she inspires to abandon his "wild and gay" ways, and to look rather "to the Word for what was right than to the world."[84] Although she is only "a quiet woman of discreet years and small riches" – nobody of importance in the eyes of the world – Margaret's influence extends through her foster-children to encompass the tenants of two large estates.[85]

Aldersyde replaces *Margaret Maitland*'s religious concerns with an exploration of the gendered inequities of inheritance law. After her father's death, Janet Nesbit must leave Aldersyde, her ancestral home, because of a "cruel, cruel law that winna let a man leave his hame tae his lassies" but instead entails it upon a male cousin, Hugh Nesbit, who has no affection for the house that she cherishes and from "whom all animals and helpless things shrank."[86] Yet Janet's lot is preferable to that of her friend Mary, whose father "values the pomp of the world above the happiness and well-being of his child" and forces her to marry the domineering Hugh.[87] Left with an annual income of £60, Janet brings up Walter, the fruit of Hugh and Mary's brief and unhappy marriage, and by selling hand-made lace pays down the debts that Hugh has mortgaged on Aldersyde. With the support of Marget, the faithful housekeeper of her Aldersyde days, Janet later adds Netta, the orphaned and impoverished daughter of her younger sister, to the household. Like Oliphant's Margaret Maitland, Janet finds fulfillment in the role of foster mother, even though some feel that "she had missed the chief joy and completeness of womanhood" in devoting herself to the care of others' children.[88] When Walter comes into the inheritance of Aldersyde and marries Netta, Janet feels that "the crown of her life had come to her now in the consecration of her bairns to the service of the Lord, in the building up of the house of her fathers, and in the blossoming of lovely hopes for the future."[89] Not only has she regained a home at Aldersyde, but Janet has also ensured that its new owners and their lineage are morally worthy of their inheritance. Like Margaret Maitland's, Janet's fostering reforms the manners and mores of the gentry, aligning wealth and virtue in the tradition of sentimental fiction reaching back to the eighteenth century.

The resemblances between *Margaret Maitland* and *Aldersyde* are too marked to be coincidental, and Swan acknowledged in her autobiography

---

[84] Oliphant, *Passages*, 240.   [85] Oliphant, *Passages*, 1.

[86] Annie S. Swan, *Aldersyde: A Border Story of Seventy Years Ago* (Edinburgh: Oliphant, Anderson, & Ferrier, 1883), 20, 19.

[87] Swan, *Aldersyde*, 317.   [88] Swan, *Aldersyde*, 317.   [89] Swan, *Aldersyde*, 317.

that her early novels were "frankly modelled on the Border stories of Mrs. Oliphant."[90] But while Swan looked to Oliphant as a literary foster-mother of sorts, Oliphant disavowed any maternal responsibility for Swan. In a review essay published in *Blackwood's Magazine* in 1889, Oliphant dismissed Swan's novels as "cheap," "silly," and "narrow," although she disdainfully allowed them to be "perfectly well adapted, with their mild love-stories and abundant marriages, for the simpler classes, especially of women."[91] Swan was taken aback by what she described as Oliphant's "virulent attack," perhaps because it reflected not just on herself but also on her readership, of whom Swan was very protective and by whom she was deeply beloved. Swan prided herself on knowing how to please readers who spent their days in the stuffy din of a jute mill or cleaning other woman's homes before seeking a harmless escape in the "mild love stories" that Oliphant so condescendingly dismissed. Quite possibly Oliphant belittled Swan precisely because she recognized that the younger woman's stories bore some superficial resemblances to her own and wanted to distance herself from someone who wrote for popular weekly magazines rather than more elite monthlies.

Stylistically, *Margaret Maitland* and *Aldersyde* reflect the different audiences for which the two women wrote, demonstrating that Swan had far too much awareness of her readership to slavishly imitate Oliphant. Episodic and rather sprawling in its structure, *Margaret Maitland* explores the events of a small community through the perspective of a central character. It thus looks back to John Galt's *Annals of the Parish* (1821) and forward to Kailyard novels such as J. M. Barrie's *A Window in Thrums* (1889). Through the garrulous middle-aged narrator that shares her first name, Oliphant softens Galt's pawky humor with a touch of the sentiment that would become the dominant tone of Kailyard fiction. The middle-class Margaret's narrative contains only a sprinkling of Scots – easily recognizable words like "bairns," "aye," and "auld" that would be comprehensible to her Anglo-British readership. Here, as in her other Scottish novels, Oliphant reserves broad Scots for servants and laborers, rendering it as a marker of class difference. In *Aldersyde*, by contrast, the gentle-born Janet somewhat incongruously speaks in the same broad Scots as her housekeeper Marget. The two women share a dialect and a moral equality. As they walk arm-in-arm through the grounds of Aldersyde at the novel's conclusion, Janet remarks, "Eh, wummin, but ye hae been a faithfu' freen

---

[90] Swan, *My Life: An Autobiography*, 40.
[91] Margaret Oliphant, "The Old Saloon," *Blackwood's Magazine* 146 (Aug. 1889): 266.

an' pillar o' strength tae me a' my days!"[92] And indeed, Marget's participation in the upbringing of Janet's foster-children is crucial to the moral
reformation of the gentry. Janet's speech allies her not only with Marget
but with Swan's working-class readership. Similarly, the novel's compact,
linear narrative, in the words of Swan's editor, "enables those who run to
read and understand."[93] It is not intended for leisurely contemplation, in
other words, but for quick ingestion by busy readers.

Oliphant's denigration of Swan's novels in *Blackwood's* reveals that
relations between literary foster-mothers and daughters could be agonistic
as well as affectionate. There would be no strolling arm-in-arm with
"Marget" for Swan, and Jane Findlater's depiction of the hateful Mrs.
Marjorybanks in *The Green Graves of Balgowrie* (1896), to which I will
return in Chapter 3, also suggests a vexed relationship with Oliphant.
While Scotswomen writing in the mid- to late nineteenth century were
very much aware of each other's work, it was perhaps only in the interwar
period that Scottish women writers became visible to readers as a distinct
community. The existence of an active, self-aware community of Scottish
women writers was documented by Marion Lochhead, poet, journalist,
and founder of Scottish PEN, in a series of articles she wrote for the *Scots
Bulletin and Pictorial* during the late 1920s and early 1930s. Each article
featured a living woman writer, providing information that Lochhead
gleaned through the exchange of letters with her subjects.[94] Lochhead's
series was capacious, featuring women working in a range of genres, from
historian Rosaline Masson to poet Marion Angus. It included those who
were well-established figures, such as Anna Buchan and the Findlater
sisters, and those who were then just beginning their literary careers, such
as Dot Allan and Willa Muir. Lochhead's celebration of Scottish women
writers marks the end point of this study, which focuses on the writers
whose lives and works made possible the emergence of this self-
aware community.

Lochhead's series stands as a memorial to tradition that was about to be
lost to literary history. It ran at precisely the historical moment when
writers of the Scottish Renaissance such as Hugh MacDiarmid and Edwin
Muir were advocating a more trenchant Scottish literary nationalism. In
reassessing their nineteenth-century predecessors, they charged Scott's
romances with popularizing sentimental images of Scotland that had

---

[92] Swan, *Aldersyde*, 317.
[93] Andrew Stewart, "Annie S. Swan," *The People's Friend* 1306 (7 Jan. 1895): 4.
[94] The correspondence is held by the National Library of Scotland. See Marion Lochhead, MS 26190.

inhibited the development of a more robust and oppositional Scottish identity. Muir bitterly described Scott and Robert Burns as "sham bards of a sham nation," and accused the former of transforming all of Scottish "history into legend, mainly tawdry."[95] The domestic fiction produced by nineteenth-century Scotswomen presumably did not register as Scottish enough in its subject matter to be worthy of recognition by the almost exclusively male writers of the Scottish Renaissance. At the same time, modernist writers such as Virginia Woolf, James Joyce, and Lewis Grassic Gibbon took the realist novel's exploration of subjectivity to new lengths in their stream-of-consciousness writing. High modernism embraced complexity, originality, and depth as paramount literary values, holding that art and literature ought to challenge and possibly even shock readers rather than comfort and entertain them. Judged by the aesthetic and political standards of the Scottish Renaissance and elite modernism, the body of fiction I discuss in this book was found wanting – neither authentic or nationalist enough for the former nor complex or original enough for the latter.

Between the middle of the nineteenth and the beginning of the twentieth century, Scotswomen participated in creating a literary tradition in which the commodification of literature is not an evil to be lamented, and originality and difficulty are not the highest conceivable artistic values. In fact, the commodification of literature was central to their understanding of the novel's purpose: to bring pleasure to readers. Deidre Shauna Lynch has shown that during the nineteenth century, novel reading, and particularly rereading, acquired a therapeutic function. Her research suggests that readers returned repeatedly to the same novel, as if to an old friend, taking comfort in its familiarity.[96] Scottish women writers understood well the pleasures of the familiar, deftly drawing on oft-used narrative conventions and well-worn character types to retell the "same" story in a somewhat different form and to represent to readers a slightly enhanced version of the mundane domestic life within which their novels were consumed. The commodification of literature, particularly through serialization, permitted Scottish women writers to create variations on their – and their readers' – favorite themes, limited only by the speed with which they could write. Reading these fictions provided the comforts of repetition and the novelty of small departures from the familiar. Moreover, reading was part

[95] Muir, *Scott and Scotland*, 71.
[96] Deidre Shauna Lynch, *Loving Literature: A Cultural History* (Chicago: University of Chicago Press, 2015), 179–92.

of everyday routines: it could be incorporated into the spaces between daily tasks and provided a revitalizing escape from those tasks.

Lynch posits that the professionalization of literary studies has rendered therapeutic reading a dubious practice in the eyes of scholars, leaving "feeling and pleasure without a history."[97] This professionalization has also contributed to the forgetting of the writers I discuss in this book, helping to explain their absence from classrooms, reading lists, conferences, and journals. In exploring their novels, the following chapters also participate in the recovery of a tradition of therapeutic reading, in which books are pastoral entities, offering readers affective comfort.

Paradoxically, given their aim to provide pleasure, Margaret Oliphant, the subject of Chapter 1, and Annie S. Swan, the focus of Chapter 2, represented novel writing in matter-of-fact terms as a form of skilled labor. They joined Scotswomen such as Henrietta Keddie, Isabella Fyvie Mayo, and Lucy Bethia Walford in turning to authorship as an employment, whether because they needed money or because they desired an occupation. Disclaiming any aspirations to literary genius, Oliphant and Swan declared themselves competent craftswomen rather than inspired artists. They found periodical publication particularly congenial to this understanding of literary production because even the most elite magazines, such as *Blackwood's*, could not claim to be high art. Periodicals, by definition, require a steady supply of new writing, and when producing an installment for the next issue, the author of a serialized novel could not wait around for inspiration to strike.

Although practices of anonymous or pseudonymous publication allowed women to disguise the extent of their labors, the justification of literary production as work was not without problems at a time when middle-class women's identity depended very much on privileging domestic duties over remunerative employment. In the pages of *Blackwood's*, Oliphant legitimated her own understanding of novel writing as a skilled craft by tracing it to the endeavors of Walter Scott, who, like Oliphant and many another Victorian woman, wrote to pay off debts. Her novels *The Quiet Heart* (1852), *Harry Muir* (1853) and *Kirsteen* (1889) feature artist figures – painters, writers, and needleworkers – who similarly understand themselves as skilled craftsmen rather than creative geniuses, but who nonetheless take a great deal of pleasure in their work. Through these artist figures, Oliphant feminized the conventions of Scott's romances and demonstrated that writing to a pattern could be a form of art. While

---

[97] Lynch, *Loving Literature*, 12.

rejecting a Romantic and masculine ideal of genius as an isolated and autonomous creative force, Oliphant's best-known novel, *Miss Marjoribanks* (1865), defines feminine genius as an aptitude for the careful management of the details of everyday life. In this novel she explores an aesthetics of the ordinary that her successors would develop into a philosophy of sorts.

Swan too wrote a pattern, as indeed she must have in order to produce two or more novels for serialization each year, in addition to countless short stories and magazine articles. She perfected this pattern through years of practice, with the specific aim of bringing some affordable and harmless pleasure to her working-class readers, among whom her motherly persona made her a celebrity. Unlike Oliphant, the comparatively affluent Swan did not write to support her family, but she too sought to reconcile her prodigious literary output and her extensive public engagements as a celebrity author with a middle-class ideal of domestic femininity that proscribed remunerative employment for women, especially outside the home. Each of her primary venues of publication – the *People's Friend*, the *Woman at Home*, and *The British Weekly* – required her to negotiate the tensions between public authorship and domestic duty differently. In the pages of the *People's Friend* and the *Woman at Home*, Swan served as a mentor to her readers and a model of the domestic femininity she valorized in her fiction. She embodied for these publications' female readers a version of themselves as they wanted to be rather than as they were, appearing in their pages as a literary fairy godmother who offered a temporary escape rather than a magical transformation and dispensed advice and comfort rather than ball gowns and carriages. But by writing under the pseudonym David Lyall for *The British Weekly*, Swan imagined for herself a literary career free from the pressures of feminine propriety.

While Swan aimed to write popular fiction, Scottish women writers also experimented with more elite fin-de-siècle literary movements. Jane and Mary Findlater stand out as Scotland's "female aesthetes," to borrow Talia Schaffer's term.[98] Chapter 3 examines the Findlaters' use of tropes and techniques from aestheticism – impressionistic reveries, abrupt shifts in mood or perspective, and elaborate symbolism – to explore the intellectually and materially circumscribed lives of middle-class women in rural Scotland. The protagonists of novels including *The Green Graves of*

---

[98] Talia Schaffer, *The Forgotten Female Aesthetes: Literary Culture in Late-Victorian England* (Charlottesville: University of Virginia Press, 2000), 64.

Balgowrie (1896), *The Rose of Joy* (1903), and *Crossriggs* (1906) are strong-minded Scotswomen whose struggles for self-realization are hampered by their genteel poverty, the bleakness of their surroundings, and their obligations toward their less competent family members and dependents. These women find temporary liberation from a lifetime of domestic drudgery in the contemplation of beauty, whether they find it in nature, art, literature, or even domestic trivia. The Findlaters propose aestheticism as a form of escape for middle-class Scotswomen much as Swan offered romance as an escape for their working-class counterparts. Yet the Findlaters sometimes published in the same venues as Swan, suggesting that there was less distance between aestheticism and romance or the elite and the popular than we might think.

The end of the nineteenth century saw the proliferation of new varieties of fiction intended for popular consumption, including the adventure story or imperial romance. Whereas Oliphant, Swan, and the Findlaters confined themselves primarily to domestic fiction, Flora Annie Steel and Violet Jacob, the subjects of Chapter 4, participated in the development of the imperial romance. A genre generally preferred by male writers such as H. Rider Haggard, Rudyard Kipling, and Robert Louis Stevenson, the imperial romance is directly descended from Scott's Waverley novels. Like them, it often takes as its protagonist a young man on the cusp of adulthood and dramatizes his loyalties and rivalries as he undertakes a quest to prove his worthiness to other, often older or more powerful, men. Steel and Jacob did not simply imitate the generic conventions developed by Scott, Kipling, Haggard, and Stevenson but instead challenged the romance's cult of manliness. Steel foregrounded women's participation in the adventures of empire-building, critiquing the masculine exclusivity of adventure fiction, but not the imperial ideologies it propagated. In contrast, Jacob's novels take male adventurers as their protagonists but turn the imperial romance's focus on conflict and conquest inward from Britain's overseas empire to its Celtic peripheries, and from physical to psychological struggle. Adventure stories, with their fast-paced action and exotic settings, might seem to offer few opportunities for metacritical reflection. But in explicitly revising Scott's *Waverley*, both Steel, in *On the Face of the Waters* (1894), and Jacob, in *Flemington* (1911), wrote themselves into a Scottish romance tradition, acknowledging the anxieties of influence and the vexed literary heritage they shared with other Scottish women writers.

In their circumscribed circumstances, the Findlaters' protagonists are the antithesis of the female adventurers depicted by Flora Annie Steel, who on occasion venture unaccompanied into the mazes of an Indian bazaar or find themselves the only white woman in a part of the Punjab distant from any British cantonments. Yet Steel and the Findlaters responded in different ways to the same cultural phenomenon: the emergence of the New Woman. The Findlaters, like the better-known New Woman novelist Mona Caird, explored the conditions preventing Scotswomen from cultivating the New Women's intellectual and economic autonomy, specifically indicting the cultural proscription of imaginative creativity in Scotland. Scotland's New Woman, they suggested, must be an artist.

Chapter 5 focuses on O. Douglas and Catherine Carswell, the former of whom has all but disappeared from Scottish literary history and the latter of whom is often hailed as Scotland's foremost female modernist. While Carswell is usually represented as the origin point of a twentieth-century efflorescence of Scottish women's writing that includes works by Willa Muir, Nan Shepherd, Nancy Brysson Morrison, Dot Allan, and Jessie Kesson, to name just a few, I position her as the terminus of the earlier lineage beginning with the works of Oliphant. For despite her groundbreaking reputation, Carswell arguably shares as much in common with her middlebrow Scottish contemporary O. Douglas as with modernists such as Virginia Woolf and Rebecca West.

Like Mary and Jane Findlater's, Douglas's novels reveal and revel in the beauty of everyday life. Their seeming artlessness promotes an aesthetics of the ordinary by asserting the ethical value of mundane forms of beauty – a verdant garden, a becoming hat, a nicely laid table, or an apt metaphor. In *Penny Plain* (1920), *Pink Sugar* (1924), *The Proper Place* (1926), and other novels, Douglas suggests that it is the responsibility of a declining gentry to bring small beauties to a formative Scottish middle class and to teach them how to appreciate the pleasures such ordinary beauty affords. By offering their readers instances of everyday beauty, Douglas's novels participated in this educative process, helping to shape a coherent middle-class Scottish identity. Carswell's *Open the Door!* (1920) and *The Camomile* (1922) eschew the subtle didactic push of Douglas's novels, but they too feature protagonists who feel oppressed by the dreary confines of their middle-class urban lives and who are deeply sensitive to unexpected moments of beauty. Like Oliphant and the Findlaters before her, Carswell takes artists as her protagonists, and their struggles to come to terms with the limitations of their talents perhaps reflect Carswell's own coming to terms with the Victorian literary tradition of which her novels are a part.

The Conclusion very briefly explores the afterlife of the aesthetics of the ordinary in the works of Scottish women writers from Muriel Spark to

Kathleen Jamie, examining both the attractions and the problems that this philosophy continues to pose. The women I discuss in the following chapters turned to the everyday for the raw materials of their literary creations, and as the realm in which the stuff of romance – the extraordinary – is to be found. They robustly affirmed that it is possible, and perhaps necessary, to take pleasure in performing daily tasks and to find beauty in contemplating mundane objects. And they offered up their own novels as examples of the delights of the everyday, not claiming to offer complexity or profundity, but making what is surely a deeply meaningful acknowledgment: that most of us must learn to find our joys in the everyday or else do without. These Scotswomen's novels, then, are as important now as they were on their initial publication. They encourage us to appreciate our own here and now by allowing us to experience someone else's. Indeed, these women insisted that reading – and reading their novels in particular – is the best way to learn to enjoy everyday life. Their novels both describe the pleasures of reading – escape, solace, entertainment, cheer – and provide those pleasures through their sumptuous descriptions of dress and manners, their slyly knowing narrators, their humorous use of type characters, and their satisfying plots. What more could anyone want from a novel, really?

CHAPTER I

Oliphant, Scott, and the Novelist's Trade

The obituary notices announcing Margaret Oliphant's death in 1897 frequently compared Oliphant not to her female contemporaries such as George Eliot, Dinah Craik, or Mary Elizabeth Braddon, but instead to her early nineteenth-century predecessor Walter Scott. The comparison seems to have been suggested neither by the two novelists' Scottish origins nor by their phenomenal productivity, but rather by their abilities as storytellers. In a review of Oliphant's posthumously published autobiography, Meredith Townsend declared that Oliphant's knack for "telling a story . . . makes the only just comparison one with Scott . . . She had so much of Scott's special power in descriptions of nature, in strong situations, and, curiously enough, in depicting individuals of the lower kind."[1] A review in *Blackwood's* written some years earlier made the same point, describing Oliphant "as specifically a story-teller – as Walter Scott and the Homer who wrote the Odyssey were story-tellers." Stylistically, the reviewer continues, Oliphant is "never so slovenly as Scott can be when he likes; but we learn when we read her books, as we do when we read his, that there is something better than style."[2] Through this backhanded compliment, the reviewer suggests that if Oliphant's and Scott's novels occasionally lack the exquisitely nuanced word choices of George Eliot's or Henry James's, they are nonetheless absorbing and entertaining.

Oliphant was only too well aware of her place in nineteenth-century Britain's literary hierarchy. "No one will mention me in the same breath with George Eliot," she gloomily predicted in her posthumously published autobiography. "And that is just. It is a little justification to myself to think how much better off she was. Should I have done better if I had been kept,

---

[1] Meredith Townsend, "Mrs. Oliphant," *The Cornhill Magazine* 79 (June 1899), 778. Obituaries comparing Oliphant to Scott included "Mrs. Oliphant," *The Athenaeum* 3636 (July 3, 1897): 35–6; and "Mrs. Oliphant," *Blackwood's Edinburgh Magazine* 162 (July 1897): 161–64.
[2] "A Little Chat about Mrs. Oliphant," *Blackwood's Edinburgh Magazine* 133 (Jan. 1883): 77.

like her, in a mental greenhouse and taken care of?"[3] George Levine has rightly warned us against taking Oliphant's self-deprecating remarks as an accurate reflection of the merit of her work.[4] They do, however, reveal that she was haunted by the belief that she could have written better novels had she written fewer of them, and she frequently lamented that the necessity of writing for money had prevented her from developing her literary talents to their full extent. With ninety-odd novels and about as many short stories to her name, Oliphant felt deeply the irony of what Pierre Bourdieu, in his account of the inverse relationship between economic and aesthetic value, describes as the "game of loser wins."[5] Oliphant sold far more novels than Eliot simply because she wrote far more. But if she "won" in economic terms, she lost out on the place in the canon of Victorian fiction to which her best novels arguably entitle her.

Although she would dearly have loved to rank with Eliot, Oliphant would surely have been gratified by the obituaries comparing her own writing to that of a man whose works, but even more so whose life, she venerated. For, in Walter Scott, Oliphant found a precedent that legitimated her very pragmatic understanding of authorship and enabled her to preserve a sense of her dignity as a professional novelist, one who made a living by entertaining readers rather than one who sought to convey spiritual truths or create great literature. Scott was an omnipresent influence on Oliphant from the beginning to the end of her career. *Katie Stewart* (1852), the first novel she published in *Blackwood's Edinburgh Magazine*, takes place during the 1745 Jacobite rebellion, featuring a heroine who is as impervious as Edward Waverley was susceptible to the romance of the exiled Stuart monarchy. Elsie Michie, Pam Perkins, and Anne Scriven have shown that *Kirsteen* (1889–90), published in *Macmillan's* almost forty years later, also paid tribute to *Waverley* (1814), although it is arguably more deeply indebted to the female-centered *Heart*

[3] *The Autobiography of Margaret Oliphant*, ed. Elisabeth Jay (Peterborough, Ont.: Broadview, 2002), 50. Oliphant's niece Annie Coghill published a bowdlerized version of this autobiography along with a selection of Oliphant's correspondence shortly after her aunt's death: *Autobiography and Letters of Mrs. Margaret Oliphant*, ed. Mrs. Harry Coghill, introduction by Q. D. Leavis (Leicester: Leicester University Press, 1974). All of my references to Oliphant's autobiography are to Jay's edition unless otherwise noted. In addition to Oliphant's own account of her life, there are several excellent biographies: Vinetta Colby and Robert A. Colby, *The Equivocal Virtue: Mrs. Oliphant and the Victorian Literary Marketplace* (Hamden, CT: Archon Books, 1966); Elisabeth Jay, *Mrs Oliphant: "A Fiction to Herself." A Literary Life* (Oxford: Clarendon, 1995); and Merryn Williams, *Margaret Oliphant: A Critical Biography* (London: Macmillan, 1986).
[4] George Levine, "Reading Margaret Oliphant," *Journal of Victorian Culture* 19.2 (2014): 232–46.
[5] Pierre Bourdieu, *The Field of Cultural Production: Essays on Art and Literature*, ed. Randal Johnson (New York: Columbia University Press, 1993), 39.

of Midlothian (1819).[6] But the personal and professional significance that Scott held for Oliphant is clearest in the numerous essays she wrote about him and in the frequent mention she makes of him in her autobiography. In these works, Oliphant transforms Scott into a prototype of the professional woman writer, looking to his commodification of literature to legitimate her own approach to writing as a skilled trade.

In adapting Scott's biography for her own ends, Oliphant also revised previous accounts of his life. The most famous of these, John Gibson Lockhart's *Life of Scott* (1837–8), depicted the Magician of the North as something of a paradox – a congenial family man and an inspired literary genius, a gentleman and a child of nature. By contrast, Thomas Carlyle, in a lengthy and scathing review of Lockhart's *Life* for the *Westminster Review*, represented Scott as a hack who churned out novel after novel to pay his bills. Carlyle's assessment troubled Oliphant because she admired Carlyle almost as much as she did Scott. Perhaps, too, Carlyle's criticisms hit close to home. In any case, Oliphant "admitted with astonishment and regret" that Carlyle "has failed to appreciate Sir Walter. We cannot tell why, nor pretend to solve that amazing question."[7] Oliphant and Carlyle saw similar characteristics embodied in Scott, but they valued these characteristics very differently. Where Carlyle lamented the mechanization of art by a well-meaning philistine, Oliphant lauded Scott for transforming authorship into a skilled trade and novels into commodities that could be produced in finite quantities by artisanal authors. She suggested that in doing so, Scott had opened up the way for women like herself to make a living by writing.

Oliphant's revision of previous narratives of Scott's life began with an essay published in *Blackwood's* in August of 1871, the centenary of Scott's birth, in which she explored his popular appeal. She arrived at a verdict similar to the one that appeared so repeatedly in her own obituaries, namely, that Scott was an entertaining storyteller rather than a refined stylist or profound thinker. For all of Wordsworth's talk of writing in the language of common men, Oliphant argued, Scott's poetry is much more authentic and less artificial. Wordsworth's poetry is like the Thames, a

---

[6] Pamela Perkins, "'We who have been bred upon Sir Walter': Margaret Oliphant, Sir Walter Scott, and Women's Literary History," *English Studies in Canada* 30.2 (2004): 90–104; Anne Scriven, "Introduction," in *Kirsteen: The Story of a Scotch Family Seventy Years Ago*, ed. Anne M. Scriven (Glasgow: Association for Scottish Literary Studies, 2010), 6–15; Elsie Michie, "History after Waterloo: Margaret Oliphant Reads Walter Scott," *ELH* 80.3 (2013): 897–916.
[7] Margaret Oliphant, *Royal Edinburgh: Her Saints, Kings, Prophets and Poets* (London: Macmillan, 1890), 470.

"well-trained, useful, majestic stream, which carries trade and wealth into the very bosom of the land."[8] By contrast, Scott's poetry is like a "wayward" mountain stream, "rushing against its rocks with wreaths and dashing clouds of spray … flowing on strongly, brightly, picturesquely, charming all eyes that look upon it, and delighting all hearts."[9] The tradition of representing Scottish poetry as natural and spontaneous dates back at least to the publication of James Macpherson's *Ossian* in 1760, but it is rather unusual to find Scott situated in this tradition of primitive poets, which more often includes Robert Burns and James Hogg. The natural spontaneity of Scott's verse, in Oliphant's view, accounts for its outstanding popularity. Wordsworth, she observes, spoke in his poetry to "a small class of people able to appreciate the loftier flights of poetry."[10] Scott, meanwhile, was "ever and at all times a minstrel and nothing more": he "took up his harp and sang" for "the "myriads who were too busy, too joyous, too sick and sorrowful, too hardworking and worn with care, to have any power to enter in the depths or ascend to the heights of that divine philosophy which speaks in music."[11] In contrast to Carlyle, who declared that Scott's poetry was suited only to "harmlessly amusing indolent languid men," Oliphant finds nothing ignoble in writing simply to entertain an audience.[12] On the contrary, she suggests that one of literature's highest ends is to give pleasure, to provide a temporary respite from "the flatness of [our] own particular lives," as Scott's "thrilling tales" do.[13]

In her *Autobiography*, Oliphant represents herself as, if not primitive, then untutored, a writer by nature rather than by education. Describing her novels as "perfectly artless art," she repeatedly positions herself as an unsuspecting consumer of her own fiction, as if she were surprised and entertained by the turns her stories took.[14] Oliphant explains that she began writing her first novel merely "to secure some amusement and occupation" while attending her mother during a prolonged illness.[15] Rather than regarding her novels with authorial detachment as aesthetic objects, she explains, "I wrote as I read, with much the same sort of feeling."[16] In other words, she was as emotionally invested in her fiction as she hoped her readers would be as they waited to find out what would

---

[8] Margaret Oliphant, "A Century of Great Poets, from 1750 Downwards: No. II Sir Walter Scott," *Blackwood's Edinburgh Magazine* 110 (Aug. 1871): 237.
[9] Oliphant, "Great Poets," 237.   [10] Oliphant, "Great Poets," 240.
[11] Oliphant, "Great Poets," 237, 240.
[12] Thomas Carlyle, "Memoirs of the Life of Scott," *Westminster Review* 6 (Jan. 1838): 334.
[13] Oliphant, "Great Poets," 241.   [14] Oliphant, *Autobiography*, 149.
[15] Oliphant, *Autobiography*, 60.   [16] Oliphant, *Autobiography*, 164.

happen in the next issue of *Blackwood's* or *Macmillan's*. Indeed, she preferred sending her serial stories to her editors at *Blackwood's* in install-ments rather than as a completed manuscript because "it seems to succeed better that what is read bit by bit should be written the same way. One looks more carefully to one's points, and by dint of requiring to keep up one's own interest, has a better chance of keeping up the reader's."[17] Yet her declarations of spontaneity and authenticity founder a little when she concludes, "I have written because it gave me pleasure, because it came natural to me, because it was like talking or breathing, besides the big fact that it was necessary for me to work for my children."[18] Writing for Oliphant may have been as natural and unpremeditated as breathing, but it was also her way of earning a living. Any natural inclinations coexisted with a businesslike approach that did not permit her to wait for inspiration to strike or to linger long over sentences.

Smarting under persistent criticisms of what Elisabeth Jay describes as her "businesslike attitude to the literary trade,"[19] Oliphant found in Scott a legitimating precedent: an author who wrote for a living and who regarded novel writing as a means to an end rather than an end in itself. If the education of her sons was the end for which Oliphant wrote, the building of Abbotsford and then the repayment of his debts were the aims of Scott's labors. Oliphant's review for *Blackwood's* of *The Letters of Walter Scott* in 1894 has very little to say about Scott's writing, focusing instead on his love affair with Abbotsford, where she imagines him "dropping his acorns into the ground, dreaming of his woods to come."[20] Scott's literary productivity enabled him to surmount financial ruin in the late 1820s, when the market crash left him owing over £100,000 to various credi-tors.[21] Rather than declare bankruptcy, the mere idea of which offended his sense of honor, Scott set up a trust deed and paid off his debts gradually from the sales of his works, writing with greater speed than ever before. Scott's efforts "to preserve the dear home which had so long been the delight of his heart" may have recalled to Oliphant her equally prodigious attempts to hold together her much more humble home.[22] Widowed at the age of thirty-one, Oliphant repaid her late husband's debts and singlehandedly supported her children and several nieces and nephews, while also contributing to the upkeep of her lackadaisical older brothers.

[17] Coghill, ed., *Letters*, 179.   [18] Oliphant, *Autobiography*, 48.   [19] Jay, *Mrs. Oliphant*, 278.
[20] Margaret Oliphant, Review of *The Letters of Walter Scott*, *Blackwood's Edinburgh Magazine* 155 (Jan. 1894): 20.
[21] See Eric Quayle, *The Ruin of Sir Walter Scott* (London: Rupert Hart-Davis, 1968).
[22] Oliphant, "Great Poets," 256.

She acknowledged in a letter to Isabella Blackwood, "My money is almost always spent before I get it, or received only just in time for pressing necessities, so that the pleasant sensation of feeling even three months clear before me is one which very rarely occurs."[23] Her debts were smaller than Scott's, but so were her earnings, topping out at £1,500 from *Blackwood's* for *The Perpetual Curate* (1863), one of the Chronicles of Carlingford. Because Oliphant often did not know when or how much she would be paid for her work, she wrote incessantly to meet her financial obligations.[24] However, with several novels appearing simultaneously or proximately in different formats and venues, she was frequently in danger of undercutting the value of her own work by overproduction. And she knew that quantity meant the sacrifice of quality, lamenting, "I must resign myself to do second-class work all my life from lack of time to do myself full justice."[25] In short, Oliphant felt that economics and aesthetics were at odds. Because she wrote for money, she could not produce great literature.

In Scott, Oliphant saw a novelist who had managed to reconcile aesthetics and economics to some to degree, one who had written for money while still managing to write well. Scott's own anxieties about being known to write for money may have contributed to his decision to publish his novels under a series of pseudonyms, beginning with "the Author of Waverley." However, he is perhaps less likely to have worried that writing for money might compromise the artistic integrity of his work than that it might undermine his claims to gentility. In choosing not to declare bankruptcy, Oliphant observed, Scott subjected himself to another form of dishonor, "the degradation which, in the public eye, attends the author who works for his bread."[26] By the time Lockhart wrote his biography, it was no secret that Scott's authorial "ambitions were worldly."[27] Scott's delight in "worldly things, wealth among others," was for Lockhart at the root of his achievements; for without "the perpetual spur of pecuniary demands, he who began life with such quick appetites for all its ordinary enjoyments would never have devoted himself to the rearing of that gigantic monument of genius, labour, and power, which his works now constitute."[28] Lockhart held that Scott's need for money was an incidental incentive to the creation of works of great artistic integrity. By contrast,

[23] Coghill, ed. *Letters*, 237.
[24] For an account of Oliphant's financial struggles, see Colby and Colby, *The Equivocal Virtue*, 142–75.
[25] Oliphant to John Blackwood in Coghill, ed., *Letters*, 238.   [26] Oliphant, "Great Poets," 256.
[27] John Gibson Lockhart, *The Life of Sir Walter Scott* (London: J. M. Dent, 1912), 485.
[28] Lockhart, *Life*, 485, 497.

when Carlyle accused Scott of "writing daily with the ardour of a steam-engine, that he might make £15,000 a-year and buy upholstery with it," he implied that the Waverley novels were mere formula fiction, machine-made commodities.[29] For Carlyle, Scott's economic motives for writing divested his creations of artistic integrity. Scott's betrayal of literature's spiritual purpose definitively demonstrated for Carlyle his "vulgar worldinesses," his enjoyment of material pleasures over the life of the mind.[30]

Where Lockhart excused and Carlyle condemned Scott's transformation of authorship into a trade, Oliphant praised Scott's ability to write himself out of debt. But she stopped well short of Carlyle's machine metaphor, instead figuring Scott as a trained craftsman or artisan. She remarks that although he was a gentleman, "Scott laboured at the highest mental work as if it had been weaving or carpentering, only with energy ten-fold greater than is ever employed at the bench or the loom."[31] The distinction between mechanized and skilled labor is an important one at this historical juncture, when industrialization increased the value of handicrafts. As Talia Schaffer explains, "the craft paradigm offered a ... culturally enshrined alternative to commodity culture and industrial capitalism."[32] An artisan or skilled craftsman makes a limited number of goods that, although they may be similar, are not identical. These handicrafts differ, on the one hand, from machine-made commodities, which are identical and depersonalized, and, on the other hand, from the work of art, which is unique and seems to transcend the workings of the marketplace. While an artist must wait for inspiration to strike, an artisan can make the objects of their trade on demand. Scott, as a skilled craftsman, achieved what was for Oliphant an acceptable compromise between economics and aesthetics.

Significantly, Oliphant construed Scott's heroic repayment of his debts, rather than his novels and poems, as his highest accomplishment, declaring that "the greatest works of his genius pale before this work of his life."[33] Oliphant values "work" in the sense of toil or labor over the literary work as an object of enduring aesthetic value – the work of genius. She transforms the financially ruined Scott into the questing hero of his own romance when she writes that "never was battle against the most chivalrous of foes on the noblest field more splendidly fought than this dark and desperate battle against the modern demons whose grip is ruin, and whose

[29] Carlyle, "Memoirs," 334.   [30] Carlyle, "Memoirs," 301.
[31] Oliphant, "Great Poets," 243–4.
[32] Talia Schaffer, *Novel Craft: Victorian Domestic Handicraft and Nineteenth-Century Fiction* (New York: Oxford University Press, 2011), 10.
[33] Oliphant, "Great Poets," 256.

conquest gives no fame."[34] Like Carlyle, Oliphant saw Scott as a flawed man rather than a literary deity, but his failures only endeared him to her more: "in the face of every misfortune, broken in health, in hope, in power, a lonely man where he had been the centre of every joy in life, an enchanter with his magic wand broken and his witchery gone – then, and only then, does Scott attain his highest greatness."[35] Divested of his "magic wand," Scott, the great Magician of the North, resembles the many nineteenth-century women like Oliphant who took up authorship to make a living.

Oliphant returned repeatedly to Scott's example to reflect on her position as a professional author in the Victorian literary marketplace. But their positions were not identical, for although Scott may have felt that writing novels was incompatible with his position as Clerk of the Court of Session, Oliphant knew that her claims to middle-class femininity were incompatible with working for money, or, at the very least, with working outside the home. To work because of financial necessity was to endanger this middle-class status; to work for other reasons was to beg the question why. In addressing this issue, Oliphant employed a feminized version of the discourse of craftmanship that she used to describe Scott's work as a novelist, comparing her writing to the making of domestic handicrafts. Schaffer explains that domestic handicrafts "made women's separate-sphere virtues visible . . . [and] testified to the woman's skills in management, thrift, industry, and ornamental talent."[36] The creation of high art took women away from family life, and so was seen as selfish, while domestic handicrafts "added to the comforts of the home."[37]

Oliphant's autobiography consistently emphasizes the workaday nature of her writing, and its compatibility with her other domestic duties. For instance, she recalls sitting "at the corner of the family table with my writing-book, with everything going on as if I had been making a shirt instead of writing a book."[38] Compared with the fancy work with which some middle-class Victorian women passed the time, making a shirt is a relatively utilitarian and rule-governed occupation, requiring little creativity. Most shirts look a lot like other shirts, and, as Oliphant tacitly acknowledged, approaching authorship as a trade rather than an art meant that her novels too tended to resemble each other to a certain extent. She wrote to a pattern but could also embellish and individualize her creations.

---

[34] Oliphant, "Great Poets," 256.   [35] Oliphant, *Royal Edinburgh*, 479.
[36] Schaffer, *Novel Craft*, 5.   [37] Schaffer, *Novel Craft*, 33.   [38] Oliphant, *Autobiography*, 66.

Oliphant did not enjoy the luxury of a room of her own in which to write, and she capitalized on this fact to reconcile her career with middle-class ideals of domestic femininity even as she lamented that it had prevented her from achieving her full potential as an author.

Oliphant departed from her preferred metaphor of writing as domestic handicraft after the death of her adult son Cyril in 1890 left her with only one living child, Frances, who would die four years later. Always desperate for money, Oliphant returned to her work almost immediately after Cyril's death, relating in her autobiography that she wrote

> steadily, a chapter a day, I suppose about twenty pages of an octavo book. Sir Walter when he was labouring to pay off his debts, speaks of writing a volume in twelve days I think. I have done it steadily in sixteen.... I am a wonder to myself, a sort of machine, so little out of order, able to endure all things, always fit for work whatever has happened to me.[39]

If, according to Carlyle, Scott wrote "with the ardour of a steam engine," Oliphant has become the engine itself, mechanically producing ever more writing regardless of life's vicissitudes. Yet Oliphant accords herself little of the heroism that she attributed to Scott, owning that "the product is very different indeed – and the object so small beside his grand big magnificent struggle – this is for butter upon the daily bread – and little debts which I hope to have cleared."[40] Neither her novels nor her needs were as great as Scott's; nevertheless, she took comfort in his example. Oliphant's description of herself in this singular instance as "a sort of machine" highlights the distinctions between mechanized and artisanal creation – one dehumanized and dehumanizing, the other skillfully bringing personal creative touches to an everyday domestic object.

Oliphant's obsessive concern with the relationship between aesthetic and economic value was not limited to her autobiographical reflections on her own writing but is also a constant theme of her fiction. Her novels are full of both working women and artists of various sorts. Some of Oliphant's novels, such as *The Melvilles* (1852) and *Hester* (1883), feature women who are the primary support of their family, at once caretakers and wage-earners, and who are saddled with ineffectual or downright troublesome men, as was Oliphant herself. An alcoholic brother, an absent father, a loving but thoughtless husband, and two underachieving sons left Oliphant with a poor opinion of male competency. Other novels, such as *Miss Marjoribanks* (1865–6) and *Phoebe, Junior* (1876), take as their

---

[39] Oliphant, *Autobiography*, 96.   [40] Oliphant, *Autobiography*, 96.

protagonists middle-class women who do not need to work for money, but whose talents and intellect require an occupation beyond the daily running of the household. These novels humorously celebrate what Elisabeth Langland calls the "managerial woman," whose influence extends beyond the home through her ability to unobtrusively shape the actions and opinions of men.[41] Still others, such as *The Three Brothers* (1869), *At His Gates* (1872), and *Mr. Sandford* (1888), feature characters – men and women – who are artists by profession, or who engage in artistic forms of labor – painting, writing novels, or even embroidery – to support themselves or their families.

Oliphant's concern with the connection between aesthetic and economic value runs through her lesser-known novels, particularly those I call her Scottish romances, and her better-known forays into domestic realism, the Chronicles of Carlingford. This commonality suggests that Oliphant's relationship to Scottish culture was more complex than her biographers Robert and Vinetta Colby have suggested. She did not merely exploit "her native land as marketable literary material," although twenty-six of her novels are set primarily in Scotland or feature Scottish protagonists.[42] Oliphant's obsessive concern with the aesthetic and economic value of her own writing suggests that she, like the other writers in this study, was influenced by nineteenth-century Scotland's Presbyterian capitalist ethos, with its suspicion of ornamental decoration and imaginative creativity, on the one hand, and its valorization of industriousness, on the other.[43] Art has value for Oliphant in part *because* it is created through work.

Oliphant's belief in the psychologically and morally redemptive value of work recalls Thomas Carlyle's *Sartor Resartus*, which poses work as an antidote to despair, or the spiritual crisis of the Everlasting No: "Whatsoever thy hand findeth to do, do it with thy whole might. Work while it is called To-day, for the Night cometh wherein no man can work."[44] On realizing the spiritual value of work, Teufelsdrockh chooses

---

[41] Elizabeth Langland, *Nobody's Angels: Middle-Class Women and Domestic Ideology in Victorian Culture* (Ithaca, NY: Cornell University Press, 1995), 148–81.

[42] Robert Colby and Vinetta Colby, "Mrs. Oliphant's Scotland: The Romance of Reality," in *Nineteenth-Century Scottish Fiction*, ed. Ian Campbell (New York: Barnes & Noble, 1979), 89.

[43] Oliphant's autobiography reveals that, in Merryn Williams's words, she "passionately identified with the Free Church" at the time of the Great Disruption, which occurred when she was fifteen, and which features in some of her early novels. See Williams, *Margaret Oliphant*, 6; and Jay, *Mrs. Oliphant*, 143–51.

[44] Thomas Carlyle, *Sartor Resartus*, ed. Kerry McSweeney and Peter Sabor (Oxford: Oxford University Press, 2008), 149.

a pen as his "wonder-working Tool" and turns to the task of writing, recognizing that through words, "man, thereby divine, can create as by a *Fiat.*"[45] For Carlyle, however, the "omnipotence" of "the WORD" and of words renders writing an "Art, which whoso will may sacrilegiously degrade into a handicraft."[46] While Oliphant shared Carlyle's beliefs that work gives spiritual meaning to human existence, and that writing was a form of work, she knew herself guilty of this sacrilege. The literary marketplace, she felt, needed handicrafts as much as masterpieces.

As the following discussion of *The Quiet Heart* (1853) and *Miss Marjoribanks* (1866) illustrates, female artists in Oliphant's novels function much like the figure of Walter Scott, allowing her to reflect metafictively on the aesthetic and economic value of her work In the first of these novels, Oliphant argues for the superiority of skilled craftmanship to inspired genius as source of artistic production and defines the realist aesthetic that she would perfect in the Chronicles of Carlingford. Whereas *The Quiet Heart* privileges the domestic handicraft over the work of genius, *Miss Marjoribanks* transforms domestic management into an art form for which its protagonist demonstrates a special genius.

"Artless Art" in *The Quiet Heart* and *Miss Marjoribanks*

Oliphant regarded authorship as a skilled trade well before her husband's death required her to support her family entirely through her literary labors, and well before she wrote her 1871 commemorative essay for the centenary of Scott's birth. *The Quiet Heart* (1853), one of her earliest novels to be serialized in *Blackwood's*, reveals that from the very beginning of her career, she denied the necessity of genius to the successful novelist. This novel also indicates the centrality of the periodical press to her understanding of novel writing as a craft rather than art. Serialization shaped Oliphant's writing practices as much as it did her audience's reading habits.[47] *The Quiet Heart* challenges the Romantic myth of autonomous masculine genius by taking as its protagonist a female artist skilled in portraiture. Drawing was not only a traditional female accomplishment that could be transformed into a source of income; it was also a mimetic art form through which Oliphant could reflect on her own

---

[45] Carlyle, *Sartor Resartus*, 150, 151.   [46] Carlyle, *Sartor Resartus*, 151.

[47] On the impact of serialization practices on writers and readers, see Linda K. Hughes and Michael Lund, *The Victorian Serial* (Charlottesville: University of Virginia Press, 1991); and Laurel Brake, *Print in Transition, 1850–1910: Studies in Media and Book History* (Houndmills, Basingstoke: Palgrave, 2001).

aesthetic aims as a novelist. *The Quiet Heart* embodies a more sentimental form of realism than *Miss Marjoribanks*, which is generally considered among Oliphant's best novels, and which is particularly celebrated for its irony. Yet despite its marked difference in tone, *Miss Marjoribanks* is not as far removed in its concerns from *The Quiet Heart* as it might at first seem to be. It too features an artistic heroine, albeit one whose talents lie in what might be called domestic design, for which, we learn, Lucilla Marjoribanks has a "genius." Whereas Oliphant reflects on her own aesthetic aims through Menie Laurie's drawings, she explores social value of women's artistry through Lucilla Marjoribanks's domestic design.

The Quiet Heart pits artistic genius against skilled craftsmanship in the characters of Randall Home and Johnnie Lithgow – two Scots who have recently moved from a small village near Dumfries to London. Randall, who has just published a stunning first novel, is lionized by the public and regarded by all his friends and family back in Scotland as an "ideal genius."[48] Johnnie is initially employed as a compositor setting type on a printing press, but he is soon "writing [for] the paper he once printed" and attracting "fame and notice" for "his popular articles" (74). When Menie Laurie, who is engaged to marry Randall, asks him if Johnnie is now "a great writer," he answers ambiguously, "Johnnie Lithgow is quite a popular man, Menie – one of the oracles of the press." But he is "only a literary workman after all. He does his literature as his day's labour – he will tell you so himself – a mere craft for daily bread" (121). By Randall's manner of speaking, Menie can tell that to be popular is a "derogation" (121), although she doesn't fully understand why this should be so. Johnnie, for his part, sustains the myth of Randall's genius, admitting,

> I do my day's work ... thanking God that it is very sufficient for the needs of the day; but between Randall and myself there is no comparison. I deal with common topics, common manners, common events, like any other laboring man. But Randall is an artist of the loftiest class. What he does is for the generations to come, no less than for today. (273)

Johnnie regards writing for the press as very little different from typesetting in that both are skilled trades, or crafts that can be learned. The necessity of producing copy for the next issue of the paper requires Johnnie to take a more businesslike attitude toward writing than Randall does. Randall's great genius unfortunately prevents him from beginning work on another

---

[48] [Margaret Oliphant], *The Quiet Heart*, by the Author of "Katie Stewart," 2nd ed. (Edinburgh: William Blackwood, 1854), 73. Subsequent references to this edition will be made parenthetically.

novel, as he is paralyzed by the fear that his second attempt will not be as well received as the first. By contrast, Johnnie "who had no fame to lose . . . did an honest day's work in every day" and soon saves up enough money to marry his sweetheart (139). Johnnie's pragmatic approach is more productive than Randall's, even if what it produces is of lesser quality.

When Randall's increasing contemptuousness toward his "simple Menie" eventually compels her to break off their engagement, she turns to portraiture to support herself and her mother. Menie approaches drawing much as Johnnie does writing, asserting that "this shall be my trade" (202). While Mrs. Laurie is concerned that working for money will undermine Menie's claims to gentility, Menie needs an occupation to fill the void left by her broken engagement even more than she and her mother need money. And so, the narrator relates, drawing was "exalted from the young lady's accomplishment to the artist's labour" as Menie "worked at this which she harshly called her trade with great zeal and perseverance" (253). Within five years she is earning enough to purchase "little comforts and elegancies" for the small cottage where she and her mother live (300). Moreover, "constant occupation has restored health and ease to Menie's mind," so that she feels "soberly, happily contented" with her lot (300). Having attained financial and intellectual independence, Menie is granted the concluding marriage that many of Oliphant's hard-working heroines are denied or voluntarily reject, as a reformed and repentant Randall returns to Scotland to seek her hand.

Critics have seen in *The Quiet Heart* a fictionalized version of Oliphant's marriage to an artist whose unrealized dreams of greatness she supported through her literary toil.[49] Undoubtedly, these autobiographical resemblances exist, but perhaps more interesting are the self-reflective insights that *The Quiet Heart* offers into Oliphant's sense of her own artistic aims as a writer. For instance, when young Jessie sits for her portrait, the child is impressed that Menie "just looks at me . . . no a thing mair. Just looks, and puts it down like writing on a sclate" (264). This comparison between drawing and writing emphasizes the mimetic nature of Menie's portraits; she records rather than creates. The resulting portrait of Jessie is, according to the narrator, "not a very fine picture; the execution is a woman's execution, very likely no great thing in the way your critics judge; but one can see how very like it is, looking at these little simple features – one could see it was still more like, looking into the child's sweet generous heart" (265). Naomi Schor has shown that women's art has long been

---

[49] See Jay, *Mrs. Oliphant*, 251–2, 260–2.

dismissed as "mere" copying rather than original creation.[50] Oliphant subscribes to this critical tradition, equating "a woman's execution" with the realistic reproduction of detail, but she also implies that such naïve reproduction at the very least entails a kind of artistic authenticity, as superficial details inadvertently reveal hidden depths. Menie's drawings are authentic in that they are faithful both to life and to her own feelings, and in that they are spontaneous creations rather than the product of prolonged planning.

Menie's inability to separate herself completely from her art is a testament to her drawings' lack of artifice – perhaps, indeed, their lack of artistry. When Randall comes across a portfolio of her drawings, they reveal to him, without any intention on Menie's part, that she still loves him. The authenticity of Menie's drawings, their embodiment of her feelings, is at once a weakness and a strength, for while it precludes them from attaining the transcendence proper to works of genius, it also enhances their appeal to viewers, giving them a popularity that Randall's more heavily revised work lacks. For, in contrast to Menie's spontaneity, Randall "lingered a long time polishing and elaborating, and retouching his second book, expecting, no doubt, a universal acclamation," but producing instead "a dead failure" (279). Barbara Onslow's analysis of the essays that Oliphant wrote about art for *Blackwood's Magazine* suggests that, for Oliphant, "the value of art lay in its impact upon people" and in its "cohesive social function."[51] Menie's simple portraits perform this function in its most literal sense, enabling Randall and Menie to mend their broken engagement.

Menie's drawings bring pleasure to those who see them because they are true to life and produced by a skilled observer but are nonetheless spontaneous rather than overthought or overwrought. The same might be said of Oliphant's best novels. But *The Quiet Heart* is unlikely to be counted among these because of its sentimentalism. A degree of sentimentalism infects all of Oliphant's novels about Scotland, and the earlier ones more than the later ones. This sentimentalism was perhaps the coloring of expatriate nostalgia, reflecting Oliphant's affection for her childhood home, but regardless of the reason, Oliphant seems to have associated Scotland with the kind of emotional authenticity that animates Menie's

---

[50] Naomi Schor, *Reading in Detail: Aesthetics and the Feminine*, 2nd ed. (London: Routledge, 2007), 1–15.

[51] Barbara Onslow, "'Humble comments for the ignorant': Margaret Oliphant's Criticism of Art and Society," *Victorian Periodicals Review* 31.1 (1998): 60.

drawings. Thus she praised in extravagant terms the "extraordinary literal truth" of J. M. Barrie's depiction of Scottish domesticity in *A Window in Thrums* (1889) – describing as "full of the highest restrained emotions, love, trust, and sublime faith" scenes that later critics would deride as unbearably sentimental.[52] By contrast, the novels that critics have singled out as Oliphant's best, the Chronicles of Carlingford, are notable for their irony rather than their sentimentalism. Indeed, Elsie Michie describes the tone of the Chronicles of Carlingford as decisively "antiromantic" and "antisentimental."[53] The sentimental clichés that the narrator voices in *The Quiet Heart* become the object of mockery in *Miss Marjoribanks*. For instance, Oliphant pokes quiet fun at the eponymous heroine for processing her mother's death through the lens of *Friends in Council*, a work "brimful of the best sentiments" and a special favorite of her teachers the Misses Blounts.[54] The strong association between Scotland and sentiment in Oliphant's work suggests that what Joseph O'Mealy praised as "the sustained artistry of Oliphant's ironic technique"[55] in *Miss Marjoribanks* and the other Chronicles of Carlingford might have its roots in her position as an outsider to the insular English community that these novels depict.

Miss Marjoribanks pays tribute to another representation of insular English community, *Emma* (1815), which Oliphant considered the best of Jane Austen's novels.[56] Like Emma, Lucilla Marjoribanks is a young woman seeking scope for her considerable creative energies in a limited social sphere. More than in its premise, though *Miss Marjoribanks* pays tribute to *Emma* by emulating Austen's achievement in making "commonplace events into things more interesting than passion."[57] Oliphant admired Austen because she, and to a lesser extent Susan Ferrier and Maria

---

[52] "The Old Saloon," *Blackwood's Magazine* (August 1889), 264. For an analysis of Oliphant's review of *A Window in Thrums*, see Andrew Nash, *Kailyard and Scottish Literature* (London: Brill, 2007), 17–22.

[53] Elsie B. Michie, *The Vulgar Question of Money: Heiresses, Materialism, and the Novel of Manners from Jane Austen to Henry James* (Baltimore, MD: Johns Hopkins University Press, 2011), 147.

[54] Margaret Oliphant, *The Selected Works of Margaret Oliphant*, vol. 17: *Miss Marjoribanks*, ed. Joseph Bristow (London: Routledge, 2014), 7. Subsequent references to this edition will be made parenthetically.

[55] Joseph H. O'Mealy, "Mrs Oliphant, *Miss Marjoribanks*, and the Victorian Canon," *Victorian Newsletter* 82 (1992): 49.

[56] For extended comparisons of *Miss Marjoribanks* and *Emma*, see Amy Robinson, "Margaret Oliphant's *Miss Marjoribanks*: A Victorian *Emma*," *Persuasions* 30 (2008): 67–76; and June Sturrock, "*Emma* in the 1860s: Austen, Yonge, Oliphant, Eliot," *Women's Writing* 17.2 (2010): 324–42.

[57] Margaret Oliphant, *The Literary History of England in the End of the Eighteenth and the Beginning of the Nineteenth Century*, 3 vols. (London: Macmillan, 1897), 3: 171.

Edgeworth, represented "life, not in its extraordinary accidents, but in the most common phases of every day."[58] Through its mock-heroic tone *Miss Marjoribanks* explores the import of the commonplace, at once acknowledging the limitations of the "common phases of [the] every day" as the realm in which Lucilla exercises her artistic talents and recognizing the momentous importance of mundane happenings to the inhabitants of Carlingford.

A number of readers have remarked on the mock-heroic register through which Oliphant represents Lucilla's activities. By describing Lucilla as a "young revolutionary" (40) or as one of the "great generals or heroes of romance" (29), Oliphant emphasizes the disjunction between Lucilla's abilities as a leader or manager and the scope to which she must limit their use.[59] Less frequently noted is that Lucilla is also an artist of sorts, specializing in what Emily Blair terms "domestic artistry, or the elevation of what we might call 'homemaking' into an art form."[60] Lucilla's talents as a "managerial woman" and as a domestic artist are closely linked. When she returns to Carlingford after completing her schooling and spending a year on the Continent, Lucilla's aims are at twofold: to "be a comfort to poor papa" (58) and to "revolutionise society in Carlingford" (16) – a revolution that commences with "new paper, [and] new curtains" in the drawing-room (43). The first of these aims is one of the sentimental clichés in which Lucilla specializes, and which she rolls out whenever it helps to justify actions that others might find questionable in an unmarried young woman – such as the wholesale redecoration of her father's drawing-room. To call this redecoration a "revolution" might seem hyperbolic, but in peaceful Grange Lane, where the wealthier inhabitants of Carlingford live, Lucilla's return is an event of great moment, and her redecoration of the drawing-room does in fact mark the beginning of a new social order. The revolutionary hyperbole extends to the state of affairs before Lucilla's arrival, which, we learn, "were

---

[58] Oliphant, *Literary History*, 3: 206.

[59] See, for instance, Monica Cohen, "Maximizing Oliphant: Begging the Question and the Politics of Satire," in *Victorian Women Writers and the Woman Question*, ed. Nicola Diane Thompson (New York: Cambridge University Press, 1999), 102; Margaret Homans, *Royal Representations: Queen Victoria and British Culture, 1837–1866* (Chicago: University of Chicago Press, 1998), 77; O'Mealy, "Victorian Canon," 48; Melissa Schaub, "Queen of the Air or Constitutional Monarch?: Idealism, Irony, and Narrative Power in *Miss Marjoribanks*," *Nineteenth-Century Literature* 55.2 (2000): 196; Andrea Kaston Tange, "Redesigning Femininity: Miss Marjoribanks Drawing Room of Opportunity," *Victorian Literature and Culture* 36 (2008): 174.

[60] Emily Blair, *Virginia Woolf and the Nineteenth-Century Domestic Novel* (Albany: State University of New York Press, 2007), 162.

in an utterly chaotic state at the period when this record commences," as "there was nothing which could be properly called a centre in the entire town" (20). While the denizens of Carlingford evidently had managed to cope without such a center for years before Lucilla's Thursday evenings established one, her accomplishment is nonetheless considerable. It is no less than to make "a harmonious whole out of the scraps and fragments of society" or to consolidate a social elite among the town's inhabitants, with herself at its head (21). Lucilla succeeds in this task, Elisabeth Langland and Susan Zlotnick have argued, by modeling exclusive standards of taste as "a moral and aesthetic predisposition" that distinguishes between the vulgar and the refined.[61] Under Lucilla's reign, to wear a high-necked white dress becomes in Carlingford a sign of good taste – a marker of socioeconomic, moral, and aesthetic distinction.

Rather than writing novels or drawing portraits, Lucilla's "grand design" as an artist is to combine the "chaotic elements of society in Carlingford into one grand unity" (122). She values others for the qualities they bring to her composition and "contemplates with the eye of an artist the young men of Grange Lane who were her raw material" (110). In this, she resembles Rose Lake, an aspiring artist and teacher at Carlingford's School for Design, who regards the inhabitants of Grange Lane as "raw material" for her art in much the same terms as Lucilla does, observing that they "were all good subjects more or less" (112). As Zlotnick remarks, Rose and Lucilla are both "aesthetic missionaries or tastemakers," but Rose reveals Lucilla's self-interestedness through her own "genuine commitment to art." Lucilla wants to be seen as having good taste because it consolidates her social status, whereas Rose dedicates herself selflessly through her teaching to cultivating "the aesthetic tastes of the nation."[62] Rose's naïve belief that artists "have a rank of our own" and transcend social distinctions cannot withstand Lucilla's appropriation of aesthetic discourses to enforce such distinctions (114).

Nonetheless, Lucilla's endeavors demand some self-sacrifice. To establish a social elite in Carlingford, with herself at its head, Lucilla must privilege "her great work" – that is, the success of her gatherings – over "her personal sentiments," a feat that, the narrator notes sardonically, "is generally considered next to impossible for a woman" (79). She seeks to promote the pleasure of her guests even when this requires her to downplay her own talents, as, for instance, when she persuades Barbara Lake to

[61] Langland, *Nobody's Angels*, 168; Susan Zlotnick, "Passing for Real: Class and Mimicry in *Miss Marjoribanks*," *Victorian Review* 38.1 (2012): 174.
[62] Zlotnick, "Passing for Real," 186–7.

sing with her. Lucilla's willingness to join her own fine voice with Barbara's equally impressive contralto rather than singing alone is, according to the narrator, a "sacrifice ... a weaker woman would have been incapable of making" (34). Indeed, the sacrifice arguably loses her a proposal of marriage from Mr. Cavendish, who becomes besotted with Barbara, but the poor taste revealed by his preference suggests that he would not have suited Lucilla anyway.

While Rose may be a more disinterested artist than Lucilla, Oliphant suggests that Lucilla's domestic artistry may be fundamentally more valuable than the fine arts that Rose and Barbara practice. On visiting the Lakes' house in Grove Street, Lucilla silently disdains Barbara's uselessness, feeling that "to be sure, the possession of a fine contralto (which is, at the same time, not fine enough to be made use of professionally) is not a matter of sufficient moment in this world to excuse a young woman for not knowing how to give her father a comfortable cup of tea" (194). It is not simply that Barbara fails to fulfill her filial duty here but that she fails to recognize the aesthetic potential of the ordinary, or to elevate the mundane into the artistic. Lucilla maintains her position at the head of Carlingford's elite in large part by administering to the comforts of others and by making sure her guests enjoy themselves. She recognizes that the aesthetic pleasures of a high-necked white gown, an impressive contralto, or a carefully lit garden in the late summer are not very far removed from the bodily comforts of a well-made cup of tea or the expensive dinners for which Dr. Marjoribanks is renowned. And the cup of tea is arguably more important than Barbara's beautiful contralto because it is more integral to everyday life.

Oliphant attributes Lucilla's domestic artistry to a kind of "genius," a term that she denies other female artist figures in her fiction. Yet her repeated references to Lucilla's "genius" in *Miss Marjoribanks* suggest that the term means little more than instinct or natural inclination. It certainly does not describe a creative power that transcends social context or the forces of the marketplace, as it does in *The Quiet Heart*. After the first of her Thursday evening gatherings, for instance, Mrs. Chiley declares to Lucilla, "I never realized before what it was to have a genius. You should be very thankful to Providence for giving you such gifts. I have given dinners all my life ... but I never could come up to anything like that" (49). The effect of Lucilla's genius is a kind of social harmony, the resolving of all the parts of her social gathering into a unified whole. Her inclinations, which have been honed through the reading of etiquette books, domestic manuals, and tracts on political economy, are evidently reliable. For, as the narrator explains, "what people took for the cleverest calculation" in

Lucilla's social successes "was in reality a succession of happy instincts, by means of which, with the sovereignty of true genius, Miss Marjoribanks managed to please everybody by having her own way" (89). So, for example, when Lucilla's instincts tell her Mr. Ashburton is the "right man" to become the new MP for Carlingford, she manages to persuade others that this so by attributing the sentiment to them and disclaiming any understanding of politics herself. Her "genius" lies in pleasing others, so that they do not realize how far she is extending the reach of her own influence. Effecting a reconciliation between the Archdeacon and Mr. Cavendish so that the former can marry the widowed Mrs. Mortimer is one of Lucilla's greatest challenges, but there, too,

> the difficulties were only such as stimulated her genius; and then it was not any selfish advantage, but the good of her neighbour in its most sublime manifestation – the good of her neighbour who had injured her, and been insensible to her attractions, which, according to the world in general, is the one thing unpardonable to a woman – which Lucilla sought. (171)

As it turns out, Lucilla's relinquishment of both Cavendish's and the Archdeacon's attentions is a relatively insignificant hardship, as she prefers her cousin Tom Marjoribanks all along. But the mock-heroic language of self-sacrifice again serves to emphasize the purported ends of Lucilla's efforts: to promote the happiness of others. Oliphant further divorces the term "genius" from any sort of autonomous creative power when we learn that Tom will make a good husband for Lucilla because he has "a perfect genius for carrying out a suggestion," which is to say that his inclination is to do what Lucilla tells him to (367).

The effect of describing Lucilla's social and political interventions in aesthetic terms is to bring them within the realm of feminine propriety. But the aestheticization of her projects becomes more difficult toward the end of the novel. The second "fytte" of *Miss Marjoribanks* (247) – a term that, as Melissa Schaub observes, positions her as the questing hero of romance – invites us to pity Lucilla as we see her world narrowing with the want of opportunities to exert her creative talents.[63] After spending ten years as a "comfort to dear papa," Lucilla has arrived at the moment when the "female intelligence, not having the natural resource of a nursery and a husband to manage, turns inwards, and begins to 'make a protest' against the existing order of society, and to call the world to account for giving it no due occupation – and to consume itself" (290). When Lucilla's

[63] Schaub, "Queen of the Air," 208.

involvement in Mr. Ashburton's campaign is disrupted by her father's death, her sphere of influence seems likely to narrow even further, as she must renounce her Thursday evening gatherings. A proposal of marriage from her cousin Tom happily supplies "a new sphere … where her influence might be of untold advantage, as Lucilla modestly said, to her fellow creatures" in the nearby estate of Marchbank, which Tom purchases, at Lucilla's suggestion, so that she can occupy herself in improving Marchbank village and its inhabitants, both of which badly need to be taken in hand (361). Tom Marjoribanks, too, will require careful management if he is to extend Lucilla's sphere of influence as she hopes by eventually winning a seat in Parliament. Lucilla envisions "a parish saved, a village reformed, a country organized, and a triumphant election at the end, the recompense and crown of all, which should put the government of the country itself, to a certain extent, into competent hands" (368). To pose these possibilities as a matter of "influence" resolves social reform into an aesthetic project, and given that Lucilla has been less successful in managing Rose and Barbara Lake, the lowly denizens of Grove Street, than she has the more class-conscious inhabitants of Grange Lane, it is questionable whether it will be as easy as she believes to effect this reform. But with this problem projected safely beyond the novel's end, Oliphant invites us to celebrate Miss Marjoribanks's triumphant acquisition of a broader sphere in which to exercise her genius.

Still widely recognized as one of Oliphant's best novels, *Miss Marjoribanks* was a touchstone for later Scottish women writers as different as Anna Buchan, Jane Findlater, and Muriel Spark. It articulated an aesthetics of the ordinary, the idea that a well-made cup of tea could bring as much pleasure, if not more, than fine art. It affirmed the vast importance that seemingly mundane events occupy in the lives of most people. And it represented social and political reform in terms of aesthetics, as questions of taste. But despite its influence on her successors, *Miss Marjoribanks* was not one of the novels through which Oliphant defined her own relationship to Scottish literary tradition. Indeed, much of the humor of *Miss Marjoribanks*, and perhaps too some of the bitterness or coldness that critics have detected in its tone, stems from Oliphant's position as an outsider, mimicking the tradition of the provincial English novel as exemplified by Austen, Trollope, or Eliot.[64] By contrast,

[64] On the novel's "chilling tone," see Colby and Colby, *The Equivocal Virtue*, 63–4; and Williams, *Margaret Oliphant*, 81.

Oliphant's Scottish romances, in which she revises the masculine tropes of Scott's novels, share the sentimental warmth of *The Quiet Heart*.

Stitching up Romance in *Harry Muir* and *Kirsteen*

Written thirty-five years apart, *Harry Muir; A Story of Scottish Life* (1853) and *Kirsteen: The Story of a Scotch Family Seventy Years Ago* exemplify Oliphant's indebtedness to Scott's Waverley novels and illustrate the tendency she shared with her literary hero to represent Scotland through the lens of romance. Pam Perkins and Anne M. Scriven have read *Kirsteen* as a loose rewriting of *Waverley*, in both its historical distance from the time of its setting – approximately two generations – and its inversion of the cultural estrangement experienced by Edward Waverley during his journey north into the Highlands.[65] *Kirsteen*'s subtitle, *The Story of a Scotch Family Seventy Years Ago*, echoes the subtitle of *Waverley; or, 'Tis Sixty Years Since*, and its setting during the Napoleonic Wars encompasses the publication of *Waverley* in 1814, which the dressmaker Miss Jean reads aloud to a group of rapt seamstresses that includes Kirsteen. Arguably, though, *Kirsteen* is more deeply reminiscent of Scott's *Heart of Midlothian* than of *Waverley*, as Kirsteen's solitary journey to London and the sacrifices she makes on behalf of her wayward sister recall the quiet courage of Jeanie Deans. Yet more immediately than either *Waverley* or *The Heart of Midlothian*, *Kirsteen* is a rewriting of Oliphant's own earlier novel *Harry Muir*, which, in turn, revises Scott's *Bridal of Triermain*. By taking Scott's works as intertexts, *Harry Muir* and *Kirsteen* challenge Scott's redefinition of romance as a masculine genre. Romance, for Scott, was a narrative of familial and national origins,[66] and in the Waverley novels, the protagonist's heroic deeds help to restore political order and secure the patrilinear transmission of property. *Harry Muir* and *Kirsteen* represent women's labor, and particularly their artistic labor, as a form of chivalric heroism that sustains the transmission of property between men. Not only are the heroines of these novels excluded from the patriarchal socioeconomic system that their work underwrites, but they are also denied marriage, the conventional culmination of female maturation and the Waverley hero's reward. While Martha Muir finds satisfaction in her role as a

---

[65] Pamela Perkins, "'We who have been bred upon Sir Walter'"; and Scriven, "Introduction."

[66] See Walter Scott, "Essay on Romance," in *The Miscellaneous Prose Works of Sir Walter Scott, Bart.* Volvol. 6 (Edinburgh: Cadell, 1827), 153–256.

foster-mother to her siblings, Kirsteen finds meaning primarily in her work as an artist.

In *Harry Muir* and *Kirsteen*, Oliphant displaces questions about the economic and aesthetic value of literary production onto needlework, which, like novel writing, was a distinctly feminized form of cultural production. In fact, needlework is literally a form of writing in these novels, where embroidered words and letters are keys to the plot. In *Harry Muir*, the lawyer Cuthbert Charteris finds the clue that restores their patrimony to the Muir family in an old sampler on which the name "Rose Allender" is stitched. When questioned about the sampler, Rose Muir acknowledges that "there is not much art in it," but explains that she values it for the sake of the grandmother who stitched it and after whom she is named.[67] Although its aesthetic value is minimal, the sampler turns out to have great economic, as well as sentimental, value when it reveals Harry Muir to be the missing heir of Allenders. Like the sampler, an embroidered handkerchief in *Kirsteen* also conveys more than it seems to. Kirsteen pretends that the handkerchief on which she embroiders the initials R.D., using her hair as thread, is for her brother Robbie Douglas to take to India, but, in fact, it is a gift for her beloved Ronald Drummond and serves as a token of their secret betrothal. When Drummond is killed in India, the handkerchief is found next to his heart, and the newspaper report describing the initials embroidered on it in red-gold hair confirms for Kirsteen that her suitor is dead. The meaning of these embroidered texts exceeds the superficially apparent, even when, as in Oliphant's novels, there is "not much art" in them.

Needlework, as Carole Shiner Wilson explains, was in the nineteenth century "the site of intense debates" concerning the propriety not only of women's "artistic and political expression" but also of their employment within and beyond the home.[68] Seamstresses, milliners, and other needle-workers blurred the boundaries between feminine pastime and employment, transforming domestic tasks into paid work. For Oliphant,

---

[67] Margaret Oliphant, *Harry Muir; A Story of Scottish Life* (New York: Appleton, 1853), 1: 143. Subsequent references to this edition will be made parenthetically.

[68] Carol Shiner Wilson, "Lost Needles, Tangled Thread: Stitchery, Domesticity, and the Artistic Enterprise in Barbauld, Edgeworth, Taylor, and Lamb," in *Revisioning Romanticism: British Women Writers, 1776–1837*, ed. Carol Shiner Wilson (Philadelphia: University of Pennsylvania Press, 1994), 169. See also Rozsika Parker, *The Subversive Stitch: Embroidery and the Making of the Feminine* (London: Women's Press, 1984). On the professionalization of domestic work, see Mary Poovey, *Uneven Developments: The Ideological Work of Gender in Mid-Victorian Britain* (London: Virago, 1989); and Monica Cohen, *Professional Domesticity in the Victorian Novel: Women, Work, and Home* (Cambridge: Cambridge University Press, 1998).

needlework constituted a particularly useful analogy for literary production in that it was a skilled trade, the products of which embodied varying degrees of artistry. If, in *The Quiet Heart*, Oliphant sought to justify female artistry by representing it as a form of work, in *Harry Muir* and *Kirsteen*, she justifies women working for money by representing their labor as a form of art.

The extensive descriptions of needlework in these novels indicate Oliphant's attentiveness to the socioeconomic implications of women's remunerative labor. Well aware that working for money was generally incompatible with middle-class ideals of femininity, she emphasized both the artistry and domesticity of needlework in order to assert her protagonists' claims to gentility. The various forms of needlework described in *Harry Muir* distinguish among the social standing of its characters. Martha and Rose Muir turn to needlework to supplement the meager salary of their brother Harry, who is clerk to a prosperous merchant in Glasgow. By opening "the collars and cuffs and handkerchiefs of richer women," Martha and Rose transform embroidery, ordinarily the pastime of leisured, well-to-do women, into a source of income (1: 38). "Opening," Oliphant explains, requires "filling up the centre of … embroidered flowers with delicate open-work in a variety of 'stiches' innumerable. Very expert, and very industrious workers at this could, in busy times, earn as much as ten weekly shillings" (1: 38). Martha and Rose's skill at this fine embroidery reflects their genteel social origins, which are revealed to them only when Harry is discovered to be the heir to Allender Place. Even before this revelation, however, it is obvious that the Muir sisters are more refined than Aggie Rodgers, who lives beneath them in a tenement building and earns money by attaching elaborately embroidered collars and cuffs to factory-made dresses. The ground floor of the tenement building houses a small shop, on the stoop of which Maggie McGillivray often sits, "'clipping,' with a web of tamboured muslin on her knee and scissors in her hand" (1: 66–7). Oliphant explains clipping as "another feminine craft peculiar to the 'west country,' where many young girls, of a class inferior to the workers of embroidery and spinning, are employed to clip the loose threads from webs of worked muslin" (1: 66). Her use of footnotes to explain these forms of needlework recalls the heavily footnoted Magnum Opus edition of the Waverley novels and suggests that they might be as unfamiliar to Oliphant's readers as the heraldry or obscure customs that Scott sought to explain to his. The type of "craft" in which women are employed signifies their class status, yet all of these forms of needlework can be done at home, in the domestic sphere to which women supposedly belonged by nature. Unlike the mill work through which many Glaswegian women would have earned a living in the nineteenth century, needlework allows women to support themselves without endangering their feminine purity.

Needlework in *Harry Muir* is a source of female community, and scenes of sewing feature in the novel as aesthetic set-pieces or tableaus. The Muirs' tenement building is a symphony of sewing and song. On the top floor, as Rose and Martha work at their embroidery, their younger sister Violet "poured forth page after page of the Bridal of Triermain" (1: 111). Downstairs, Aggie Rodgers "stayed her needle in mid-course while she accompanied the Ro-o-se of A-ah-allandale" (1: 112), and on the stoop outside, Maggie McGillivray sings Robert Burns's "The Lea Rig," "with a gay flourish of her shears accompanying ... every verse" (1: 111). The scene emphasizes the commonality of these women's lot, as they are all engaged in forms of needlework to support themselves and their families, so that the tenement has become a domestic factory of sorts. There is no romance in their unremitting toil, but they find it instead in the stories and songs of courtship that accompany their work and that reflect their social standing. Walter Scott's *Bridal of Triermain* (1813), a chivalric romance, indicates the Muir sisters' refined literary taste, whereas "The Lea Rig" describes a lovers' tryst with Burns's typical bawdiness. "The Rose of Allendale" describes a suitor's fidelity to his beloved and foreshadows Cuthbert Charteris's prolonged courtship of Rose Muir, who, upon Harry's inheritance, becomes Rose Allender.

Oliphant depicts a second scene of female community in Ayrshire, where the lawyer Charteris, looking for clues that might link the Muir family to the estate of Allenders, finds himself in a large garden filled with

> apple-trees in full blossom, and a bright congregation of all the flowers of spring ... homely produce ... climbing plants, roses and honey-suckles, which, in a month or two would be as bright and fragrant as now they were green ... But the animate parts of the picture were still more remarkable ... a number of girls, from fourteen to twenty, working the Ayrshire work as it is called – to wit, the fine embroideries on muslin, which the Muirs "opened." (1: 173–4).

In this scene, women's needlework is rendered natural, a visibly "animate" part of the garden's luxurious growth. The surrounding beauty alleviates the monotony of the girls' work, much as song does in the earlier scene. The two set-pieces reveal the magnitude of work that goes into making garments for the wealthy, as the embroidery begun by the Ayrshire girls will be "opened" and completed by more skilled needleworkers such as the

Muirs. Oliphant shows how the textile industries for which the west of Scotland was renowned in the nineteenth century are supported by a network of women woven together by the threads of their shared work.

In *Kirsteen*, needlework similarly registers socioeconomic status and artistic sensibility. Dressmaking, the trade adopted by Kirsteen, "constituted the higher end of female employment with the needle" in the nineteenth century, according to Beth Harris.[69] Nonetheless, it is a significant step down in the world for the daughter of a Highland laird, no matter how poor her family might be. Long before she considers dressmaking as a trade, Kirsteen is known to be "accomplished with her needle according to the formula of that day," but sewing is just part of the drudgery of her life at home in Drumcarro, where she and her sisters are regarded as "handmaids who might be useful about the house, but who had no future, no capabilities of advancing the family, creatures altogether of no account."[70] Although the laird of Drumcarro treats Kirsteen and her sisters little better than the slaves on his West Indian plantation, she shares her father's pride in the Douglas name and his "concern with the aggrandizement of his family" (84). On joining Miss Jean Brown's dress-making establishment in London, she chooses to go by the name "Miss Kirsteen" rather than "Miss Douglas," explaining, "I think no shame of my work, but I will not put my father's name in it, for he is old-fashioned, and he would think shame" (194). Kirsteen flees to London to avoid a forced marriage to a man she does not love but whose wealth her father covets. Although her father treats her as chattel he can sell in order to shore up his property, Kirsteen remains loyal to the patriarchal system that dehumanizes her, and is determined to avoid degrading the name of Douglas.

While class and gender cannot be entirely disaggregated in Victorian debates about women's work, Kirsteen is certainly much more concerned that pursuing a trade might seem degrade her rank than that it might seem to sully her feminine purity. When Kirsteen declares that she wants to "make my fortune if I can," Miss Jean warns her, "that's all very well in a lad – and there's just quantities of them goes into the city without a penny and comes out like nabobs in their carriages – but not women, my dear, let alone young lassies like you" (188). The story of the Scottish "lad o'

---

[69] Beth Harris, "Introduction," in *Famine and Fashion: Needlewomen in the Nineteenth Century*, ed. Beth Harris (Burlington, VT: Ashgate, 2005), 4. See also Arlene Young, "Workers' Compensation: (Needle)Work and Ideals of Femininity in Margaret Oliphant's *Kirsteen*," in ibid., 41–51.

[70] Margaret Oliphant, *Kirsteen; The Story of a Scotch Family Seventy Years Ago*, ed. Anne M. Scriven (Glasgow: Association for Scottish Literary Studies, 2010), 71, 55. Subsequent references to this edition will be made parenthetically.

pairts" who goes to London or abroad to the colonies to make his fortune was a common one, but in envisioning a "lass o' pairts," Oliphant, as Linda Peterson has observed, revises the typical trajectory of the female bildungsroman.[71]

Dressmaking is a marginally acceptable trade for Oliphant's proud protagonist only because it requires taste, or the refined artistic sensibility that distinguishes the well-born woman from those who have "have money and nothing else" (250). Kirsteen is first introduced to the idea that dressmaking could be considered an art by Miss Macnab, the only dress-maker in the "wilds of Argyllshire" (21). When Miss Macnab remarks to Kirsteen that dressmaking, "is just like a' the airts I ever heard tell of, a kind of epitome of life," Kirsteen is confused, for she "knew very little of any art, but thought it meant painting pictures" (78). She initially looks down on Miss Macnab as a mere tradeswoman, who, although she is descended from a good family, must work for a living. But as she watches the dressmaker at work on a simple muslin gown, Kirsteen is impressed by her "devotion to her art," recognizing that "it was as terrible to her as a mistake on the field of battle to a general, to send forth into the world a gown that did not fit, a pucker or twist in any garment she made" (77). Miss Macnab's attention to the smallest details elevates dressmaking from a trade into an art and "an epitome of life," in which attention to details also matters. "Take a' the trouble ye can at the beginning," Miss Macnab advises, "and the end will come right of itsel'" (78). Her advice underlies Kirsteen's success in London as a dressmaker and a businesswoman. Despite her businesslike approach to her trade, Kirsteen also brings to the designing of dresses "much of the genuine enjoyment which attends an artist in all crafts, and liked to handle and drape the pretty materials and to adapt them to this and that pretty wearer, as a painter likes to arrange and study the more subtle harmonies of light and shade" (197). Kirsteen's artistic sensibilities, like Lucilla Marjoribanks's, manifest themselves in her ability to harmonize parts into a whole, and her keen awareness of what is fitting (here literally) to a given individual or situation. These sensibilities elevate her above other seamstresses, and she "soon developed a true genius for her craft" (196). As in *Miss Marjoribanks*, Oliphant understands "genius" as an aptitude or inclination that can be cultivated and improved.

---

[71] Linda Peterson, "The Female *Bildungsroman*: Tradition and Subversion in Oliphant's Fiction," in *Margaret Oliphant: Critical Essays on a Gentle Subversive*, ed. D. J. Trela (Selinsgrove, PA: Susquehanna University Press, 1995), 66–79.

Kirsteen's aesthetic tastes reflect her birth and breeding, but they are honed through the practice of her art.

Harry Muir revises Scott's romances by taking as its chivalric hero a woman who performs great feats of economy through her work. Although its title suggests otherwise, the real protagonist of the novel is Harry's eldest sister, Martha. It is Martha's self-sacrifices, as foster-mother to her brother and younger sisters, that lift the family above poverty and rescue its reputation. By shouldering the family's economic burdens, moreover, Martha leaves Rose free to marry and Violet to pursue a literary career. Harry, with his "weak and yielding" mind, and "the rapidly-changing projects which he took up and threw down as toys of a day" (3: 181), is frequently "led away" – the euphemism the Muir women use to refer to his episodes of drunkenness. Accordingly, Martha has long been "the support, the guardian, the protector" of the family, the roles Harry might be expected to fulfill (2: 74). When he inherits Allenders, Martha is silently reluctant to exchange her tacit position as head of the household for that of "Harry's dependent sister" (2: 74–5). "Labouring for Harry . . . seemed to Martha a thing so natural as never to disturb her everyday life for a moment," as she is inured to self-sacrifice, but the prospect of relying on Harry to run the economic concerns of the household "required a stronger exertion" (2: 72). When Harry dies unexpectedly after falling from his horse, he leaves Allenders mortgaged for thousands of pounds of debt, and with its tenants' livelihoods disrupted by half-completed improvement projects. In the course of rehabilitating the estate, Martha also repairs Harry's reputation by repeatedly affirming to his creditors and tenants that she is only carrying out his intentions: "Gradually, these people came to look upon him with a visionary reverence – this spirit of the dead whose intentions lived in a will so strong and unvarying; and his own weakness passed away, and was forgotten, in the strength which placed itself like a monument, upon his grave" (3: 261–2). Like the managerial women of the Chronicles of Carlingford, who quietly exert their sway over their menfolk, Martha cloaks her own ambitions in the shroud of Harry's authority. She will run the estate until Harry's infant son comes of age but is happy to let Harry take posthumous credit for her endeavors.

Martha Muir's heroic undertakings to rescue Allenders from debt recalls Oliphant's claim that the "great work" of Scott's life was not his novels but his repayment of his debts. In her own life and her fiction, Oliphant insisted that women too were capable of such great work. In *Harry Muir*, she represents the economic and artistic maturation of Violet, the youngest of the Muir sisters, through the language of romance, describing her dreams of contributing to the support of the family as a form of chivalric endeavor. Violet, who recites *The Bridal of Triermain* while her sisters are busy with their embroidery, has read all of Scott's works by the age of eleven, and is fascinated by tales of chivalry and romance. When Harry inherits Allenders, Violet is quick to rewrite the family's history as a romance, declaring their new home "an enchanted castle" and casting Rose as "the princess" and the lawyer Mr. Charteris as "the knight" (2: 53). She is delighted to find that the old retainer of Allenders goes by the name of Dragon because of his fiery temper, as he too can be incorporated into her romance narrative.

In the legend of the Lady's Well, which Dragon recounts for Violet, *Harry Muir* again recalls *The Bridal of Triermain* in its depiction of a disappointed and abandoned woman. The Lady's Well was a favorite haunt of an earlier Violet, the daughter of one of the Lords of Allender, who came "ilka day" to sit by the spring and make "ballants and sangs out of her ain head" (2: 249–50). When her heart was broken by the dissolute conduct of her betrothed, Lord Harry, Lady Violet dressed herself in her wedding gown, set out for the well, and was never seen again. Lady Violet's disappointment in the feckless Lord Harry prefigures Violet's displeasure with her brother Harry, who is similarly dissolute and unreliable. And further like her aristocratic ancestor, Violet turns out to have poetic gifts. When Harry's death leaves the family impoverished, she is "chivalrously determined to win, by some unknown means, a fortune and fame for her sisters, far better than Harry's" (2: 76). She fashions the story of the Lady's Well into a ballad that is published in a magazine, much to her sisters' pride and astonishment. Like Scott, whose works she so loves, Violet takes traditional lore and transforms it into literature. Instead of viewing women merely as the objects of chivalry, she claims the right to tell her own tales of chivalry, and through her "gracious, womanly, beautiful triumph," she perpetuates her family's "fame and honour" (3: 309). By positioning women as chivalric heroes, striving to recoup their family's fortune, *Harry Muir* reclaims and feminizes the traditionally masculine genre of romance, and it does so while paying tribute to the great romancer, Scott.

Like *Harry Muir*, *Kirsteen* reveals the patrilinear transmission of property that in Scott's novels ensures national stability to rest on women's self-sacrificial labor. But this later novel is not so much a feminizing revision as it is a cynical rejection of Scott's chivalric romances. Although *Kirsteen* is effectively disowned by her father after she runs away to London to avoid the marriage he has arranged for her, she nonetheless uses the money she earns as a dressmaker to buy back some of the land that the Douglas family lost after "the disastrous conclusion of the Forty-Five" (54). Kirsteen's father had attempted to recoup the family's fortunes by working as an overseer on a plantation in Jamaica, where, despite his "dogged and fierce determination," he gained only "enough to buy a corner of his old inheritance, the little Highland estate and bare house of Drumcarro" (54). Soured by his experiences in the West Indies, Drumcarro returns to Argyle "a fierce, high-tempered, arbitrary man, by no means unworthy of the title of 'auld slave-driver,' so unanimously bestowed upon him by his neighbors" (54) and proceeds to treat his "feeble" wife and his "useless" daughters as if they too were slaves (54, 56). He looks to his sons to redeem the rest of the family's former estate and considers a "lass" with "siller at her command" to be an indication that "everything in this country is turned upside down" (382). Kirsteen, who has always dreamed of being "a help to everyone that bore her name" (190), purchases her family's former land "on terms that would cripple her for years" (384). Yet even this sacrifice does not atone in her family's eyes for the crime of adopting what her father calls a "dirty trade" (382), and she remains an unwelcome "visitor in the house she had redeemed" (385).

Kirsteen is denied the marriage with which the female bildungsroman usually concludes, and with which Scott rewards Jeanie Deans after her long trek to London to secure a pardon for her sister. Kirsteen is not only deprived of the consolations of domestic affection, but is also excluded from the historical life of the nation, the sphere in which her brothers, her suitor Ronald, and Scott's questing heroes find purpose and meaning. Kirsteen's double exclusion constitutes a rejection rather than a rewriting of romance. Oliphant reminds readers of the importance of marriage in Scott's chivalric romances when Miss Jean reads *Waverley* aloud to her seamstresses, who are accustomed to listening to didactic tales about "Ellen as an example of youthful indiscretion, or Emily as a victim of parental cruelty" (258). Their primary interest in *Waverley* is the marriage plot; for although the seamstresses "were greatly stirred by the Highland scenes and Fergus MacIver's [*sic*] castle … nothing in it was so important to the imaginations of the workwoman" as whether Edward would marry Flora or Rose (258). "This was not the chief point of interest in the book perhaps," the narrator acknowledges, "but these young women regarded it from that point of view" (259). Oliphant takes care to emphasize that the seamstresses are not poor interpreters. Rather, as Elsie Michie observes, "Oliphant shows that *Waverley* provided a narrative that taught readers to experience both history and fiction as romance" and to expect the narrative trajectory of both to move "toward a liberatory or redemptive end."[72] This ending entails not just the resolution of military conflict and the restoration of political order, but also marriage, which rewards the hero and heroine for the trials they have endured. While the seamstresses look forward to marriage as their "redemptive end," Ronald's death robs Kirsteen of this "liberatory" conclusion to her life's story.

The scene in which Miss Jean reads *Waverley* to the seamstresses should remind Oliphant's readers that they too are reading a historical novel, one set at the time of *Waverley*'s publication, toward the end of the Napoleonic Wars. Yet history, understood as large-scale military and political events, is always happening somewhere else in *Kirsteen* – Spain, Portugal, Belgium, India, wherever British troops are stationed. As each of Kirsteen's brothers comes of age, he is sent to join a regiment and enter into this history, "with good blood and plenty of pride and no money, the Quentin Durwards of the early nineteenth century" (26). But the women who remain at home, including Kirsteen and her sisters, experience time as circular rather than linear: there is always the "dinner to think of, and the clean clothes to be put into the drawers, and the stockings to darn" (44). The narrator remarks, "Nothing accordingly could exceed the dullness, the monotony of their lives, with no future, no occupation, except their work as almost servants in their father's house, no hope even of those vicissitudes of youth which sometimes in a moment change a young maiden's life" (58). Kirsteen and her sisters cannot expect to escape from the cyclical repetitions of domestic time into the linear time of history, as their brothers do. Indeed, the political and military events of their day are accessible to them only in mediated form through letters and newspapers; as the narrator reminds us, "In those days there was no thought of the constant communications we have now, no weekly mails, no rapid courses overland, no telegraph for an emergency. When a young man went away he went for good – away – every trace of him obliterated as if he had not been" (38). This passage implies that by the late nineteenth century, the time of *Kirsteen*'s publication, advances in communications technology had made history more accessible to women, even those living far from urban centers. Oliphant's readers had been brought, if not into history, at least much closer to it. The utter isolation that Kirsteen and her sisters experience is for these readers the stuff of fiction.

---

[72] Elsie Michie, "History after Waterloo," 898.

Oliphant suggests that women's virtual exclusion from the historical life of the nation might account for the importance that marriage holds in their narrative imagination, and for the seamstresses' shared obsession with Edward Waverley's marriage prospects. This exclusion has shaped Kirsteen's vision of her own future. When she promised to marry Ronald on his return from India, she understood that this might mean

> waiting for interminable years – waiting without a glimpse or a word. Nor did this depress her spirits: rather it gave a more elevating ideal form to the visionary bond. All romance was in it, all the poetry of life. He would be as if he were dead to her for years and years. Silence would fall between them like the grave. And yet all the time she would be waiting for him and he would be coming to her. (39)

Kirsteen's fortitude in Ronald's absence is her own form of heroism, her sacrifice for the national good in a time of war. Envisioning her life as a romance, she has believed that her long wait would ultimately be rewarded with marriage to the man she loves; for this end, she has disobeyed her father's wishes and left home and family forever. The news of Drummond's death radically alters the genre of her life story, as the narrator remarks, "And thus life was over for Kirsteen; and life began. No longer a preparatory chapter, a thing to be given up when the happy moment came.... The worst had happened to her that could happen. No postscriptal life of new love was possible to her" (278). If Kirsteen has understood her life thus far as a "preparatory chapter," full of trials she must endure before she and Ronald can marry, his death forces her to acknowledge that she will never achieve this happy ending. She is left without a narrative pattern through which to interpret her life experiences.

In drawing attention to the new formlessness of Kirsteen's life, Oliphant highlights the originality of her novel's form – a female bildungsroman in which work rather than marriage gives meaning to the protagonist's experiences. Whereas *Harry Muir* feminizes romance, *Kirsteen* marginalizes it, much as it marginalizes history. This symmetry should be unsurprising, if, as Ian Duncan suggests, "romance and history name either side of a common border, the site of narrative experience."[73] Duncan has shown that the exclusion of romance from history is often expressed through the "topos of the domestic idyll," or through the family estate understood as "a domestic space set apart from public life, from politics, and ... from

---

[73] Ian Duncan, *Modern Romance and Transformations of the Novel: The Gothic, Scott, Dickens* (Cambridge: Cambridge University Press, 1992), 60.

historical process."[74] Thus *Waverley*'s protagonist escapes from the dangers of war, which he has shown himself less than capable of navigating, to join Rose Bradwardine at the rehabilitated estate of Tully Veolan; in *The Heart of Midlothian*, Jeanie Deans retires with Reuben Butler to a lodge on the Duke of Argyle's estate of Roseneath after successfully seeking a pardon for her sister. For Kirsteen, no such consolation is available; not only does she reject the idea of a "postscriptal" love after Ronald's death, but she is also virtually excluded from the family estate of Drumcarro, shunned by her relations, and written out of the Douglas lineage.

If romance and history are both marginalized in *Kirsteen*'s narrative, what remains are the repetitive cycles of everyday life, the substance of which is work – whether that entails her domestic duties as foster-mother, "the stand-by for the whole house" at Drumcarro in her youth (303), or "the activity and occupations" of dressmaking after her flight to London (210). Work is "congenial" to Kirsteen's "energetic and capable spirit," and although it is not the destiny she had imagined for herself, it gives her life meaning. After years spent cultivating her skills as a dressmaker in a successful partnership with Miss Jean, Kirsteen retires to "one of the most imposing houses, in one of the princeliest squares of Edinburgh," where "her hospitality was almost boundless, her large house running over with hordes of nephews and nieces, her advice, which meant her help, continually demanded from one side or other of a large and widely extended family. No one could be more cheerful, more full of interest in all that went on" (385). Beyond her family, Kirsteen is known "as the friend of the poor and struggling" and takes pleasure in the "activity and occupation" that helping others provides. Oliphant reflected in her autobiography that, thanks to her early widowhood, she had enjoyed a broader range of experience than many of her contemporary female novelists and had learned "to feel that the love between men and women, the marrying and giving in marriage, occupy in fact so small a portion of either existence or thought."[75] Her most interesting heroines either do not marry at all, like Kirsteen, or, like Lucilla in *Miss Majoribanks,* approach marriage as a form of employment, seeking a husband through and on whom they can exercise their talents.[76] *Kirsteen*, like Carlyle's Teufelsdrockh, embraces a philosophy of work for work's sake, suggesting that a profession or trade can be a source of fulfillment for women as much as for men. If that work

---

[74] Duncan, *Modern Romance*, 15, 53.   [75] Oliphant, *Autobiography*, 44.

[76] On marriage as a means rather than an end for women in the Chronicles of Carlingford, see Langland *Nobody's Angels*, 152–81; and Michie, *Vulgar Question*, 155–75.

should be artistic, bringing aesthetic pleasure to consumers, so much the better.

Harry Muir and *Kirsteen* are versions of the same story, the story of a woman who supports her family – as both a lineage and a domestic unit – through artistic labor at no small personal expense. Yet *Kirsteen* constitutes a more thoroughgoing rejection of romance than the earlier *Harry Muir*, perhaps reflecting Oliphant's fatigue with her role as her own family's chivalric hero or perhaps reflecting her narrative fatigue – her frustration with the limited stories available to women. Given the number of novels that Oliphant authored, it was perhaps inevitable that she would write the "same" story over again, or at least write variations on a theme. For instance *Merkland: A Story of Scottish Life* (1850) and *Hester: A Story of Contemporary Life* (1883) feature versions of the same character – a strong but flawed matriarch seeking a deserving heir for her property and who in both novels happens to be named Catherine. But where *Merkland* is sentimental in tone and at times melodramatic, *Hester*'s narrator shares the ironic detachment of *Miss Marjoribanks*'s. The differences in tone and style through which these Catherines are represented cannot be attributed solely to Oliphant's development as a writer over a thirty-year period. Rather, they differentiate the two distinct modes – Scottish romance and English realism – in which Oliphant worked.

Oliphant's Scottish romances have been devalued because their sentimental tone, occasional melodrama, and critique of the marriage plot do not fit comfortably in the English tradition of the domestic realist novel. They seem much less anomalous when situated in a Scottish tradition originating with Scott's Waverley novels. In this tradition, as Oliphant's celebration of Scott's life and works reveal, the commodification of literature is not an evil to be lamented; originality is not the highest conceivable artistic value; and literary production is part of everyday life rather than a hallowed and mysterious process. For Oliphant, writing to a pattern – as if she were making a shirt – was a necessity and a virtue: it enabled her to reliably produce the novels through which she supported herself and her family. Yet she rightly claimed a degree of artistry even when writing to a pattern, and she demonstrated great facility in embroidering her narratives, or in experimenting with tone and style. As she revised and feminized Scott's romance plots, Oliphant also turned from Scott's sweeping historical vistas and intense political crises to the mundane world of women's work – domestic and artistic. Her romances of everyday life, as much as her outsider's take on English domestic realism, deeply influenced the Scotswomen who followed in her literary footsteps.

Her instrumentalist approach to authorship and her success in legitimating novel writing as a skilled trade provided a precedent that made their forays into the literary marketplace easier. Indeed, Oliphant unwittingly occupied the position of self-sacrificial foster-mother for these women. While she was never able to transform her own life, with its financial struggles, familial disappointments, and literary frustrations, into romance, she could imagine alternative realities through her fiction.

CHAPTER 2

Annie S. Swan's Friendly Fiction

In her autobiography, Annie Shepherd Swan declares of the *People's Friend*, "The hold of that unpretentious magazine on the public, not only in Scotland, but wherever Scots folk are to be found, is one of the romances of the newspaper world."[1] Swan played a leading role in this romance, as her reputation grew along with the magazine's circulation until she became the *Friend's* celebrity author. Her remarkable longevity as a popular writer, this chapter contends, was due to her understanding of what her primary readership of working- and lower middle-class women wanted from fiction: to escape the dullness and fatigue of factory work, house cleaning, and childcare. Swan sympathized with and was able to meet these readers' needs largely because their world was familiar to her.

Swan was born into a farming family just outside Edinburgh in 1859, and the *People's Friend* was born in Dundee a decade later as the literary offspring of the populist weekly newspaper the *People's Journal*. Swan grew up reading the *People's Friend* and the *People's Journal* along with *Good Words*, *Chambers's*, and the *Sunday Magazine*.[2] The intended readership of these magazines – working- and middle-class evangelical families bent on self-improvement – accurately reflects Swan's origins. Despite her parents' endorsement of "sound" or morally and intellectually improving reading, Swan relates in her autobiography that "authorship was not then, in certain circles, at least, considered a very respectable occupation" and that "art was also looked upon askance."[3] When Swan began to write her own stories, she worked "largely in secret and in holes and corners," hiding the manuscript for her first big success, *Aldersyde: A Border Story of Seventy Years Ago* (1883), inside a footstool.[4] By January of 1895, when the editor of the *People's Friend* hailed her as Scotland's foremost novelist, Swan had

---

[1] Annie S. Swan, *My Life: An Autobiography* (London: Ivor Nicholson, 1934), 283.
[2] Swan, *My Life*, 25–30.   [3] Swan, *My Life*, 32.   [4] Swan, *My Life*, 31.

published twenty-nine novels, fourteen of which had been serialized in the *Friend*, with others running in the Glasgow-based *Christian Leader*.

Swan would maintain this rapid pace of publication well into the 1930s, publishing a prodigious 200 novels and countless short stories and essays during her lifetime. But as her celebrity grew, she struggled to reconcile her prolific literary career with her image as the embodiment of middle-class domestic femininity – an image on which her celebrity depended.[5] Margaret Oliphant, thirty years Swan's elder, had spent much of her career attempting to reconcile professional authorship with middle-class domestic femininity. Unlike Oliphant, Swan could not claim economic necessity as her motive for writing novels. Following her marriage to James Burnett Smith in 1883, Swan supported the couple through her writing while her husband studied medicine at Edinburgh University. But after he opened a medical practice in London, the Burnett Smiths seem to have been consistently comfortable, even affluent, living first in Camden and then in Hampstead until they eventually moved to Hereford. Nonetheless, it was likely Oliphant's struggles to reconcile professional authorship with middle-class domestic femininity that that Swan referred to when she described the experience of reading Oliphant's autobiography: "it gave me such a strange sensation, almost as if I read my own life, written by another hand. Of course the facts are all different, and she was much abler in every way than I, but her point of view regarding many things was quite the same as mine."[6]

One of the "many things" in which Swan and Oliphant shared a "point of view" was their pragmatic approach to literary creation, or their understanding of novel writing as a skilled craft rather than an art. With somewhat less rue than Oliphant, Swan acknowledged that none of her books was "likely to prove immortal" nor even become "a best seller" because her "public [was] mainly a serial one" – that is, one that accessed her fiction in magazine rather than book form.[7] She wrote to feed "a great public, which cannot afford, or which has never been educated to buy books, but which nevertheless must be fed," and which could be fed "through the pages of magazines and newspapers."[8] Over the course of her long career, Swan developed a deep knowledge of what her public wanted and perfected the practice of writing serial fiction that met its

---

[5] On the development of celebrity authorship in the 1890s, see Philip Waller, *Writers, Readers, and Reputations: Literary Life in Britain, 1870–1918* (New York: Oxford University Press, 2006), 364–97.

[6] *The Letters of Annie S. Swan*, ed. Mildred Robertson Nicoll (London: Hodder and Stoughton, 1946), 45.

[7] Swan, *My Life*, 280.   [8] Swan, *My Life*, 283.

needs. Her readership was communicative, sending so many letters to the offices of the *People's Friend* that when Swan became the primary contributor to the *Woman at Home*, she instituted a correspondence column, "Over the Teacups," to formalize her responses to readers' letters.

In her autobiography, Swan recounted what she had learned over the years about writing serial fiction, which she described as "a profession, by itself," distinct from other forms of writing.[9] Her carefully thought-out prescriptions indicate that we should not be too quick to dismiss the practice of writing to a pattern. For Swan, following the guidelines that she had developed was the way to ensure her readers' satisfaction, and to experiment too widely would be deprive them of a bright spot in their week. In writing for weekly serialization, Swan asserted, a fast-paced plot was important. She explained that "there must be no discursive meditations in a serial – the story is the thing, and if the author does not get on with it, he will have no vogue."[10] In addition, the story should allow readers to escape the confines of the familiar because "the majority of those who are avid readers of serial fiction do not want stories about people in their own rank of life."[11] Swan's novels do in fact include a number of working-class characters, but they are upwardly mobile, ascending the social ladder through marriage, inheritance, or sheer hard work. She insisted that serial fiction must "satisf[y] the primal need for happiness. Denied to the reader, possibly he, or more likely she, finds some assuagement in contemplating the happiness of others in an imaginary world." Swan perhaps intuited that reading had for her audience what Janice Radway in her now-classic study of women romance readers called a "compensatory function."[12] Reading was a form of escape that allowed women to identify with characters leading lives different from, and generally better than, their own, and it was a form of what we might now term "self-care" that allowed them to take a break from fulfilling others' emotional needs in order to fulfill their own.

Swan did not save most of her voluminous correspondence, but one letter that she did save, now held at the National Library of Scotland, illustrates the compensatory function that her fiction performed for readers and attests to the importance of happy endings. It responds to *The Ne'er Do Well*, which ran in the *People's Friend* in 1897 and in which the protagonist Donald despondently marries a scheming and unworthy

---

[9] Swan, *My Life*, 283.   [10] Swan, *My Life*, 283.   [11] Swan, *My Life*, 285.
[12] Janice Radway, *Reading the Romance: Women, Patriarchy, and Popular Literature*, revised ed. (Chapel Hill: University of North Carolina Press, 2009), 89.

woman because he mistakenly believes that his true love, Fiona, does not care for him. Undated and unsigned, the letter calls Swan "the most cruel hearted writer I ever read" and charges her to "lay it to yourself could you like any of your family used the same way as you are treating fiona [*sic*] and the way you are treating Donald." The letter-writer concludes threateningly, "I have wrote to the People's friend warning them a great many of there [*sic*] readers are going to give up reading the paper if you don't alter your strain of writing."[13] This reader clearly was very upset that Swan had denied happiness to her characters, leaving both Donald and Fiona miserable. Happily, the situation was rectified by the novel's end, when the death of Donald's deranged first wife leaves him free to marry Fiona, who had always been true to him. "If one has the power to act as a minor Providence," Swan asked, "why not?" – especially if one could thereby ensure readers' contentment.[14]

Perhaps most importantly, Swan wanted to offer her readers spiritual sustenance, and leave them feeling uplifted rather than downcast. The religious bent of her fiction reflected her upbringing in the Evangelical Union Church at Leith, which, according to Swan, preached "free grace for every man, and pardon for all repentant sinners" and helped to shape Swan's self-proclaimed "immoveable faith in the inherent . . . goodness of human nature."[15] Swan drew on evangelical discourse to explain her aims as a novelist, expressing a hope that she might "salve some of the ills of our time" through her work.[16] In an allusion to the parable of the laborers in the vineyard (Matthew 20:1–16), she described her fiction as intended to help "working women and on occasions working men to stand up to the burden and heat of the day."[17] Yet Swan never preaches at readers. She eschews heavy-handed didacticism and overt indoctrination of any kind. Sermonizing, or what Swan called "discursive meditations," would both interrupt the plot and disrupt the reader's absorption in the story. By instead providing readers with eventful and engrossing stories in which both virtue and middle-class manners are generally rewarded, she enabled working-class readers to temporarily and vicariously escape the hardships of their lot, and subtly encouraged them to better themselves spiritually and materially.

The numerous author-figures who appear in Swan's fiction reflect her understanding of her role as a mentor to her readers. For instance, in *The Gates of Eden: A Story of Endeavour* (1887), she represents the writer's work

---

[13] National Library of Scotland, Acc. 6003 Box 1 folder 1.e.   [14] Swan, *My Life*, 286.
[15] Swan, *My Life*, 13.   [16] Swan, *My Life*, 249.   [17] Swan, *My Life*, 297.

as a kind of spiritual offering by contrasting twins Sandy and James Bethune. Sandy, the eldest by a matter of minutes, is destined for the church, while James, an autodidact, works on the family farm until through "sheer industry and force of character" he establishes himself as a journalist.[18] James reflects that "if God has given me the gift of a writer, and I sometimes think He has, I should like to use it for good; to write what would help others as well as myself in the higher life."[19] James's aims as a writer resemble what Sandy's aims ought to be as a clergyman. Yet his early hardships have made James much more sympathetic to suffering and sin than Sandy, who is proud to the point of arrogance despite never having had to work for anything he has received. In *The Gates of Eden*, as in her other novels, Swan provides her own readers with the type of story that inspired James, the story of an individual from a background like their own who achieves success through hard work. She also reflects on her aims in telling this kind of story: to "help" and inspire her readers.

Swan was as devoted to the predominantly working-class female readers of the *Friend* as they were to her, and she took her responsibilities toward them seriously enough to develop a theory of serial fiction. Yet scholars have summarily dismissed her as a Kailyard writer whose novels are not worth studying, even in sociological, let alone literary, terms.[20] "Kailyard" has become a pejorative term in Scottish literary studies, although, as Andrew Nash has shown, this was not always the case.[21] Critics have derided the so-called Kailyard school for its celebration of rural parochialism, which they have tended to see as a nostalgic response to the socio-economic problems arising from urbanization and industrialization.[22] In Kailyard fiction, the Scottish village is a bastion of genuine Christian feeling, with middle-class domestic femininity enshrined at its heart. The

---

[18] Annie S. Swan, *The Gates of Eden* (London: Oliphant & Ferrier, 1949), 44. The novel ran in *The People's Friend* in 1887.

[19] Swan, *The Gates of Eden*, 143.

[20] See Beth Dickson, "Annie S. Swan and O. Douglas: Legacies of the Kailyard," in *A History of Scottish Women's Writing*, ed. Douglas Gifford and Dorothy McMillan (Edinburgh: Edinburgh University Press, 1997), 329–46; and Samantha Walton, "Scottish Modernism, Kailyard Fiction, and the Woman at Home," in *Transitions in Middlebrow Writing, 1880–1930*, ed. K. MacDonald et al. (Houndsmills: Palgrave, 2015), 141–59.

[21] Andrew Nash, *Kailyard and Scottish Literature* (London: Brill, 2007).

[22] On the conventions of Kailyard literature, see Gillian Shepherd, "The Kailyard," in *The History of Scottish Literature*, vol. 3: *The Nineteenth Century*, ed. Douglas Gifford (Aberdeen: Aberdeen University Press, 1988), 309–20. For uses of the term as synonymous with a stifling sentimentalism, see Ian Campbell, *Kailyard* (Edinburgh: Ramsay Head, 1981); and Thomas D. Knowles, *Ideology, Art and Commerce: Aspects of Literary Sociology in the Late Victorian Scottish Kailyard* (Göteborg: Göteborg University Press, 1983).

Kailyard label ignores the diversity of Swan's fiction, and particularly of her representations of women. Those who, like Samantha Walton and Beth Dickson, categorize Swan as a Kailyard writer see her depictions of femininity as sentimental, nostalgic, and above all deeply conservative. Yet in both her fiction and her personal life, Swan engaged with the tensions surrounding the issue of women's work, within and without the home. Any assessment of Swan's representations of domestic femininity must take into account Swan's own attempts to reconcile its ideals with professional authorship.

Swan's identity as Mrs. Burnett Smith, wife and mother, was arguably as much a careful construction as her literary personae, Annie S. Swan and David Lyall. In her nonliterary life as Mrs. Burnett Smith, Swan was active in the temperance and women's suffrage movements and was involved in a variety of church missions; in 1906 she was president of the Society of Women Journalists; during the First World War she spoke to British soldiers stationed in France, offering them "a message of gratitude and encouragement from the women at home";[23] from 1916 to 1918, she served as spokeswoman for the Food Administration, writing and giving speeches across Britain and the United States on the importance of food conservation; and in 1922 she stood for Parliament as Liberal candidate for the Maryhill division of Glasgow, losing to the Labour party.

With such an array of public commitments as Mrs. Burnett Smith, how did Swan manage to write 200 novels? Her autobiography asserts that it was certainly not by neglecting her duties as wife and mother. Swan averred that her writing "never obtruded" on her family because "it was done mostly in the early morning, while others were asleep."[24] "My home has always taken precedence of my work," she declared, "and when anything had to go by the board, it was not my home."[25] It is highly unlikely that Swan's autobiography is an entirely accurate source of information, but, as her final attempt to cement her public image as she wanted to be remembered, it is important. Over her fifty-year writing career, Swan repeatedly attempted to reconcile her prolific literary output and her extensive public commitments with a middle-class ideal of domestic femininity. While the magnitude of the problem may have been different, many of Swan's readers would have faced a version of the tension she embodied, whether because they were forced to work outside the home to support themselves or their family, or because they sought independence and fulfillment beyond what they could find in their domestic duties.

---

[23] Swan, *My Life*, 147.   [24] Swan, *My Life*, 273.   [25] Swan, *My Life*, 225.

Although she was unable to resolve the contradictions between her private identity as Mrs. Burnett Smith and her public authorial identity as Annie S. Swan, the different audiences addressed by Swan's primary venues of publication allowed her to explore the tensions between women's public work and domestic duty from a variety of angles. Swan began publishing fiction in the *People's Friend* before she married, and she continued to use her maiden name throughout her career with the magazine. In the pages of the *Friend*, Swan encouraged working-class women who might aspire to upward mobility to embrace middle-class mores and manners by taking pleasure in their roles as wives and mothers. It was also as Annie S. Swan that, in 1894, William Robertson Nicoll appointed her as the "principal contributor" of the *Woman at Home: Annie S. Swan's Magazine*, which built on the celebrity that Swan had already acquired among readers of the *Friend*. Whereas Swan encouraged her working-class readers to emulate a middle-class model of domestic femininity, she warned middle-class women against imitating their social superiors, whose wealth left them with leisure to engage in pursuits outside the home. In both these publications, then, Swan suggests that working outside the home should be either the resort of economic necessity or the privilege of wealth.

If Swan's valorization of domestic womanhood in the *People's Friend* and the *Woman at Home* seems at odds with her own literary career and public activities, it is possible that she may have considered "Annie S. Swan," the advocate of middle-class domestic femininity, to be quite distinct from Mrs. Burnett Smith, the public speaker and activist. In other words, Annie S. Swan was perhaps as much a fiction as David Lyall, a name under which she contributed to *The British Weekly: A Journal of Christian and Social Progress*. As William Donaldson explains, the London-based *British Weekly* dominated "the prosperous middle-class middlebrow Nonconformist market in England" in the last decade of the nineteenth and the first decade of the twentieth century and regularly featured fiction by Swan's male contemporaries, J. M. Barrie, Ian Maclaren, and S. R. Crockett.[26] Through her pseudo-autobiographical account of Lyall's development as a writer in the pages of *The British Weekly*, Swan imagined for herself a literary career free from the pressures of middle-class ideals of feminine domesticity, one in which she did not have to disguise or downplay the time and energy she devoted to her work. Ironically, writing

---

[26] William Donaldson, *Popular Literature in Victorian Scotland: Language, Fiction and the Press* (Aberdeen: Aberdeen University Press, 1986), 146.

as Lyall also allowed Swan to address frankly and without fear of person-alization or repercussion the difficulties faced by working women.

Swan as a Friend of the People

The *People's Friend* was the literary offspring of the *People's Journal*, a weekly penny newspaper run by John Leng that was, as Donaldson has shown, "in the forefront of advanced Liberalism," supporting the abolition of slavery in the United States, and Home Rule for Ireland.[27] The *Journal* ran intermittent literary competitions, encouraging readers to submit poems, stories, and songs, the best of which would be published in its pages.[28] When the Christmas competition of 1868 garnered 265 short stories and 605 poems, the sheer volume of contributions inspired Leng to start the *People's Friend* as a forum for the literary "contributions of the working men and women of Scotland."[29] Swan won the *People's Journal* story competition in 1879, and her first serial story for the *Friend*, titled *Wrongs Righted*, ran in 1881. From then on, she published a serial story in the *Friend* almost every year until her death in 1943 and was easily its top-selling and most highly paid fiction writer.[30]

Because there is so little archival material remaining from the *Friend*'s early years, Swan's own account of the magazine and her contemporaries' commentaries on it are our best source of information about its readership. These sources suggest that although the *Friend* began as a family magazine, by the 1890s its readership was primarily, although by no means entirely, working-class women. At a Poets, Essayists and Novelists (PEN) reception held for Swan in Edinburgh in 1935, Lord Provost Buist of Dundee observed that "the mill girls of Dundee vied with their employers' daughters in looking forward to the delivery of the *People's Friend*," while another speaker located the magazine's readership in "the mills of Dundee, the tenements of Glasgow, [and] the fishermen's rows in their fishing villages."[31] As a penny weekly, the *Friend* was priced for these working-class readers.

---

[27] Donaldson, *Popular Literature*, 28.

[28] Kirstie Blair discusses the poetry generated by these competitions in *Working Verse in Victorian Scotland: Poetry, Press, Community* (Oxford: Oxford University Press, 2019).

[29] John Leng, "Annie S. Swan," *The People's Friend* 5 (1870): 1. For the history of *The People's Journal* and *The People's Friend*, see Donaldson, *Popular Literature*, 23–33.

[30] D. C. Thomson, the current publisher of the *People's Friend*, holds a ledger recording payments to Swan between 1895 and 1943 that shows her earning between £400 and £650 per serial, with additional payments for book rights.

[31] "Scottish Novelist. A Public Tribute to Annie S. Swan. P.E.N. Reception," *The Scotsman*, January 10, 1935, National Library of Scotland, Acc. 6003 Box 2.

Why might Swan's stories have been so popular among the *Friend's* readership of working-class women? For a start, her fiction was at least as good as and usually better than that of authors cultivated by the *Friend*. Its superiority is evident if we compare it to the serial stories of Adeline Sergeant, a competition winner who also began writing for the *Friend* in 1881 and who also became something of a celebrity among the magazine's readers. Swan's fiction relies less on sensational plot moves, such as bigamous marriages, shipwrecks, and the swapping of babies at birth than does Sergeant's, and the worlds that she creates in her stories are richer and more fully realized. While setting rarely matters much to Sergeant's stories beyond a basic distinction between urban and rural, local economies and customs impact Swan's characters and shape their experience. For instance, *Mary Garth: A Clydeside Romance* (1902) is set in a mining village in Lanarkshire, and the debates between pit-owners and workers over the drawbacks and benefits of unionization are central to the plot; Mary Durie, protagonist of *The Inheritance* (1908), works in a Dundee jute factory to support her ailing mother and, remarkably, does not end up marrying the factory owner's handsome son; and *McLeod's Wife* (1923) tells the story of woman who has grown up in genteel poverty on Mull and struggles to adjust to middle-class life in Glasgow after marrying an aspiring surgeon. Swan's stories allowed readers to see versions of themselves and their world in print in a way that Sergeant's stories did not.

However, aesthetic or literary value alone is unlikely to account for the extent of Swan's celebrity among readers. I suggest that Swan's greater popularity may have been due to her nuanced understanding of and sympathy for the audience for which she wrote and the *Friend's* careful shaping of her authorial identity to fulfill the desires of that audience. Swan offered herself to the magazine's readers as motherly mentor, some-one who understood readers' struggles, shared their hopes, delighted in their successes, and offered comfort and counsel to support them in their disappointments. The *Friend* allowed readers to enjoy a semblance of closeness to Swan, granting them access to details about her life through interviews, puff pieces, and portraits or photos. After the birth of her son Edward, for instance, the *Friend* included portrait of mother and baby with the installment of *A Son of Erin*, published on October 3, 1899. Congratulatory letters and presents for the new baby poured in from readers.

Swan's authorial identity as a foster-mother to the *Friend's* readers was predicated on her embodiment of a middle-class ideal of feminine domes-ticity that she encouraged them to emulate, but that her very visible work as a novelist always threatened to undercut. Accordingly, Andrew Stewart, editor of the *People's Friend*, managed Swan's authorial image carefully. In a puff piece from 1895 he emphasizes the continuities rather than disparities between her roles as author and as wife and mother when he asserts that she owes her popularity to

> the tenderness infused into all she writes. She writes from a warm and loving and heart. She feels what she writes, and she lives the gospel she seeks to teach. For it must not be lost sight of, that there is an earnest purpose in all her stories, and that purpose is to make all who read them rise from their perusal better than they sat down.[32]

Swan's fiction here is a spontaneous expression of the love she feels for her readers, as if they were indeed her own children.

When Mrs. Burnett Smith's public activities challenged Annie S. Swan's maternal image too much, readers noted it. In January of 1923 one Jeannie Rough, a loyal reader of the *People's Friend* for forty years, wrote from Sawyerville, Quebec, to express her relief at Swan's defeat in the parliamentary race in Glasgow: "All through the years you belonged to us, but when we heard you were 'running for Parliament' we felt we were going to lose you and when you were defeated we said 'Praise be! She did not get in'! – We do not want our gracious womanly Annie Swan at Westminster. Three cheers for the Scotch mothers who did not vote for her!" Rough implies that Swan's ability to offer spiritual counsel to her readers, an ability predicated on shared experiences and ideals of womanhood, would have been comprised by her participation in the dirty world of politics. Rough seems to have wanted to reassure Swan that her usefulness to others did not depend on her political power or lack thereof, explaining that "in this Dominion there are those of your countrywomen who love you because you have helped them."[33] Swan "helped" the *Friend*'s readers not only by providing them with a harmless and inexpensive escape from the irritations of daily life but also by legitimating their value as wives and mothers, both in her public embrace of those roles and in her stories of women who found happiness in them.

In the fiction Swan wrote for the *People's Friend*, the home is not a space of confinement but a space of privilege and protection for women. In many of her stories the middle-class female protagonist learns that her foremost duty is to ensure the well-being of her family before turning her

---

[32] Andrew Stewart, "Annie S. Swan," *The People's Friend* 1306 (Jan. 7, 1895), 3.
[33] National Library of Scotland, Acc. 6003 Box 1 file 1.e.

energies farther afield. For instance, in *Mistaken* (1889), Margaret alienates her siblings, parents, and fiancé by devoting her time to Christianizing "Arabs" in Hackney while her mother's health fails and the children are left to scramble for themselves. Joyce, the eponymous heroine of *Wyndham's Daughter* (1898), leaves her comfortable Hampstead home, where she feels stifled and useless, and joins a workers' commune in East London. She soon learns that she is virtually unemployable, and when her mother grows ill, realizes that her proper employment is in making home a happy place for her parents and brother. These stories suggest that women who *can* enjoy the privilege of devoting themselves exclusively to their duties as wives and mother should do so. Yet they are not simply cautionary tales. They also affirm women's domestic significance in ways that might have been gratifying for Swan's readers. When Margaret and Joyce turn their energies outward, their family members suffer, and they gratefully welcome back these prodigal daughters on their return. These stories illustrate the value of women's unpaid domestic labor, providing a source of emotional validation that readers might not have received from their own families.

The Guinea Stamp: A Tale of Modern Glasgow, which ran in the *People's Friend* from January to June of 1892, offers a more complicated exploration of the issue of women's work by incorporating working- and middle-class characters who engage in a variety of paid and unpaid labor.[34] This novel promotes for a working-class readership an ideology of middle-class domesticity that Swan would revisit from another perspective when writing for the middle-class readership of the *Woman at Home*. But it also asserts the importance of character over rank, as its titular allusion to Robert Burns's "A Man's a Man for A' That" would suggest. *The Guinea Stamp* affirms that "The rank is but the guinea's stamp, / The man's the gowd for a' that" defining a uniform standard of moral conduct for all women, regardless of social class. Through the novel's metafictional representations of serial stories, moreover, Swan reflects on her own role as a writer for the *People's Friend* in helping her female readers to hew to that standard, regardless of the work they perform.

---

[34] *The Guinea Stamp* was syndicated and ran on varying schedules the same year in *The Burnley Express, The Daily Gazette for Middleborough, The Cheshire Observer, The Lancashire Evening Herald,* and *The Morpeth Herald.* See www.victorianresearch.org/atcl/show_title.php?tid=8152&aid=2606. On the development of syndication in the late nineteenth century, see Graham Law, *Serializing Fiction in the Victorian Press* (Houndsmills: Palgrave Macmillan, 2000), 65–91. The novel was issued as a single volume late in 1892 by the publishing house Oliphant, Anderson & Ferrier.

Gladys Graham, the protagonist of *The Guinea Stamp*, strives to embody the ideals of domestic femininity even though she lives in a dingy warehouse and is so poor that she often does not have enough to eat. As housekeeper for her uncle Abel, an oil and tallow dealer, she is protected from the dubious influences to which working girls are exposed, such as the music hall that Liz and her friend Teen like to frequent. Liz and Teen are foils to Gladys and represent different degrees of exposure to the ills of city life. When Gladys first meets Liz, she is lying in front of the fire, wrapped in shawls, "with a copy of the *Family Reader* in her hand, open at a thrilling picture of a young lady with an impossible figure being rescued from a runaway horse by a youth of extraordinary proportions."[35] Liz has been reading to Teen a story called "Lord Bellew's Bride; or the Curse of Mountford Abbey" (52) while Teen adds sleeves, neckbands, and button-holes to men's coats for a penny per coat. Liz and Teen club their money together to buy the *Family Reader* each week so that they can follow the fortunes of Lord Bellew and his bride. As they eagerly discuss the story, Gladys

> wondered at the familiarity of the two girls with dukes and duchesses, and other persons of high degree, of whom they spoke familiarly, as if they were next-door neighbours. Although she ... knew nothing of their life, she gathered that its monotony was very irksome to them, and that they were compelled to seek something, if only in the pages of an unwholesome and unreal story, to lift them out of it. It was evident that Liz, at least, chafed intolerably under her present lot, and that her head was full of dreams and imaginings regarding the splendours so vividly described in the story. (54)

Sure enough, Liz declares that although she may be only a mill worker at present, she will one day live in a big house, ride in a carriage, and wear silk dresses, pointing out to Gladys, "Lord Bellew's bride in the story was only the gatekeeper's dochter, an' that's her on the horse look, after she was my Lady Bellew" (53). *The Family Reader* does not simply offer Liz a much-needed escape from what Gladys describes as "the terrible realism of city life" (56); it also leads her to believe that her own life might read like a romance – that she too might be raised from ignominious origins to enjoy a life of luxury. It comes as no surprise when, shortly after Gladys's visit, Liz disappears – ostensibly to seek her fortune in London, but in fact to become mistress to her wealthy employer at the paper mill. If Liz is a poor reader who mistakes fiction for real life, the fictive author of "Lord Bellew's

---

[35] Annie S. Swan, *The Guinea Stamp: A Tale of Modern Glasgow* (Edinburgh: Oliphant, Anderson & Ferrier, 1892), 49. Subsequent references to this edition will be made parenthetically.

Bride" is perhaps also at fault in misleading her. By figuring "Lord Bellew's Bride" as a dangerous influence on the impressionable Liz, Swan differentiates her own wholesome fiction from the fantasy offered in *The Family Reader*, which entertains readers without offering them guidance.

Swan's critique of "Lord Bellew's Bride" defines the limits of the escapism her own fiction offers readers. Yet *The Guinea Stamp* is not without its own improbabilities, as Swan mixes a welcome dose of romance into its depictions of poverty, and the attendant ills of alcoholism and prostitution, in Glasgow's East End. When Uncle Abel dies, he unexpectedly leaves his business to his shop-boy Walter and a substantial fortune to Gladys, who, like Bellew's bride, is raised into a higher sphere of existence. With her inheritance, Gladys purchases Bourhill, a house in Ayrshire that she plans to transform into a holiday home for "working girls in Glasgow ... those poor creatures who sew in the garrets and cellars," and Teen is her first visitor (176). At Bourhill, young women like Teen will have "nothing to do but eat and sleep, and walk in the country" while they enjoy some time away from their soul-sapping employment in the city (194). The unexpected inheritance is plot device that originates in romance. Indeed, Mrs. Fordyce, who takes Gladys under her maternal wing after Uncle Abel's death, compares Gladys's life to a "fairy story" (129). What is particularly interesting about Swan's use of this device in *The Guinea Stamp* is that it is posed as a resolution to an intractable social problem – the moral dangers and physical ills experienced by young working-class women in the city.

Gladys's plan comes in for a great deal of criticism from both her middle-class and working-class acquaintances. The wealthy women of Glasgow's West End have little sympathy with her desire to "brighten life a little for those [who] ... have had so very little brightness" (201). Mrs. Fordyce points out that Teen "is not even interesting – nothing could be more hopelessly vulgar and commonplace" (200). Yet Mrs. Fordyce is by no means an unsympathetic character. She does "a great many good deeds, though on strictly conventional lines. She was the clever organizer of Church charities, the capable head of the Ladies' Provident and Dorcas Society, to which she grudged neither time nor money; but she did not believe in personal contact with the very poor, nor in the power and efficacy of individual sympathy and effort" (201). Teen, on the other hand, has benefited greatly from Gladys's attention, but she is highly skeptical of the possibility that any kind of charitable organization could achieve on a larger scale what "personal contact" with Gladys has done for her. When Gladys explains that she wants Teen's "advice and help" in "establish[ing] a kind of friendly Club" for working girls in Glasgow, a place that would be safer and more wholesome than the music hall, Teen points out that there are already Christian associations where girls can go to read or sew but acknowledges that many girls "gang just to serve themselves, because they get a lot frae the ladies. My, ye can get onything oot o' them if ye ken hoo to work them" (205). When she visited one such organization with Liz, Teen found that "there was ower muckle preaching, and some of the ladies looked at us as if we were dirt" (204). Leslie Orr Macdonald's work on women's religious charities in Scotland suggests that these Christian associations would have been supported by middle-class women like Mrs. Fordyce, who regarded it as a religious duty to protect the morals of working-class girls.[36] But Teen's experiences suggest such associations benefit neither the women who run them nor those who attend them, as the former's moral and social snobbery brings out the worst in the recipients of their charity.

All this is so much "cold water" thrown on Gladys's "bright enthusiasm" (205), but it is Liz's unfortunate demise that finally squelches her plan to establish a holiday house for working girls. Liz, who is dying of consumption, confesses that it was Mrs. Fordyce's son George, owner of the paper mill at which she worked, "that led me awa' first . . . He said he wad mairry me, an' I believed it" (367). When Gladys attempts to lure Liz to Bourhill, telling her "my own fortune is very nearly as wonderful as that of 'Lord Bellew's Bride,'" (287) Liz is uninterested, replying ,"Eh, sic lees there is in papers! It shouldna be printed. Things like yon never happen in real life – never, never!" (287). Yet something "like yon" has happened to Teen; for, if Uncle Abel is Gladys's Lord Bellew, then Gladys is Teen's. Once removed from her sordid surroundings, Teen undergoes a gradual transformation. Formerly discontented, sullen, and withdrawn, she blossoms into a trusted friend for Gladys, and wins over everyone at Bourhill with her "unpretentious, willing, cheerful ways" (368). It is not surprising that Teen adores Gladys, speaking of her benefactor, according to Liz, "the way I've heard lassies speak aboot men" (314). While the transformation of Teen might be counted a success, Gladys is dismayed by her failure to save Liz, who had "deliberately chosen a wicked life" (348) These very different outcomes teach Gladys that she cannot save those who do not want to be

---

[36] Leslie Orr MacDonald, *A Unique and Glorious Mission: Women and Presbyterianism in Scotland, 1830–1930* (Edinburgh: John Donald, 2000), 33–52. See also C. G. Brown and J. D. Stephenson, "Sprouting Wings? Women and Religion in Scotland, c. 1890–1950," in *Out of Bounds: Women in Scotland in the Nineteenth and Twentieth Centuries*, ed. E. Breitenbach and E. Gordon (Edinburgh: Edinburgh University Press, 1992), 95–120.

saved and persuade her that "personal contact" and "individual sympathy and effort" are more effective modes of social reform than large-scale charitable organizations or institutions.

Gladys's quiet renunciation of her grand plans to brighten the lives of working girls is part of her maturation and signals her readiness to become a good wife and mother. Her marriage to the morally upstanding Walter Hepburn rather than the wealth libertine George Fordyce provides Swan's readers with the satisfying ending they desired. In Gladys's maturation, *The Guinea Stamp* illustrates a variation on the pattern common to *Mistaken* and *Wyndham's Daughter* whereby young women learn that charity begins at home, turning their energies from the wider world to their domestic circle, where they can make an appreciable difference in others' lives. Again, it is possible to read this pattern as highly conservative, encouraging readers to embrace a middle-class ideal of domesticity, that might very well be out of the reach of a woman who must make a living by working in a factory or a paper mill. But certain moral aspects of this ideal *were* accessible to working-class women, and these open up the possibility of a less punitive reading of *The Guinea Stamp*. Although Gladys enjoys circumstances very different from the workaday lives of most readers of the *People's Friend*, she is the character with whom readers are encouraged to identify and through whom they can vicariously enjoy a miraculous change of fortunes. Unflaggingly industrious, considerate, and cheerful, Gladys's character does not change throughout the novel, even though her rank does. She not only enables Teen's transformation but also encourages a new manliness in Walter when she demands a husband who is morally worthy of her, one who embraces hard work and takes pride in his humble origins instead of trying to disguise them. While Gladys begins the story as a middle-class woman in working-class circumstances, she ends it as a middle-class woman surrounded by wealth and privilege. She is the "gowd" that takes the guinea stamp.

If *The Guinea Stamp* offers readers a potentially empowering model of womanhood in Gladys, it also reflects Swan's sense of her authorial responsibilities to nurture her readers as Gladys nurtures Teen – by providing them with an escape from daily toil. Gladys's understanding of charity as an individualized and intimate form of mentorship recalls Swan's authorial identity in the *People's Friend* as spiritual counselor to her readers, one who wrote for them from the heart. Her desire to impart through her fiction what the *Friend's* editor Andrew Stewart described as "strength to the weak and tempted, and blessing to the desolate and outcast" construes authorship as a mediated form of "personal contact," a form of charity stemming from "individual sympathy" rather than an abstract sense of obligation.[37] Swan not only wrote her fiction at home, but, if we take Liz and Teen as the imagined readers for whom she wrote, she also envisioned it being read at home. By figuring her highly paid work as a circumscribed and personalized form of charity, Swan drew readers into her domestic circle and smoothed over the tensions between her literary career and her image as a model of middle-class femininity.

Swan as a Woman at Home

Given the ideal of middle-class domestic femininity that Swan endorsed in the fiction she wrote for the *People's Friend*, it seems fitting that in 1894, she became the figurehead of a newly established magazine for middle-class women called the *Woman at Home: Annie S. Swan's Magazine*.[38] The glossy pages, numerous illustrations, and price of sixpence per monthly issue marked the *Woman at Home* as something of a luxury for most of the *Friend*'s readership. Whereas the *Friend* included household hints and recipes, readers of the *Woman at Home* were perhaps less likely to do their own cooking and cleaning. Instead, it offered a fashion column, albeit one illustrated with black-and-white rather than expensive color plates, and addressed issues pertinent to middle-class women, such the difficulty of obtaining servants in Canada or the propriety of wives keeping a "private purse" separate from their husband's money. In the *Woman at Home*, Swan's role as motherly mentor to her readers was formalized in the column "Over the Teacups," in which she responded to readers' letters. Here, she could write more frankly about the difficulties of balancing career and family than she could in the *People's Friend*, where her literary career was configured as an extension of her domesticity. Swan may have been, as Kate Krueger has argued, an "ideal role model for readers who were attempting to bridge the gap between women's domestic and professional roles," but the magazine itself was less successful in bridging this gap.[39] According to its founder and proprietor William Robertson Nicoll, the *Woman at Home* was created for "women who were married or expected to marry,"[40] yet its readership appears to have significantly

---

[37] Andrew Stewart, "Annie S. Swan," *The People's Friend* 958 (May 9, 1888), 291.
[38] For the publication history of *The Woman at Home*, see T. H. Darlow, *William Robertson Nicoll: Life and Letters* (London: Hodder and Stoughton, 1925), 111–12.
[39] Kate Krueger, "*The Woman at Home* in the World: Annie Swan's Lady Doctor and the Problem of the Fin de Siècle Working Woman," *Victorian Periodicals Review* 50.3 (2017): 517.
[40] Darlow, *William Robertson Nicoll*, 111.

exceeded this category, including, if Swan's correspondence is an accurate indicator, single women who had no desire to marry and women who were interested in pursuing careers.[41] Nicoll acknowledged uneasily that "numbers of the best women now live independent lives and that their tastes and needs must also be taken into account."[42] But the very title of the *Woman at Home* signifies its ideological allegiances, and its efforts to appeal to women living "independent lives" while openly advocating marriage as women's natural state must have created some cognitive dissonance among readers.

Swan's commentary on women's work in the *Woman at Home* often took a more direct form that it did in the *Friend* but was similarly complicated by considerations of social class. The *Woman at Home* regularly showcased a range of perspectives on gendered questions by publishing responses from contributors to prompts such as "Should widows remarry?," "Is platonic friendship possible?," "Should long engagements be encouraged?," and "Should married women engage in public work?" In these debates, Swan regularly represented a self-consciously middle-class perspective in contrast to more socially elite contributors, and as in the *People's Friend*, hers was the perspective with which readers were expected to identify.

In response to "Should married women engage in public work?," Swan is the only one of four contributors to answer the question with an emphatic "no." The other three respondents – Lady Mary Murray, Lady Isabel Margesson, and Lady Laura Ridding – uniformly agree that participation in public work benefits the women who undertake it and the community in which they work.[43] By "public work," however, they mean "work which is given freely, for the common good, by those whose time and strength are not absorbed in the daily struggle to obtain a livelihood," in other words, unpaid charity work, not remunerative labor of the sort performed by Liz and Teen, or indeed by Swan herself. Lady Murray further distinguishes "individual charity," one of "the duties of private life," from what she rather awkwardly calls "combined philanthropic effort," or participation in organized charities.[44] "Individual charity," the

[41] On the demographics of the *Woman at Home*'s readership, see Margaret Beetham, *A Magazine of Her Own? Domesticity and Desire in the Woman's Magazine, 1800–1914* (London: Routledge, 1996), 158, 170–1.
[42] Darlow, *William Robertson Nicoll*, 111.
[43] "Should Married Women Engage in Public Work?," in *Woman at Home*, vol. IV (London: Hodder and Stoughton, 1895), 112.
[44] "Public Work?," 112.

sort of assistance that Gladys spontaneously offers to Teen, and that Swan aimed to offer her readers, is for Murray a responsibility for women of all classes. It is the propriety of "combined philanthropic effort" that is up for debate in the *Woman at Home*. For, as Dorice Elliott has observed, the bureaucratization of philanthropy made it difficult to configure charity as an extension of womanly nurturing and thus to naturalize women's participation in it.[45] Organized charity work came dangerously close to working outside the home in any other capacity, except that it was unpaid. Lady Ridding, who helped to found the National Union of Women Workers, an organization for women involved in charitable endeavors, responded positively to the question of whether married women should engage in public work. In contrast to Lady Murray's suspicion of "combined philanthropic effort," Ridding asserts that "service on philanthropic committees" is an antidote to "feminine sins of morbidness, frivolity, self-concentration, [and] narrowness."[46] Ridding, as Swan's response makes clear, imagines a woman who has little to do other than care for herself rather than one who is occupied in running a household and caring for a family.

The respondents to the question "Should married women engage in public work?" contributed to an ongoing debate about whether women's philanthropy would, in Elliott's words, "jeopardize the separation between the domestic and public spheres that seemed to Victorians to be the foundation of social order."[47] For instance, Lady Margesson asserted that "a woman's faculty of tenderness was meant for the comfort and alleviation of the human family, not only for one family."[48] Blurring the distinctions between private and public, she reconfigures society as a family in order to legitimate women's philanthropic interventions in its management. In contrast to the three other contributors, whose titles suggest that they may have enjoyed a good deal of domestic help, Swan draws strict boundaries between private and public. She asserts categorically that "a woman's first duty is her home."[49] Although she does not reject the possibility that an exceptional woman might balance domestic duties with charitable endeavors, she believes that most women cannot. After all, "the average house, consisting of father, mother, children, and servants, as every

---

[45] Dorice Elliott, *The Angel Out of the House: Philanthropy and Gender in Nineteenth-Century England* (Charlottesville: University of Virginia Press, 2002), 11–12. On the problematic professionalization of philanthropy, see also Frank Prochaska, *Women and Philanthropy in Nineteenth-Century England* (Oxford: Clarendon Press, 1980); and Daniel Siegel, *Charity and Condescension: Victorian Literature and the Dilemmas of Philanthropy* (Athens: Ohio University Press, 2012).

[46] "Public Work?," 111.   [47] Elliott, *Out of the House*, 3.   [48] "Public Work?," 113.

[49] "Public Work?," 114.

tired housewife knows full well, requires no small amount of labour, thought and planning to keep it going in smooth working order."[50] Swan allows that "a certain amount" of public work "can be undertaken as a diversion, or stimulus, without encroaching in any serious degree on the claims of house and home."[51] But to indulge in this diversion is tricky, for "the fascination of this work is so great that, if it once gets a firm hold, it becomes altogether engrossing. It has also upon some natures an unwholesome effect, creating a desire for excitement and rendering irksome the 'daily round, the common task,' which is the lot of every housemother."[52] If Swan emerges as a conservative voice in this forum, it is because she embraces a middle-class ideal of domestic duty rather than a seemingly more liberal feminism founded in class privilege. Charity work stands to deter women from their primary responsibilities in a way that even novel reading does not. Rather than providing a temporary escape – one that can be picked up and put down – it may become an ongoing distraction. Swan's suggestion that charity work might render daily domestic work dull by contrast subtly acknowledges that middle-class women's lives were often monotonous and unfulfilling. Nonetheless, she asserts, these women's daily work was essential, even if it was not glamorous.

Yet Swan provides this advice as a professional – a journalist and novelist. Rather than cultivating a maternal image, as she did in the *People's Friend*, Swan in the *Woman at Home* speaks to her readers as equals so that she can define "us" middle-class women against the wealthier gentry. The very title of Swan's advice column, "Over the Teacups," figures the exchanges between Swan and her correspondents as an intimate conversation taking place within the home and suggests an equality between Swan and readers of the *Woman at Home*. But this seemingly intimate and egalitarian conversation was fraught with contradictions. Margaret Beetham, who analyses "Over the Teacups" at length in *A Magazine of Her Own*, observes that the "most persistent" problem that Swan was called on to solve for her correspondents was "how to earn a living as a middle-class woman" without engaging in work that was degrading or improper.[53] Swan emphasized that women should not be ashamed to work outside the home in order to support themselves and their families if they needed to do so. But she also recognized that the jobs middle-class women might aspire to required skill and training. Thus, despite the many letters she received from aspiring writers, Swan

---

[50] "Public Work?," 114.   [51] "Public Work?," 114.   [52] "Public Work?," 114.
[53] Beetham, *A Magazine of Her Own?*, 169.

consistently discouraged her readers from pursuing authorship or journalism as a means of earning a living, undoubtedly because of the very real challenges involved – challenges that she would address more fully in *A Woman Journalist*, a serial written under the name David Lyall and published in *The British Weekly*. In recognizing her own profession as a skilled and remunerative one Swan could not conceal the tensions between her very successful literary career and the ideal of domestic womanhood that the *Woman at Home* promoted.

In the serial fiction she wrote for the *Woman at Home*, Swan tried to please the magazine's dual audiences of women who were or hoped to be married and women who wanted to pursue a career. Her stories about working women are quite different from those she wrote for the *Friend*. Swan appears in them as herself, and the women she writes about are presented to readers as her friends. The plots are loosely episodic, designed to showcase the protagonist's work, and the tone is almost that of a documentary. In their explorations of the social ills that women's careers bring them into contact with – poverty, illness, crime – these stories reveal the impact of W. T. Stead's new journalism. In their own way, Swan's stories about professional women also provided a form of escape for readers by allowing those who were "women at home" to imagine living very different lives. While validating women's career ambitions, these stories suggest that the pursuit of skilled professions may be incompatible with marriage and thus require a sacrifice that some women are not prepared to make. Married readers could thus enjoy a temporary distraction from their domestic duties with the assurance that they had made the correct choice.

Even as Swan cautioned against long engagements in "Over the Teacups," urging women to embrace marriage as soon as possible, her serial stories depicted women pursuing professional careers in a positive and occasionally even heroic light. Nonetheless, in the very first paragraph of the first installment of *Elizabeth Glen, M.B., the Experiences of a Lady Doctor* (1894), Swan hastens to assure readers that Elizabeth is "a woman of so large a heart and so wide an experience that I have often said wifehood and motherhood could scarcely improve her in that respect."[54] Swan's working women belong to what we would now call the "helping professions," and their deep capacity for sympathy suits them for their vocations. These professions bring them into contact with the best and the worst of humanity. In *Memories of Margaret Grainger, Schoolmistress*

---

[54] Annie S. Swan, *Elizabeth Glen, M.B., the Experiences of a Lady Doctor* (London: Hutchinson & Co., 1895), 2.

(1895), the eponymous heroine, who becomes principal of Fleetwood College for girls at the tender age of thirty, is afforded many "glimpses, sometimes very near and sacred ... into the sanctuary of other lives."[55] Much of Elizabeth's and Margaret's work occurs in the private realm and engages their particularly womanly qualities.

Despite the pleasure they find in helping others, Swan makes it clear that these professional women have sacrificed their longings for the domestic affections other women enjoy. Ironically, this emotional self-sacrifice, arguably a particularly feminine characteristic, allows them to retain their claims to womanliness in conditions that might otherwise undermine them. Margaret, who began teaching to pay off her father's debts, describes herself with regret as "an old maid" who has "never even had a romance" because "the sun-time of [her] youth was spent in the interests and concerns of those committed to [her] charge."[56] And although her profession gives her many opportunities of forming friendships with others, Elizabeth acknowledges, "I am still a lonely woman, standing on the outside always."[57] Only in the last installment of Elizabeth's story do we learn that her "desire to be a doctor, and to live a more useful and a fuller life" than she thought she could as a wife and mother put an end to a youthful courtship. Her suitor Keith Hamilton "pooh-poohed" her ambitions, declaring, "[T]o me it is intolerable to think of you subjected to experiences which will rob you of that exquisite womanliness which makes everybody love you."[58] Swan's account of how medical work has nurtured Elizabeth's most womanly qualities prepares us to recognize Keith's objection as mistaken. Indeed, the spirited Elizabeth replies, "If my womanliness is to be so easily damaged, Keith Hamilton, it is a quality not worth possessing," but twelve years later she regrets her choice, and when Keith, now an MP, proposes again, she is only too happy to "settle down into a member's wife" and renounce her career.[59] The subtitle of the sequel, *Mrs Keith Hamilton, Further Adventures of a Lady M.B.*, is somewhat misleading, as Elizabeth, now retired from medicine, devotes herself to child rearing and charitable endeavors – a form of public work that her husband's wealth and status renders acceptable.

The professional women of Swan's serials for the *Woman at Home* are loved and admired by all who know them. They maintain the strictest

[55] Annie S. Swan, *Memories of Margaret Granger, Schoolmistress* (London: Hutchinson & Co., 1896), 1. *Margaret Grainger* ran in volumes 3 and 4 of *Woman at Home* in 1895.
[56] Swan, *Margaret Grainger*, 2.   [57] Swan, *Elizabeth Glen*, 202.   [58] Swan, *Elizabeth Glen*, 299.
[59] Swan, *Elizabeth Glen*, 299, 311.

standards of feminine propriety while performing public work that develops their most womanly qualities, but they are nonetheless filled with a quiet regret that they cannot enjoy both marriage and a career because each in its own, Swan suggests, is a full-time job. The *Woman at Home* ceased publication in 1919 due to what its then-editor Alice M. Head called "cataclysmic changes in magazines for women."[60] These changes in magazine culture were undoubtedly related to the equally cataclysmic transformation that war had wrought in British society, as many middle-class women began to work outside the home, taking jobs previously held by the men who had gone to fight, and as the availability of domestic help dwindled.[61] Although Head did not admit it in so many words, the *Woman at Home*'s continued emphasis on marriage and domesticity as the highest calling to which women could aspire probably was beginning to seem rather old-fashioned by the end of the Great War. The contradictions between what Annie S. Swan preached in the *Woman at Home* and the services that Mrs. Burnett Smith performed during wartime as a visitor to soldiers at the front and an advocate for the Food Administration in Britain and the United States suggests that either Swan considered her authorial persona to be distinct from her private identity or that she too may have found the ideal of domestic femininity somewhat outmoded.

David Lyall, Author-Hero

Whether she presented herself as a foster-mother to readers of the *Friend* or as an equal struggling to balance domestic and public duties in the *Woman at Home*, Swan's authorial agency was limited by the dictates of feminine propriety, which prohibited middle-class women from straying too far from home. Swan lamented that in comparison with men, "the women writers of my day worked under a handicap, being expected to stop at home, and not encouraged to make themselves conspicuous in any way," so that it was difficult for them to acquire "fresh material" to write about.[62] Several of Swan's novels feature heroes who are writers of sorts, and through these male author-figures Swan imagines a more liberated – and more liberal – version of authorship than she could enjoy in her own person.[63]

---

[60] Nicoll, *Letters*, 21–22.

[61] See Deirdre Beddoe, *Back to Home and Duty: Women between the Wars, 1914–1939* (London: Pandora, 1989); and Alison Light, *Forever England: Femininity, Literature, and Conservatism between the Wars* (London: Routledge, 1991).

[62] Swan, *My Life*, 130.   [63] See, for instance, *The Gates of Eden* (1887) and *A Son of Erin* (1898).

Swan's fantasies of authorial agency perhaps found their culmination in David Lyall, the pseudonym under which she wrote for *The British Weekly*, a London-based Nonconformist penny paper founded by William Robertson Nicoll. In addition to fiction, *The British Weekly* featured reports of church news from correspondents situated throughout Britain; essays on questions of religion, politics, and science; and reviews of books, often from evangelical presses such as Hodder and Stoughton and the Religious Tract Society. By the time Swan began contributing to *The British Weekly* in 1894, it was already known for its mutually sustaining affiliation with the Kailyard writers, Ian Maclaren, S. R. Crockett, and J. M. Barrie. Nicoll, whom Donaldson has called "the Grandfather of the Kailyard," turned to these writers to add a literary dimension to the religious concerns of *The British Weekly*;[64] in doing so, he enabled Maclaren, Crockett, and Barrie to reach a broad audience beyond Scotland, fueling their considerable commercial success. David Lyall's earliest stories, written in the wake of Barrie's *Auld Licht Idylls* (1888) and *A Window in Thrums* (1889), Crockett's *Stickit Minister* (1893), and Maclaren's *Bonnie Brier Bush* (1894), bear a stronger resemblance to these sentimental sketches of Scottish village life than to the fiction of Annie S. Swan. But Lyall soon left behind the substance and style of his Kailyard contemporaries as Swan recognized the broader potential in her use of a male pseudonym.

When Swan acknowledged her identity as David Lyall in her autobiography in 1934, she offered no explanation of why she had adopted the pseudonym, merely implying that it was at the suggestion of Nicoll. She may have invented Lyall as a way to avoid saturating the market with fiction by Annie S. Swan, or to evade restrictions imposed on her by John Leng & Co., who, as her fame grew, claimed to have exclusive rights to the name "Annie S. Swan," and requested her not to publish with Hodder and Stoughton under that name.[65] After Lyall gained a readership in *The British Weekly*, his stories sometimes appeared in the *Woman at Home* side by side with fiction by Swan; and in 1923 the *People's Journal*, parent of the *People's Friend*, began to run serials by David Lyall, regularly including one per year until Swan's death in 1943. But even if Lyall began as a way to avoid undercutting sales of Swan's work, the pseudonym also allowed

[64] Donaldson, *Popular Literature*, 145.
[65] This information comes from the correspondence between Swan and Leng, which is held by D. C. Thomson, the company that bought out John Leng in 1905, and which now publishes the *People's Friend*.

Swan to write about subjects and in a style that would not have comported with her image in the *People's Friend* as a foster-mother to readers. This is not to say that Lyall's stories were in any way racy, only that they were not for the most part romances. They tended to feature male protagonists – Free Church clergymen, factory workers, monied gentlemen – whose exciting pursuits often took them beyond Britain. Marriage features only tangentially in their development.

Writing as David Lyall, then, may have allowed Swan to enjoy the same kind of temporary escape from the conditions of her everyday life as a writer that her stories offered readers of the *Friend*. David Lyall was not merely an authorial pseudonym, but a fully fleshed out character with a history. Written in the first person, a perspective that Swan never adopts in her stories for the *People's Friend*, the initial sketches that she published as David Lyall constitute a kind of fictional autobiography, following David from the small Scottish village of Faulds to London, where he obtains a place on the *St. George's Gazette*. Like the stories about professional women that Swan wrote for the *Woman at Home*, Lyall's career reveals the influence of W. T. Stead's "new" or investigative journalism, through which newspapers and magazines became instruments of moral improvement by shocking readers into awareness of social ills and campaigning on behalf of the disadvantaged.[66] As Lyall observes the effects of poverty, alcoholism, and mental illness on other recent arrivals in London, journalism and philanthropy become inseparable for him. He describes his "life work" as "more satisfying and fruitful than most" because it has required from him "conscientious, self-denying toil."[67] For Lyall, writing is a form of social activism in a way that it could not be for Annie S. Swan, whose readers wanted happy endings.

Unlike Swan, moreover, Lyall experiences no conflicting allegiances between domestic duty and his work. In an October 1897 issue of *The British Weekly* he marries his beloved Euphan Wingate, but a sketch of 1900 casually mentions her death, which conveniently enables Lyall to set off for the Transvaal to report on the South African War without domestic complications: "a man without home ties, and with little to bind him to life except congenial work, the comradeship of tried friends, the sympathy of many, and mayhap the gratitude of some."[68] As David Lyall, Swan

---

[66] On the New Journalism, see Beetham, *A Magazine of Her Own?*, 121–4.

[67] David Lyall, *David Lyall's Love Story* (London: Hodder and Stoughton, 1897), 56. The series of sketches comprising *David Lyall's Love Story* ran sporadically in *The British Weekly* from September 24, 1896, through November 7, 1897.

[68] David Lyall, *Flowers o' the Forest* (London: Hodder and Stoughton, 1900), 4.

imagined for herself a career as a writer that was not limited by the dictates of feminine propriety or domestic duty, a career that brought her into contact with danger, put her in proximity to vice, and took her to distant parts of the world.

As David Lyall, moreover, Swan could also address issues that may have felt too volatile for her to write about under her own name. For instance, from January through June of 1899, *The British Weekly* ran a serial by Lyall titled *A Woman Journalist*, which relates the professional struggles of its eponymous woman journalist Marian East in what were for Swan quite lurid terms.[69] Marian, the daughter of a doctor from the Midlands, is depressed by the dreariness of her London boarding house and the crude manners of the other women who live there, and shocked by how hard she must work to earn enough to support herself. Most distressingly, she is shocked by the habits of her employer, Mr. Stanton, who keeps a "perfect gallery of ladies' photographs" on his mantlepiece and "sometimes he forgets that he is a gentleman" – although only, as the rather plain Marian points out, when a woman is "ridiculously beautiful."[70] Marian herself never suffers from his indiscretions, for Mr. Stanton sees her as "not a person at all, but a machine, whose value entirely depended on the capacity to turn out so much copy in a given time."[71] Compared with the other working women we encounter in the story, Marian thrives, suggesting that dehumanization is preferable to sexual harassment. Yet she hopes that "in setting down these experiences ... I shall sound a note of timely warning or encouragement in the ears of the great body of young women, who are thirsting for a career such as I took up, without the faintest idea of its trials and temptations and discouragements."[72] In *The Woman Journalist*, writing under a man's name but speaking through a female protagonist, Swan warns middle-class women about the challenges they are likely to face if they pursue a professional career in much less equivocal terms than she does in the *Woman at Home*. Her male pseudonym may have allowed her to write more frankly about these challenges, protecting her from speculation that the story was autobiographical or from the skepticism of those who might find a degree of contradiction in a woman with a highly successful career counseling other women against pursuing a profession.

---

[69] The first instalment of *A Woman Journalist* appeared in *The British Weekly* 25.636 (Jan. 5, 1899) and it ran through 26.662 (July 6, 1899). It does not seem to have been published in book form.
[70] *The British Weekly*, no. 643 (Feb. 23, 1899), 362–3.
[71] *The British Weekly*, no. 643 (Feb. 23, 1899), 363.
[72] *The British Weekly*, no. 636 (Jan. 5, 1899), 245.

However, Swan was accustomed to managing contradictions. Annie S. Swan, the celebrity writer, and Mrs. Burnett Smith, the wife, mother, and social activist, were always somewhat at odds, and the former may have been a persona that Swan adopted as easily as she did the name of David Lyall. Swan's success as a serial writer required a great deal of work – and not only the work of writing 3,000 words every morning while making public appearances in the afternoon. The work involved in visibly embodying a middle-class ideal of domestic femininity while simultaneously managing a busy literary career that threatened to undermine that ideal must have been immense. Swan's assertions of the compatibility of her literary career and her domestic duties were so frequent and vociferous as to seem performative, almost as if by saying it enough, Swan could make it true. She never fully acknowledged – at least in print or in public – the hard work that must have gone into her astounding productivity and her carefully managed celebrity. Yet she may have concealed this work from readers – and especially readers of the *People's Friend* – to avoid destroying their illusions. For these readers, Swan's own story, her authorial persona, was inseparable from the stories she published. Swan embodied for the *Friend*'s working-class female readers a version of themselves as they wanted to be rather than as they were: a working mother and wife, but much more glamorous. In addition to her other talents, Swan was a savvy businesswoman who participated actively in manufacturing her authorial persona. She was not the pawn of her publishers, nor were her identities the result of happenstance. How closely her persona reflected the real woman, we cannot know.

CHAPTER 3

The Scottish New Woman and the Art of Self-Sacrifice

By the end of the nineteenth century, women in Scotland were in some ways better off than their English counterparts. Girls and boys were educated together at public schools, and a higher percentage of Scotswomen than Englishwomen could read and write. Divorce on the grounds of adultery or desertion was easier in Scotland, and the Married Women's Property Acts of 1877 and 1881 gave wives the right to keep their own earned income and to control their personal estates.[1] Despite these advantages, though, many middle-class Scotswomen must nonetheless have faced the predicament of the eponymous protagonist of Mary and Jane Findlater's *Penny Monypenny* (1911). At school, Pen, as she is nicknamed, learns "the pleasure of working in earnest, and wanted very much to have a life worth living filled with useful energy. But at Yarnoch what was she to do?"[2] *Penny Monypenny*'s narrator has no satisfactory answer to Pen's question, acknowledging that

> To bring a girl up with just enough of education to make her an intelligent companion, yet with no single subject to occupy her mind, is virtually to admit that marriage is to be her occupation. (An ample one it is if children are included.) But then to train her to look upon marriage with distrust unless it is united with romantic passion, is probably to deprive her of the only thing that will make her life satisfactory; for romantic passions are not so common in this everyday world.[3]

Pen's predicament is exacerbated by her seclusion in a "bare and stern bit of country" in the Highlands, where she could not find suitable employment outside the home even if she wanted to, and where she encounters

---

[1] Rosalind K. Marshall, *Virgins and Viragos: A History of Women in Scotland from 1080 to 1980* (London: Collins, 1983), 279.
[2] Jane Findlater and Mary Findlater, *Penny Monypenny* (London: Thomas Nelson, 1918), 113.
[3] Findlater and Findlater, *Penny Monypenny*, 114.

very few men for whom she can feel anything resembling "romantic passion."[4]

A number of Jane and Mary Findlater's novels examine the intellectually and materially circumscribed lives of middle-class women living in rural Scotland. The Findlaters' protagonists are strong-minded women whose struggles for self-realization are hampered by their lack of money, the bleakness of their surroundings, and their obligations toward their less competent family members and dependents. At a time when the courtship plot dominated the novel, very few of these women's stories end with marriage. Instead, the Findlaters' protagonists strive unceasingly but often unsuccessfully to reconcile themselves to the "everyday world" in which comfortable contentment, let alone "romantic passion," seems difficult to attain. The Findlater sisters knew intimately the conditions of such women's lives. Daughters of a Presbyterian minister in the Highland parish of Lochearnhead, they managed to write their way out of their reduced circumstances and out of the Highlands after their father's death, moving first to Edinburgh, then further south to Sussex and Cornwall. Like so many of their protagonists, they remained unmarried.[5]

Despite their propensity for crafting narratives that pit their female protagonists against social convention, Jane and Mary Findlater's novels have been overlooked in literary historical accounts of the New Woman, a figure that Sally Ledger explains as "a discursive response to the activities of the late nineteenth-century women's movement."[6] Detractors represented the New Woman as a cigarette-smoking, bicycle-riding, freethinking adulterer. More sympathetic representations explored the New Woman's struggle for economic and moral independence – the right to earn a living, make her own decisions, and occupy multiple roles, including, but not limited to, those of wife and mother. Even the most forward-thinking New Woman novelists shared a "preoccupation with the institution of marriage," and their frequent "inability to think beyond heterosexual marriage as the only available route to happiness and fulfillment for women" accounts for the pessimism of much of their fiction.[7]

Some New Woman novels, such as Olive Schreiner's *Story of an African Farm* (1883), Sarah Grand's *The Beth Book* (1897), and Mona Caird's

[4] Findlater and Findlater, *Penny Monypenny*, 114.

[5] For further biographical details, see Eileen Mackenzie, *The Findlater Sisters: Literature and Friendship* (London: John Murray, 1964).

[6] Sally Ledger, *The New Woman: Fiction and Feminism at the Fin de Siècle* (Manchester: Manchester University Press, 1997), 1.

[7] Ledger, *The New Woman*, 20, 23.

Daughters of Danaus (1894), are thinly disguised political or philosophical manifestos, in which characters are less fully realized individuals than didactic embodiments of particular positions in the debates surrounding women's rights and capacities. Jane and Mary Findlater's novels eschew this didacticism to such an extent that Talia Schaeffer has described their novels as "disengaged from the gender debates of the 1890s."[8] Attending to their use of impressionistic reveries, abrupt shifts in mood or perspective, and elaborate symbolism, Schaeffer has argued compellingly that the Findlaters' novels belong properly to fin-de-siècle aesthetic movement rather than to New Woman fiction.[9] I contend that their works are not as politically disengaged as Schaeffer suggests. Rather, the Findlaters enter the debates surrounding the woman question in aesthetic terms – that is, through their reflections on the uses, or lack thereof, of art and literature. The Findlaters were both New Woman novelists and, as Schaeffer terms them, female aesthetes. Like the better-known Scottish New Woman novelist Mona Caird, Mary and Jane Findlater represent women's artistic and literary endeavor as a means to economic and intellectual independence. But they also recognize the peculiar impediments to artistic and literary development encountered by women in rural Scotland: poverty and domestic drudgery, distance from metropolitan centers of culture, the Presbyterian church's suspicion of ornamental beauty and imaginative creation, and the pressure to conform exerted by the censorious gaze of neighbors in a small town.

Patriarchy takes culturally and historically specific forms, so it should not be surprising that the figure of the New Woman, and the discourses of the New Woman novel, might also be culturally inflected. Given the extent to which artistic and literary endeavors in nineteenth-century Scotland were perceived as the prerogative of men, it seems particularly appropriate that Scotland's New Women novelists would employ aesthetic techniques and tropes that foregrounded their own artistry, and that the Scottish New Woman should herself be an artist. In what follows, I first examine Jane Findlater's *Green Graves of Balgowrie* (1896), and *Crossriggs* (1906), coauthored by Mary and Jane Findlater, as dramatizations of the peculiar hardships that the isolation and insularity of rural Scottish life imposed on women. These works are not New Woman novels proper. Instead, they account for the comparatively limited development of the New Woman in Scottish fiction by illustrating the circumstances impeding middle-class

[8] Talia Schaffer, *The Forgotten Female Aesthetes: Literary Culture in Late-Victorian England* (Charlottesville: University of Virginia Press, 2000), 14.
[9] Schaffer, *The Forgotten Female Aesthetes*, 64.

Scotswomen's intellectual and economic autonomy. Subsequently, I compare Mona Caird's *Daughters of Danaus*, widely recognized as a New Woman novel, with Mary Findlater's *Rose of Joy* (1903). Both novels take as their protagonist a Scotswoman who questions whether individual artistic development is compatible with marriage and motherhood. The pressures of domestic duty and social convention prevent Caird's Hadria from fulfilling her potential as composer. Her dwindling musical abilities, on the one hand, and her resentment of the conventional roles she succumbs to, on the other, leave Hadria at an impasse to which Caird can offer no resolution. By contrast, Mary Findlater's Susan finds an escape from domestic drudgery in drawing, which allows her to find small instances of beauty in sordid surroundings. When she is released from her unhappy marriage, her efforts to reproduce these small beauties enable her to achieve economic independence. Hadria's and Susan's capacity to appreciate and re-create beauty, I suggest, is the defining characteristic of Scotland's New Woman. Yet scale is important to Mary Findlater's relative optimism concerning the possibility of women's economic and moral autonomy. For Susan never aspires to be an internationally renowned artist in the way that Hadria is poised to become a world-famous composer. The comparatively small scale of Susan's artistic ambitions is reflected in the minute detail of her drawings and of the Findlaters' writing. Contentment is found in embracing limitations, they suggest, rather than in railing against them.

Tales of Two Sisters

The Green Graves of Balgowrie is a highly wrought story of two emotionally enmeshed sisters brought up in a state of isolation and deprivation by their unhinged mother. Although it is set in the mid-eighteenth century, it cannot but raise unanswerable questions about the relationship between Jane and Mary Findlater, and their own childhood in Lochearnhead. *The Green Graves* is like a pre-Raphaelite painting in novel form: richly textured and boldly colored, it mimics the pre-Raphaelites' archaic style and flat perspective that, in Tim Barringer's words, paradoxically joined "historicism and modernity or revivalism and realism."[10] In tone, *Green Graves* is very different from the comparatively understated *Crossriggs*, which is generally considered the Findlater sisters' best novel. In subject, however, the two novels are quite similar. Set in the late nineteenth

---

[10] Tim Barringer, *Reading the Pre-Raphaelites*, revised ed. (New Haven, CT: Yale University Press, 2012), 12.

century, and divested of its predecessor's sentimentalism, *Crossriggs* tells the story of two sisters who struggle with intellectual and material deprivation under the watchful eyes of their neighbors in a Lowland village. Both novels depict an amoral and senseless world in which individual effort seems to count for nothing, and characters' fates are to a great extent determined by heredity, environment, and chance.

Green Graves and *Crossriggs* join George Douglas Brown's *House with the Green Shutters* (1901) in critiquing the sentimentalized image of small-town Scotland made popular in the 1890s by J. M. Barrie and Ian Maclaren. Barrie's *A Window in Thrums* and Maclaren's *Bonnie Brier Bush* represented the Scottish village as a community of quirky individuals whose occasional misunderstandings could never destroy the religious feeling and domestic affection uniting them. In *The House with the Green Shutters*, in contrast, Brown depicts the Scottish town of Barbie as a hotbed of petty gossip and jealous rivalries. Whereas women, as the guardians of hearts and hearths, hold great sway in Barrie's and Maclaren's villages, Brown's Barbie is riven by the intense competition among men to be richer and more successful than their neighbors. For Mrs. Gourlay and her daughter Janet, home is a site of terror rather a comfortable refuge, where they suffer emotional and physical abuse. While women are peripheral characters in *The House with the Green Shutters*, they are at the center of *Green Graves* and *Crossriggs*; yet these novels do not portray the harmonious households that Barrie and Maclaren had popularized. Instead, the Findlaters explore the material and psychological burdens that domestic upkeep placed on women in small-town Scotland. Although their protagonists do not suffer physical violence, they endure the more subtle impact of geographic isolation and cultural deprivation, particularly the absence of beauty in their lives.

The Green Graves of Balgowrie pays ironic tribute to another novel of small-town life – Margaret Oliphant's *Miss Marjoribanks* – through Mrs. Marjorybanks, a character whose name obviously alludes to Oliphant's heroine despite the variant in its spelling. Like Oliphant's Lucilla Marjoribanks, Mrs. Marjorybanks enjoys managing people. But where there is ample scope for Lucilla's careful plans to bring together the people of Carlingford, the widowed and isolated Mrs. Marjorybanks turns all her energies on her daughters, Lucie and Henrietta. Most who encounter Mrs. Marjorybanks assume that "the woman must be mad!"[11] She has raised Lucie and Henrietta "in as complete isolation as any castaways on a desert

---

[11] Jane Helen Findlater, *The Green Graves of Balgowrie* (London: Methuen, 1896), 14. Subsequent references to the novel will be made parenthetically.

shore" (12), and the two girls have spent their "childhood at the mercy of whims and theories; a helpless living sacrifice ready to be offered up" to their mother's latest ideas concerning their education (36). It is tempting to blame Mrs. Marjorybanks for the emotional abuse she inflicts on her daughters, but we must allow for the possibility that her madness may be the effect of years spent in Balgowrie, "an eerie spot: rat-haunted, and with a reputation for being ghost-haunted too" (11). Henrietta and Lucie find some respite from their mother's whims in the company of Dr. Hallijohn, a local clergyman whom Mrs. Marjorybanks, an emphatic atheist, has chosen to tutor her daughters because she believes he is only "in the Church for the fat living" it provides him (31). In a grotesque revision of Jane Eyre's first encounter with Mr. Rochester, Lucie and Henrietta are introduced to Dr. Hallijohn just after he has fallen drunk from his horse. His occasional intemperance later leads Henrietta to question, "Was everyone false and disappointing? Was there anyone in the world to trust and love wholly?" (57). Henrietta and Lucie can "trust and love" only each other, and their shared experience of neglect brings them closer.

While the novel's title refers to the graves in which Lucie and Henrietta lie at the story's end, Balgowrie is from the novel's beginning a sort of grave, where the sisters exist in a state of living death. Reflecting on their upbringing at Balgowrie, Dr. Hallijohn exclaims, "What a living tomb it's been for the poor children!" (262). Lucie recognizes how limited their experience has been only when, as a young woman, she visits London with Dr. Hallijohn. Attending her first play, Lucie finds the theater-goers as much a spectacle as the drama itself:

> What a show it was! So this was life? Had all this pomp and brilliancy really been going on always? – it seemed to her a sudden creation; but when she considered the matter, she knew that of course it had always existed through the dead years of her former life, and away back and back before she had even lived. The great and noisy and moving world had been rushing on while she and Henrietta had lived unaware of it, buried as deep as if they were in their graves, at poor sleepy old Balgowrie. (186–7)

To her acquaintances in London, Lucie appears almost as if she had been raised from the dead, "a white figure ... most ghostly to behold" (223), with "a terrible, lifeless sound in her voice" (225). Her deathlike despair develops from the realization that she is completely unable to function in society. In London she sees herself for the first time "through other peoples' eyes" (227) and realizes that she and Henrietta are irreparably "queer all through" (169). Because Henrietta never leaves Balgowrie, she does not fully comprehend her own peculiarity as Lucie does, nor does she ever experience the opportunity to become part of "a great and noisy and moving world" through which she might transcend the confines of her existence. She is abstractly aware that "just beyond this life of mine is a great and wonderful world where men and women *live*; there is beauty that I cannot imagine – not if I strain my powers to cracking – for does not Locke hold that the highest imagination is a remembrance of something experienced? I have experienced so little that my imagination itself is stunted" (205). As her reference to John Locke's empirical theory of the mind demonstrates, Henrietta has tried valiantly to compensate for her lack of experience through extensive reading and study. But beauty cannot be perceived through these means; it must be experienced directly, and because she has never enjoyed things of beauty, Henrietta's stunted imagination has no raw materials to work with.

As Lucie and Henrietta die of consumption, one after the other, it is tempting to agree with Lucie's declaration that "it seems as if it were all a mistake, a blunder, that anyone should be created only to die" (273). But the seeming pointlessness of the sisters' short lives is perhaps redeemed by Henrietta's independent formulation of a divine power. She responds to Lucie, "I see that terrible things are permitted in our lives . . . but I do not think they are mistakes; the whole world moves by order, and not by confusion – they are purposed, not accidental" (273). Although she has not received any formal religious instruction, Henrietta concludes that "this life is not reason enough for our existence" (274), and that death, accordingly, "concerns the flesh, not the spirit" (279). She knows that she will never experience the "great and wonderful world" but hopes her desire "to live, live, live – " nevertheless might be fulfilled in an afterlife (205). Henrietta's independent arrival at a belief in life after death suggests that this belief is somehow natural and inevitable. It need not be taught formally because it can be divined intuitively. It is remarkable, then, that God is nowhere to be found in *Crossriggs* and that religion offers no consolation to the mundane sufferings of Alexandra Hope.

With its interweaving of Gothic conventions and aesthetic techniques, *The Green Graves of Balgowrie* seems simultaneously archaic and modern. It dramatizes in vividly hyperbolic and almost allegorical terms the isolation and deprivation experienced by women in small-town Scotland. By contrast, *Crossriggs* is understated and naturalistic, an attempt to uncover the extravagances of romance in the banalities of everyday life. The village of Crossriggs is situated in what the novel's unnamed narrator, evidently a denizen of the locale, describes as an "unromantic bit of agricultural country" an hour's train ride from Edinburgh.[12] The characters too are more commonplace in *Crossriggs* than in *Green Graves*. There is no crazed mother to blame for the intellectual isolation and material deprivation that Alex experiences, for Mrs. Hope is long dead, perhaps sent to an early grave through hard work. Alex's sufferings are by no means as spectacularly awful as Henrietta's and Lucie's. But there is a fundamental similarity among the protagonists of the two novels: they share a thwarted desire to "live, live, live – " in all the limitlessness implied by the dash at the end of this cry.

Crossriggs dramatizes the frustrations of a woman whose talents and ambitions exceed her means and environment. Spirited and strong-minded, Alex is a dour version of *Little Women*'s Jo March. She is a foster-mother to her widowed sister's children and the sole provider for a household that also includes her father Mr. Hope, or Old Hopeful as he is known in Crossriggs. As his nickname suggests, Mr. Hope's "life has been one long series of mistakes and failures, from a practical point of view, and yet his soul is alive all the time. He goes on believing and hoping and enthusing, whatever happens to himself" or, Alex adds bitterly, "*to others*" (82). Old Hopeful's insouciant optimism is endearing, but also selfish. He maintains his enthusiasm for life because he counts on Alex to ensure the family's survival. Her task is made more difficult by the glaring absence of remunerative employment for middle-class women in a village such as Crossriggs. Alex initially finds work reading to an elderly neighbor and teaching elocution in Edinburgh; eventually, though, she must resort to giving public readings, a form of work she finds humiliating, perhaps because it is too close to performing as an actress for a middle-class woman's comfort. And if employment prospects are scarce for genteel women in rural Scotland, the Findlaters suggests that marriage prospects are scarcer. Alex and her married neighbor Robert Maitland suffer from the necessity of hiding their love while living in such close proximity in the "tight little" village of Crossriggs (4).

Alex's sense of powerlessness against circumstance may illustrate the middle-class myopia of which Douglas Gifford has with some justice accused the Findlaters, but her frustration is nonetheless genuine.[13]

[12] Jane Findlater and Mary Findlater, *Crossriggs* (London: Virago, 1986), 4. Subsequent references to this edition will be made parenthetically.
[13] Douglas Gifford, "Caught between Worlds: The Fiction of Jane and Mary Findlater," in *A History of Scottish Women's Writing*, ed. Douglas Gifford and Dorothy McMillan (Edinburgh: Edinburgh University Press, 1997), 292–3.

Her weariness is palpable as she recounts the causes of her dissatisfaction to her sister:

> Our life has been all wrong from the very beginning, indeed, before that, for it began wrong before we were born, with our parents' dispositions, but we won't go into that just now – anyway, we're all wrong. I've wasted life, and youth is nearly over, and my health isn't what it used to be, and we are too poor to be dignified even in the simplest way, and our house, which ought to be the expression of the soul, is hideous, and our life is limited, and our ideas are provincial, and our neighbours are dull, and the world is full of bores, and your children are just so many responsibilities to squeeze us down, and Father is an unpractical optimist. (250)

Alex's outburst recalls Lucie's realization at the theater in London of all the joy and wonder she has missed out on simply because of the circumstances of her birth. The Findlaters' invocation of heredity and fate also recalls the naturalism, understood loosely as a literary mode that explores "the impingement of natural processes on human agency and consciousness," of George Gissing or Thomas Hardy.[14] But, among literary critics at least, middle-class women who complain of their reduced circumstances rarely meet with the sympathy that *Jude the Obscure* (1896) solicits for a stonemason who might have been a scholar.

The Findlaters suggest that the frustration expressed by Alex is shared to some degree by most middle-class women, who in *Crossriggs* spend their lives in unfulfilling toil. One of the Hopes' neighbors, Bessie Reid, lives "a monotonous life, spending much time in tending a paralyzed aunt" (11). We learn that "it was only a brave effort that kept her going at all, and she made it unceasingly" (11). Bessie's "brave effort" primarily takes the form of ridiculous personal decorations – a wreath of artificial grapevines around her hat, or a lurid bouquet of bows pinned to her dress. Despite, or perhaps because of, her questionable sartorial choices, Bessie is a sympathetic and even an admirable character; these decorations make her bleak life just a bit brighter. That minor but continual irritations are women's lot in life is clearly illustrated when Alex and Matilda are walking home in the midst of a quarrel and run into Maitland, an eminent historian who looks, Alex says, "as if you had been on some mount of transfiguration, whilst we have had such a petty and disgusting woman's day, though perhaps some of us would have liked quite as well as you to lie by the side of a burn, and

---

[14] Constance D. Harsh, "Gissing's *The Unclassed* and the Perils of Naturalism," *ELH* 59.4 (1992): 912. Gifford observes similarities between Hardy and the Findlaters in "Caught between Worlds," 294.

look at beautiful things, and come home to write history" (179). Instead, Alex and Matilda have endured "Singed soup, sodden potatoes, burnt apples, house dense with smoke, an unexpected guest to luncheon, one child ill with earache ... all the others naughty" (179). Well before Virginia Woolf suggested that a room of one's own might be necessary for serious intellectual work, Alex understands that the "petty and disgusting" problems that make up women's daily labor are not conducive to writing history. Her remark draws attention to the Findlaters' generic choices; for rather than addressing the lofty subject matter of history, they turn the familiar stuff of Alex's "petty and disgusting woman's day" into art.

Similar metafictional moments in *Crossriggs* shed light on the Findlaters' aims in transforming the unrelenting drudgery of daily domestic life in small-town Scotland into literature. When Admiral Cassilis employs Alex to read to him, he specifies that the reading materials must not include novels – not because novels are frivolous, but, on the contrary, because "life ... is sad enough without fiction" (76) and reading should offer an escape from that unhappiness. Alex, by contrast, sees fiction as presenting a distilled version of everyday trials: the sadness of life is "so long and hard and spread out, compared to the brief romantic sorrows of fiction, that it does one good to read about them, I think, and then we can imagine that [our sorrows] are going to be like that!" (76). The irony, of course, is that the Findlaters have made Alex's "long and hard and spread out" frustrations, of which "romantic sorrows" are merely one element, into the stuff of fiction. Whereas Annie S. Swan sought to offer her readers an escape from the monotony and vexations of their daily lives, Jane and Mary Findlater elevate those experiences into art, using Alex's long lists of annoyances to evoke the tedium with which readers might be familiar.

In another of *Crossriggs*'s metafictive moments, the Findlaters suggest that the novel's representations of the small sufferings of genteel poverty give it a claim to realism that other novels lack. Alex declares that "one of the weak points of novels" is "that they prefer to pretend that the outside circumstances look like the inside – the outside of the stained glass window like the window seen from within. It hardly ever does!" (214). In its depiction of Alex's mental and emotional turmoil, *Crossriggs* seeks to offer readers a glance at the inside of the stained-glass window, an angle from which the contours of the picture are not always clear. For, in addition to the married Maitland, whom Alex loves fruitlessly, she must also contend with the admiral's nephew Van Cassilis, who is desperately in love with Alex and for whom Alex feels an affection that she will not allow to ripen into love because she is nine years older and a great deal poorer than him. Readers are privy to her complicated feelings – the inside of the window – at the same time we see her efforts to conform outwardly to social conventions that frown on those feelings.

Despite her pluck, Alex is not a New Woman because she does not reject the constraints of social convention. She seeks employment because she must support her relations, not because she wants to develop her faculties or fill her time, and she eschews marriage because she cannot find a husband whom society would sanction. Both her efforts to find employment and her eschewal of marriage come to seem futile when her sister remarries, taking all of her five children away from Crossriggs, and leaving Alex to ask, "To what purpose had all her struggles been if the children did not care enough for even one of them to stay with her? All the life and brightness were leaving the house with them" (352). Unlike her fictional predecessors – Oliphant's Margaret Maitland or Swan's Janet Nesbit – Alex fails to reform social institutions or hierarchies through her fostering. The novel's last chapters strip away Alex's connections, leaving her isolated and depressed as "the round of her home duties" defining her "monotonous life" comes to feel "like the walls of a dungeon, from which she must escape or die" (334).

She escapes thanks only to the unexpected appearance of a foster-mother of her own: her aunt Clara, whom Alex had nursed through several months of illness and who leaves Alex a legacy when she dies. It is fitting that Alex's inheritance comes from a woman, given the foster-mother's typical position outside the institution of marriage and the patrilinear transmission of property it supports. Aunt Clara repays Alex in economic terms for the emotional labor she has performed for others. However, the legacy does not provide the happy ending that we might expect it to, as it does nothing to alleviate Alex's loneliness or her sense of the futility of her earlier economic and emotional struggles: "Life is over for me," she tells herself, "the best of it – the zest of it, and nothing – not all the money in the world, not anything could ever bring it back again" (374). She uses her inheritance to leave Crossriggs indefinitely, perhaps forever, setting out on a voyage around the world. Although she departs feeling "as if she had no tears left to shed, no power left to hope" (379), her name – Alex Hope – suggests the possible regeneration of this power. The ambivalent ending leaves open the possibility of future happiness for Alex, but it is unclear what form this happiness might take.

Alex's failure to become a New Woman by resisting the pressures of social conformity, whether by marrying Van, having an affair with

Maitland, or finding happiness in independence, owes much to her rural isolation and her poverty. In Crossriggs, she can never be anonymous, nor can she find sympathy in the company of like-minded women. She is constantly under the scrutiny of well-meaning neighbors who consider her an oddity. The New Woman is not only primarily a metropolitan figure; she is also a relatively affluent one.[15] The choice to shake off society's trammels in order to pursue personal desire comes with a price that only the economically independent can afford. When, at the novel's end, Alex's legacy brings her financial stability and autonomy, it is as if she does not know what to do with her new freedom. She can finally "live, live, live – " but it is not clear that she knows how to.

Portraits of the Artist as a New Woman

If Alex Hope lacks the New Woman's sense of mission, the protagonists of Mona Caird's *Daughters of Danaus* and Mary Findlater's *Rose of Joy* find their purpose in artistic creation. Their struggles to reconcile their artistic talents with their socially sanctioned roles as wives and mothers are what make Caird's Hadria and Findlater's Susan New Women rather than simply the culturally and intellectually deprived women that Henrietta and Alex are. Like many New Woman novels, *Daughters of Danaus* and *The Rose of Joy* deviate from the traditional courtship plot.[16] Rather than taking marriage as their end point and as the culmination of their protagonists' experiences, both novels focus on the protagonist's experiences after marriage, when she begins to feel the limitations imposed by her duties as wife and mother. Stylistically, however, *The Daughters of Danaus* and *The Rose of Joy* could not be more different. Caird's novel is consciously polemical: its characters represent recognizable positions in the debates surrounding the New Woman, and they perform these debates through their interactions. Hadria is at odds with virtually everyone around her, and her continual conflicts render the novel as tumultuous as her musical compositions. Mary Findlater is no less interested than Caird in exploring the tensions between individual fulfillment and social

---

[15] Alicia Carroll uncovers a rural tradition of New Woman writing in *New Women Ecologies: From Arts and Crafts to the Great War and Beyond* (Charlottesville: University of Virginia Press, 2019). However, the women she discusses resided primarily in southern England and were affluent enough that they did not need to work.

[16] On the New Woman novel's avoidance of the courtship plot, see Anne Ardis, *New Woman, New Novels: Feminism and Early Modernism* (New Brunswick, NJ: Rutgers University Press, 1990), 3–14.

obligation, but *The Rose of Joy* eschews abstract argument in favor of concrete and detailed representations of its protagonist's subjectivity and surroundings. It invites readers to find in Susan's meditations on the minutiae of the natural world around her an escape from domestic duties and stifling social conventions.

A number of New Women novels took artists or writers as their protagonists because the female artist provided a kind of limit case in discussions of the woman question – the question of whether and how women's nature might be compatible with roles traditionally reserved for men. As Lyn Pykett explains, in Victorian fiction the female artist often "serves as a compound figure for the exceptional or aspiring woman and for the obstacles that she will inevitably encounter in attempting to realize her aspirations in the face of dominant social definitions of femininity."[17] As Caird and Findlater recognized, the female artist must struggle to reconcile artistic creation with biological procreation, and the development of her talents with domestic and social responsibilities. In Scotland, moreover, the female artist had to contend with Mrs. MacGrundy, or with a religiously informed social censoriousness toward the expression of imagination and emotion. Taking artists as their protagonists allowed Caird and Findlater to reflect metafictionally on their own status as women writers and on the relationships between art and life, and between the aesthetic and the political. They join a number of other turn-of-the-century Anglo-American women who wrote *Künstlerromane*, or novels of artistic maturation, in engaging with Ralph Waldo Emerson's very masculine ideal of artistic genius as absolute self-realization.[18] For Emerson, the development of artistic genius requires the rejection of the predetermined narratives that limit us, and for the female artist, as Caird and Findlater knew well, such narratives tended to end in marriage or death.

Caird called into question both the inevitability of marriage as a narrative ending and the utility of marriage as a social institution in a polemical essay published in *The Westminster Review* in August 1888. "Marriage" brought Caird literary notoriety almost overnight, eliciting written responses from over two hundred readers.[19] Caird's novels, the first two

---

[17] Lyn Pykett, "Portraits of the Artist as a Young Woman: Representations of the Female Artist in the New Woman Fiction of the 1890s," in *Victorian Women Writers and the Woman Question*, ed. Nicola Diane Thompson (Cambridge: Cambridge University Press, 1999), 136.

[18] Novelists who engaged with Emerson's conception of genius include Kate Chopin, Olive Schreiner, Sarah Grand, and Willa Cather, among others. See Virginia M. Kouidis, "Emersonian True Romance and the Woman Novelist," *North Dakota Quarterly* 60.4 (1992): 84–104.

[19] Mona Caird, "Marriage," *The Westminster Review* 130.1 (1888): 191.

of which she published under the name G. Noel Hatton, illustrate through their protagonists' predicaments the main point of her essay "Marriage" – that women must be given the means of economic independence so that they do not need marry in order to survive. Over the past two decades, feminist critics have rescued Caird from obscurity, with Sally Ledger arguing persuasively that she "should be regarded as the most significant foremother of modern feminism at the fin de siècle."[20]

Ironically, given her criticisms of the institution of marriage, little is known about the life of Alice Mona Alison before her marriage to James Henryson-Caird. Scottish by parentage and marriage, although born on the Isle of Wight, Caird spent much of her adult life in London, leaving her husband to manage the estate of Cassencary, near Dumfries. Despite the recent attention Caird's writing has garnered, critics have overlooked the thematic importance of Scotland to her best-known New Woman novel, *The Daughters of Danaus*. Scotland inspires Hadria's musical compositions, but the pressure to conform to standards of feminine respectability in the remote and insular Highlands compels Hadria into a marriage to which she must sacrifice her talents.

The title of *Daughters of Danaus* alludes to a Greek myth in which Danaus forced his fifty daughters into marriage, and when they proceeded to kill their husbands, they were "condemned to the idiot's labour of eternally drawing water in sieves from fathomless wells."[21] Ann Heilman observes that "Caird's mythopoeia historicised the contemporary condition of women by revealing the ancient rites of woman-sacrifice on which dominant cultural discourses of turn-of-the-century Britain were predicated."[22] In *The Daughters of Danaus*, endlessly repeating domestic duties and social engagements become the metaphorical sieves through which women are doomed to fritter away their time and energy. When we first encounter Hadria she is debating with her brothers and sister the question that Emerson poses in his essay "Fate": whether human will is stronger than circumstance. *The Daughters of Danaus* explores this question in gendered terms, implicitly asking whether the Danaides might have succeeded in emptying the well if they had only been determined enough,

---

[20] Ledger, *The New Woman*, 22. Ann Heilmann was crucial in bringing renewed critical attention to Caird with her essay "Mona Caird (1854–1932): Wild Woman, New Woman, and Early Feminist Critic of Marriage and Motherhood," *Women's History Review* 5.1 (1996), 67–95.

[21] Mona Caird, *The Daughters of Danaus* (New York: Feminist Press, 1989), 467. Subsequent references to this edition will be made parenthetically.

[22] Ann Heilmann, *New Woman Strategies: Sarah Grand, Olive Schreiner, Mona Caird* (Manchester: Manchester University Press, 2004), 233.

and by analogy, whether a Victorian woman might become a successful composer despite her numerous social and domestic obligations if only she tried hard enough. Hadria is enchanted by Emerson's belief that "the soul contains the events that shall befall it, for the event is only the actualization of its thoughts" (8), but she cannot bring herself to agree that such autonomous self-realization is possible or that "circumstance can always be conquered" through effort (10). For, if Emerson "had been a girl, he would have known that conditions do count hideously in one's life" (14). While she finds Emerson's ideal of self-actualizing genius attractive, Hadria recognizes that it is implicitly gendered and that the obstacles that women must conquer before they can cultivate their talents are often too great to leave them any time or energy for self-realization.

Daughters of Danaus relates Hadria's own attempt to overcome the conditions that prevent her from developing her considerable talents as a musician and composer. Foremost among these are the numerous tedious social and domestic obligations that arise every day, and break "the good serviceable time into jagged fragments" (44) so that "her greatest effort had to be given, not to the work itself, but to win opportunity to pursue it" (109). When she finally finds an unbroken stretch of time, usually in the middle of the night, to devote to her work, Hadria often finds that she has lost "the delicate balance of thought and mood necessary for composition" (110). Many of Caird's contemporaries, including Florence Nightingale, Dinah Mulock Craik, John Stuart Mill, and Havelock Ellis, similarly remarked on the social and domestic monopolization of women's time, which precluded the pursuit of serious intellectual or artistic endeavor. In an apt metaphor, poet Augusta Webster observed that a woman's time is "reckoned needless to the owner and free to whoever takes it, like black-berries in a hedge."[23] Although Hadria at one point takes the dramatic step of leaving her husband and sons to study music in Paris, she cannot escape the socially instilled sense of guilt she feels at pursuing her own desires rather than devoting herself to meeting theirs. The conditions preventing women from realizing the full extent of their abilities are not simply imposed from without by others, Hadria finds. She has internalized

---

[23] *A Housewife's Opinions* (London: Macmillan, 1879), 130. For a sustained analysis of time in *Daughters of Danaus*, see Patricia Murphy, *Time Is of the Essence: Temporality, Gender, and the New Woman* (Albany: State University of New York Press, 2001), 151–82; and Lisa Surridge, "Narrative Time, History and Feminism in Mona Caird's *The Daughters of Danaus*," *Women's Writing* 12.1 (2005): 127–41.

society's expectations of her as a wife and mother and cannot defy them without constant and all-consuming struggle.

Daughters of Danaus is not just the story of any late Victorian woman's futile struggle to develop her musical talents; it is specifically the story of a Scotswoman's struggle. Hadria's Scottishness is an integral part of her identity as a musician. For Hadria, the "bleak and solitary" regions of northern Scotland where she grows up both inhibit and inspire her creativity (16). Throughout the novel, Hadria's musical genius is consistently associated with the Highland landscape and her "Celtic blood" (17). Hadria "seemed to have absorbed the spirit of the northern twilights," so that her compositions are haunted by a "spectral loneliness" and evoke images of "a sudden storm among the mountains," "the wind-swept heavens at midnight," and "the lonely sea" (266). Inspired by a harsh but sublime landscape, Hadria's compositions are far from the "melodious, graceful music" that, according to Phyllis Weliver, was considered appropriate for female composers.[24] While the Scottish landscape inspires Hadria's compositions, parochial Scottish society censors her originality. The narrator informs us that "in this out-of-the-way district, society smiled upon conformity, and glared vindictively at the faintest sign of spontaneous thinking" (12). Her musical compositions – described by one of her neighbors as "things without any tune that bore one to death" (66) and by a renowned French composer as "rebel music, offensive to the orthodox" (321) – are looked on askance because they are unusual.

Caird's description of Hadria's musical compositions recalls Matthew Arnold's *On the Study of Celtic Literature* (1867), which attributed to Celts a propensity to strong and volatile emotions.[25] For Arnold, Celtic sensibility was a source of exciting imaginative creativity that could become excessive and destructive if untampered by Anglo-Saxon rationality. As Arnold might have predicted, Hadria's emotiveness, never greater than when she hears music that moves her, proves her undoing. Scotland's "national music" evokes for Hadria "bewildering memories" of "some wild, primitive experiences . . . as if [she] had lived before, among some

---

[24] Phyllis Weliver, *Women Musicians in Victorian Fiction, 1860–1900: Representations of Music, Science and Gender in the Leisured Home* (Aldershot: Ashgate, 2000), 23–4. On Hadria's musical compositions, see also Anna Peak, "Music and New Woman Aesthetics in Mona Caird's *The Daughters of Danaus*," *Victorian Review: An Interdisciplinary Journal of Victorian Studies* 40.1 (2014): 135–54.

[25] Matthew Arnold, *On the Study of Celtic Literature and on Translating Homer* (New York: Macmillan, 1906), 67–8. On the nineteenth-century tendency to infantilize or feminize Celts by associating them with unregulated emotion, see Murray G. H. Pittock, *Celtic Identity and the British Image* (Manchester: Manchester University Press 1999), 61–74.

ancient Celtic people" (137). Beginning to dance, she is gradually over-powered by the feelings evoked by these inherited memories until "some mad spirit seemed to possess her" (136). It is while she is in such a state, "as if she were in the thrall of some dream" (137), that Hubert Temperley persuades Hadria to marry him by falsely claiming to share her unconventional views on the nonbinding nature of marriage and by promising that she will have more freedom as a wife than she does as a daughter. In contrast to Hadria's expansive emotional capacity, the English Hubert demonstrates a rigidity of thought and shallowness of feeling. His opinions are "of an immoveable order, with very defined edges" (77), and he is certain that marriage will soon tame Hadria's wildness by providing her with new and more appropriate duties and pleasures.

Hadria's Celtic capacity for deep emotion is the source both of her determination to pursue a career as a composer and of her inability do so. Although she recognizes the masculine bias in Emerson's claim that individual will can overcome material circumstances, it is her "intellect, rather than her heart, [that] opposed the philosophy of Emerson" (17). At a visceral level, Hadria feels that if someone "has but the spirit that can soar high enough to really be resolved upon stars, or the ambition sufficiently vaulting to be determined on kingdoms, then ... stars and kingdoms would be forthcoming, though obstacles were never so determined" (44). Hadria is alive to the romance of Emerson's theory; it is emotionally satisfying to believe that individual effort can triumph over obstacles, and Hadria is seduced by this belief to continue working at her musical compositions even after her marriage. But if her emotional capacity buoys up her belief in her abilities, her strong feelings and sensitive nature also make her reluctant to offend others by "cutting through prejudices that are twined in the very heart-strings of those one loves" (15). Hadria's fear of giving pain to others renders her particularly sensitive to the claims of her mother, husband, and children on her time and energy – claims that she must ignore if she is to pursue a career as a composer. When the emotional distress caused by Hadria's flight to Paris causes her mother to become dangerously ill, Hadria finds herself in "circumstances [that] could not be overcome by any deed that she could bring herself to do" (370). The word "circumstances" recalls the debate between Hadria and her siblings over whether circumstances or will is a stronger determinant of an individual's fate. Emerson asserts that genius can surmount circumstances of any kind in the quest for actualization, but to accept the triumph of circumstances, Hadria finds, also takes immense will. Rather than exacerbate her mother's illness, she renounces her musical studies.

In presenting readers with a New Woman who fails to realize her ambitions, Caird claims for *The Daughters of Danaus* a realism that she suggests other novels lack. Although she is an avid reader, Hadria is unable to find in books a "spiritual sanctuary" from her troubles (112). She explains, "I am oppressed by a sense of the discrepancy between the world that books disclose to me, and the world that I myself inhabit. In books, the impossibilities are all left out. They give you no sense of the sordid Inevitable that looms so large on the grey horizon" (112). Whether she is reading novels or Emerson's essays, literature offers Hadria no reflection of her own difficulties, depicting instead a world in which individual agency triumphs over circumstance and escapes the "sordid Inevitable," the pressures to conform to conventional models of womanhood. Hadria's friend, the novelist Valeria du Prel, embodies the discrepancy between life, which demands difficult sacrifices, and literature, in which sacrifice is either easy or nonexistent. Du Prel's novel, *Caterina*, features a strong-willed heroine very like Hadria who permanently leaves her husband and children to pursue her own ambitions – a feat that Hadria is unable to accomplish. But in contrast to her celebrated heroine, Miss du Prel deeply regrets that she has remained unmarried, feeling that she has sacrificed the joys of motherhood to her own authorial ambitions. She laments her own experiences of the female independence that she commends in her fiction.

In suggesting that only in a work of fiction can women achieve self-fulfillment, *The Daughters of Danaus* claims for itself what Sally Ledger describes as "an extreme form of social realism."[26] In its style and story, the novel is certainly an uncomfortable read, and stands out from so many of the other works discussed in this book in that it offers neither escape from the dismal limitations of women's everyday lives nor the comforting suggestion that such limitations might be overcome. Caird's sometimes overwrought prose and insistently obvious symbolism is perhaps the literary equivalent of Hadria's jarringly discordant music, too angry and despairing to be pleasing. In keeping with the extreme social realism that Ledger observes, Caird avoids assigning her protagonist "woman's standard fictional fates – either marital fulfilment or extra-marital sexuality, despair, and death."[27] Hadria neither dies like Schreiner's Lyndall in *The Story of*

---

[26] Ledger, *The New Woman*, 28.
[27] Margaret Morganroth Gullette, afterword to Caird, *The Daughters of Danaus*, 503. Elisha Cohn approaches Caird's rejection of the marriage plot as a revision of evolutionary theory in "Darwin's Marriage Plots: Unplotting Courtship in Late Victorian Fiction," in *Replotting Marriage in Nineteenth-Century British Literature*, ed. Jill Galvan and Elsie Michie (Columbus: Ohio State University Press, 2018), 35–54.

an African Farm nor achieves liberation from her marriage like the protagonist of Sarah Grand's *Beth Book*. Instead, the novel leaves Hadria
bleakly resigned to her lot. She learns to see her failure as a step in a
process that will enable other women to succeed. In a dream sequence that
illustrates the feverish pitch of Caird's writing, Hadria sees

> a vast abyss, black and silent, which had to be filled to the top with the
> bodies of women, hurled down to the depths of the pit of darkness, in order
> that the survivors might, at last, walk over in safety ... Hadria knew, in her
> dream, that some day it would have claimed its last victim, and the surface
> would be level and solid, so that people would come and go, scarcely
> remembering that beneath their feet was once a chasm into which throb-
> bing lives had to descend, to darkness and a living death. (451)

Hadria's acceptance of her fate as one of the bodies thrown into the pit
seems heroic, but it perhaps only indicates how far she has internalized a
socially sanctioned ethic of feminine self-sacrifice.

Susan Crawford, protagonist of *The Rose of Joy*, shares none of Hadria's
passionate longing to throw off the shackles of marriage and motherhood,
nor does she declare herself a supporter of women's rights, or even think
much about individual agency in the abstract terms that Caird's heroine
uses. Instead, Susan retreats from domestic drudgery and an unfulfilling
marriage into herself, conforming outwardly to others' expectations of her
while living an intensely rich inner life that few know of. Similarly, *The
Rose of Joy* eschews the vehement tones, performative debates, and didactic
symbolism of *The Daughters of Danaus*. It allows readers to share both the
narrator's seemingly objective gaze and Susan's artistic perspective, which
finds beauty where the narrator recognizes deprivation. Susan's claims to
be a New Woman are almost accidental. She gains the opportunity to
develop her talents as a painter by chance rather than through any
concerted effort of her own, so that *The Rose of Joy* shares the fatalistic
outlook of *The Daughters of Danaus* even though Susan succeeds where
Hadria fails. In the tiny Scottish village of Burrie Bush, where children
"know at an early age, with a flat finality of knowledge, all that there is to
be known about everyone," Susan's intellectual horizons are narrower than
Hadria's.[28] Yet even in this environment Susan develops an aesthetic and
moral philosophy that, when she is freed by a sensational plot device from
her unhappy marriage, enables her to thrive as a New Woman.

---

[28] Mary Findlater, *The Rose of Joy* (London: Methuen, 1903), 23. Subsequent references to this edition
will be made parenthetically.

The Rose of Joy takes its title from a passage in Ralph Waldo Emerson's essay, "Love," which contrasts the "actual" world – "this painful kingdom of time and chance" marked by "care, canker, and sorrow" – with the ideal world of thought that holds "the rose of joy" around which "all the muses sing."[29] It is fitting that Emerson's rose of joy appears in an essay about love, for *The Rose of Joy* is a novel about the inadequacy of romantic love as a source of happiness, especially in contrast to the pleasures to be found in the contemplation of beauty. Love, in this novel, at least, is transient and changeable. As Susan explains to her younger sister Emmy, "Anyone can't just marry anyone else . . . so many things prevent it. Circumstances – and tastes – and fate" (209). Most of the novel's characters are defeated by "circumstances," forced by economic pressures into marrying for money, or by their "tastes" resigned to a lifetime of married indifference. Among the older generation, Maurice Hamilton's unrequited love for Susan's mother created a kind of domino effect. Susan's mother, beloved by Hamilton, married Captain Crawford. Susan's aunt loved Captain Crawford but, because he loved Susan's mother, settled for marriage to Mr. Murchison, the brewer. Lady Agnes loved Maurice Hamilton but, because he loved Susan's mother, settled for Maurice's brother, William Hamilton. The younger generation seems poised to repeat the convoluted disappointments of the elder.

Like Hadria, Susan marries out of a sense of obligation and a belief that marriage is the only way out of her parental home. Dally Stair is infatuated with Susan's cousin Juliet Clephane, but proposes to Susan because her uncle Mr. Murchison has promised to make Dally a partner in his brewing company if Dally marries Susan. "There's my fortune made, you see," Dally explains (104). "Do it for my sake – do, Susan, do. I'd be so happy – I'd be such a much better man if you'd do it. I love you so" (104). If Dally mentions love only belatedly as a reason to marry, Susan, for her part, greatly doubts whether she loves Dally or not, but reassures herself, "It will be all right when once I am married. . . . After all, how could I just live on at home? I do love him – I must" (130). Susan convinces herself that she "must" love Dally because the prospect of remaining at home to care for her younger siblings is too awful. Like Alex Hope, Susan is forced into the role of foster-mother because she is the most competent person in her household. Her father is dead and her mother, who has "practically spent her life in the nursery" is faded, tired, and helpless (12), leaving Susan

---

[29] Ralph Waldo Emerson, "Love," in *Essays* (London: Fraser, 1841), 172, qtd. on the title page of Mary Findlater, *The Rose of Joy* (London: Methuen, 1903).

responsible for "doing all that had to be done" (46). Marriage will not change this domestic drudgery much, perhaps, but it promises to alleviate the sordid poverty in which the Crawfords live.

Amid the disappointment and frustration of so many mismatched unions, only Colonel Hamilton and Susan are able to take pleasure in the "indestructible joys" and "solid satisfactions" found in art and litera- ture – pleasure that transcends the vagaries of time and circumstance. Hamilton first introduces Susan to Emerson's rose of joy while reflecting on his youthful disappointment when Susan's mother turned down his proposal of marriage. Over time he has learned that "there are innumerable lights – solid satisfactions that are always to be had" next to which romantic passion pales (33). These solid satisfactions, according to Hamilton, include "friends and philosophies, and beautiful places, and books and pictures – these are the indestructible joys forever" (33). Although Susan has not yet experienced disappointment in love, she understands Hamilton intuitively because she has already learned to find in the contemplation of beauty a source of great pleasure that withstands the encroachments of domestic drudgery.

Susan can find beauty in the most humble of surroundings, such as Striven, the bleakly bare house inhabited by Dally's mother and sisters. There, in contemplating "old green linen hangings embroidered with a design of apples" she ceases to notice that she has "scarcely the commonest comforts of life in other ways; that fierce draughts blew cold through every chink in the paneling; that the glass on the dressing table was so blue and blurred she could hardly see her own face in it; that the boards of the floor were crumbling beneath her feet" (172). While other visitors to Striven might see only what it lacks, Susan's pleasure in the embroidered hangings blinds her to its discomforts. Dally observes with frustration that Susan could make "a meal off the colour of the sea" (96). Susan is able to find spiritual sustenance in contemplating beauty, because, as Colonel Hamilton observes with genuine wonder, she is "the rarest thing in the world – a woman artist" (165). Hamilton recognizes that circumstances conspire against women developing their artistic talents, and Susan's abilities are all the more surprising given the grind of her daily existence, which "followed only the ordinary course of too many women's lives" (46). But Susan has learned to feed her hunger for beauty even while she follows this course, so that "with unquestioning patience she continued to perform all the unvarying duties of the day, whilst all the time her heart was busy with its own occupation – one which no one she lived with could share" (49). After the children are in bed and her work is done, Susan turns to her drawing books, but all day while she works, she is mentally gathering material for her designs. Susan's "inner and outer life [are] disconnected" (49): the latter, a tedious round of chores, belongs to Emerson's "painful kingdom of time and chance," while the former, devoted to the appreciation of beauty, holds "the rose of joy" in its enduring pleasures.

Findlater's artistic protagonist recalls the artist-figures that are so prominent in Margaret Oliphant's fiction. Like the writers that Antonia Losano discusses in *The Woman Painter in Victorian Literature*, Findlater and Oliphant "use the figure of the woman painter not only to engage with social and aesthetic debates about art in general, but also to consider the cultural position of their own medium."[30] In her descriptions of Susan's art, Mary Findlater comments on her own practices as a writer. Susan's art is imitative, like Menie Laurie's in *The Quiet Heart*, but it is also impressionistic. Susan draws because "she wanted to fix with greater intensity the impression that the outer world made upon her when it was translated by her imagination" (51). Susan's aim is not to reproduce the world around her as accurately as possible, but rather to record her subjective "impression" of this world. Findlater's writing is similarly impressionistic, using concrete images derived from the domestic and natural environments in which her characters move to convey information about them. For instance, she describes Susan as "a young green shoot growing from a withered tree" (26) to convey the unexpectedness of her youthful bloom in the washed-out world of Burrie Bush. Her mother's youthful beauty and accomplishments, by contrast, are "gone as completely as the plating off an old spoon" (12).

Findlater also shares with Susan a predilection for minutiae, and both find much to notice within a limited scope. Susan's sketchbook includes "buds, leaves, the heads of marsh rushes, a blue beetle, a snail-shell with its black whorl design, butterflies, a twig with the purple coming of spring, sometimes a landscape so small that you could have covered it with a penny" (51). Because the scale of her drawings is so small, and the drawings are so detailed, the notebook looks "as if the richness of her observation had overflowed its borders, and must decorate everything" (51). The scale and detail of Susan's drawings resembles that of Findlater's writing. Findlater limits the scope of her impressions to the world she knows best: rural Scotland. Yet hers is not the sublime Highland scenery portrayed in the paintings of Alexander Naysmith or the novels of Walter

---

[30] Antonia Losano, *The Woman Painter in Victorian Literature* (Columbus: Ohio State University Press, 2008), 4.

Scott; for as the narrator remarks bluntly, "the sphere of the village is a small one" (23). Findlater often piles detail upon detail, as in the description of the contents of Susan's overflowing notebook or her survey of a messy room: "the litter of school-books left upon the sofa, by the boys, who had gone out to feed their rabbits; the unswept hearth; the worn, dusty carpet; the heap of purposeless sewing by her mother's chair, each added a tiny grain of discomfort to her misery" (263). The heaping-on of detail here parallels the accumulation of "tiny grain[s] of discomfort" in Susan's mind. Seemingly trifling details, Findlater suggests, can have large ramifications, and even the "small sphere" of a village can contain many stories.

Findlater and her artist-figure Susan find in this sphere a beauty and an interest that might not be readily apparent to outsiders. When Dally imagines Susan as a Madonna in an Italian painting, seated "under a spindle-stemmed tree ... with an infinitely calm sky above you, and a baby on your knee," Susan retorts that she could "make a picture like that, only with one of our own skies, and a tree that grows in Scotland" (186). Findlater too sought to demonstrate that provincial Scotland might be transformed into art, that it had beauty and interest worth capturing. She rejects the stylized conventions of the Italian painting within which Dally imagines Susan, instead tacitly siding with Colonel Hamilton, for whom Susan resembles a figure in "an old Dutch picture," certainly not beautiful, but with a "simple out-looking glance, as of a creature unafraid, looking about in a new world" (21). In nineteenth-century Britain, Dutch painting was associated with "low or humble subjects" and was considered "a low and humble form of art – the mere copying of nature without improving upon it."[31] Susan is an admirer of Dutch art – on her first visit to an art gallery she spends "half an hour" standing in front of Rembrandt's *Man in Armour* (68) – and her own drawings, like Findlater's novels, similarly represent "low and humble subjects."

Dally and Colonel Hamilton both imagine Susan the subject of a painting, albeit of different kinds, but Susan would rather be the painter than the painted, preferring the rapture of perceiving beauty to the experience of embodying it. In this she differs from her cousin, the very beautiful Juliet Clephane, who enjoys the attention her good looks bring. Yet when Susan and Juliet visit an art exhibition in Edinburgh, Juliet recognizes that "never in all her prosperous days had she known an hour of

---

[31] Ruth Bernard Yeazell, *Art of the Everyday: Dutch Painting and the Realist Novel* (Princeton, NJ: Princeton University Press, 2008), 9.

such pure delight as Susan was enjoying then; not even when she had realised the indescribable inward thrill of possession which is the secret joy of beauty" (68). While Juliet possesses beauty in the sense of embodying it, Susan simply enjoys it without the desire to possess it either in herself or in others. Neither Juliet nor Dally can understand the pleasure that Susan finds in attempting to re-create the beauty she finds in the world around her. When Dally denigrates the accomplishments of female artists, Susan tries to explain that she draws "not for the sake of anything I could ever *accomplish*; I never think of that. I don't care though they should all be buried in my coffin and nobody ever see a line of them except myself" (185). It is difficult not to read this passage as Mary Findlater's defense of her own art, as she worked on her first novel, *The Rose of Joy*. Susan feels sure that she will never amount to much as an artist because her first duties are as a wife and mother. "I'll do a little in a stupid way, because I can't help it," she acknowledges, "but the work of my life is going to be all in another direction. Pictures are just like a door to me that stands a little bit open and lets me see into another world – a world where Colonel Hamilton once told me are 'the indestructible joys for ever'" (185). Her art offers Susan a glimpse into a transcendent realm of beauty, removed from what she believes is the "work of her life," her daily domestic duties. This work is, for Susan, in many ways less real and less important than the aesthetic pleasures she glimpses through the door opened by her drawings.

Despite Susan's ability to nurture her inner life while she works, *The Rose of Joy* suggests that women's duties as wives and mothers cannot be reconciled with serious artistic pursuits. Dally articulates the conventional view that women are born to be wives and mothers when he warns Susan, "Art's a cold bedfellow...Every woman ought to be married" (185). Female artists, he contends, are "not painters," but at the same time, "they've none of the common interests of women" (185). In other words, they are neither one thing nor the other, neither proper painters nor proper women. Susan has always known tacitly that marriage might put an end to her artistic pursuits, and this is one of the reasons she feels so ambivalent about it. The day before her wedding, Susan visits her neighbor, the aptly named Miss Mitford, a spinster who "suddenly acquired a new value, a new interest" for Susan because "she had lived to be sixty and was still free" (132). Susan, who accepts Dally's proposal in large part because she cannot "just live on at home" (130), wonders of Miss Mitford, "'what should any woman want more than she has got – a home, a quiet life of her own where she can read Shakespeare and worship God in peace and freedom?' To her Miss Mitford's parlour took on an almost sacred air" (133). She envies

Miss Mitford her cottage because within its walls Miss Mitford has the freedom, if she so desires, to devote herself to the "indestructible joys" – to the pleasure to be found in reading Shakespeare or in contemplating the divine.

Susan's marriage puts the indestructability of these joys to the test, and their durability is proven when, in scene imported from sensation fiction, she learns that Dally is a bigamist. The impact of this catastrophe is to reveal to Susan pleasures that outlast grief and love. While the dramatic revelation of Dally's bigamy does seem out of place in a novel so devoted to exploring the nuances of its protagonist's perceptions and inner life, it has an important formal effect on the novel's plot. As Maia McAleavy has observed, "the bigamy plot undermines the security of a wedding as the nineteenth-century novel's inescapable ending."[32] In doing so, it allows for the telling of different stories, ones that, crucially for female characters, do not end with marriage. We learn that Dally had secretly married his mother's laundry woman several years previously, but she had gone to the United States with another man, and Dally had hoped never to see her again. However, when the first Mrs. Stair learns from her relatives in St. Fortunes of Dally's marriage to Susan, she returns home to blackmail him, and Dally is discovered stealing large sums of money from his employer, Susan's uncle Mr. Murchison. Dally and his first wife are immediately packed off to New Zealand, and Susan is left to return to her "comfortless" childhood home in Burrie Bush – a homecoming "worse than she could have ever imagined" (263). Bigamy disrupts the conventional marriage plot by doubling it, leaving Susan, the illegitimate second wife, in a kind of narrative limbo. She is "neither maid nor widow" (285), neither Susan Crawford nor Mrs. Stair. This doubling opens up new possibilities for her story's ending, enabling the rejection of predetermined narratives that, for Emerson, was crucial to the cultivation of genius.

Susan makes no claims to genius, but after her discovery of Dally's treachery, she eventually turns again to art, which offers her an escape not only from grief but also from her narrative limbo in a renewed sense of purpose and identity. Her grief manifests in a feeling of numbness, "as if her sense of beauty had been entirely lost" (270). Yet, some months after Dally's departure for New Zealand, Susan "tasted the joy of life again. She returned to the land of the living, and got out of her own grief into the gold world of Art – a world where she had a corner of her own, an aim, a

[32] Maia McAleavey, *The Bigamy Plot: Sensation and Convention in the Victorian Novel* (Cambridge: Cambridge University Press, 2015), 7.

certainty of vision, a joy that such natures as hers alone possess, which the world can neither give nor take away" (286–7). Although Susan's ability to find beauty in the mundane world around her is temporarily numbed, it is not destroyed by her shock and disappointment. Indeed, liberation from marriage allows Susan to enter "the gold world of Art," rather than merely catching glimpses of it, as if through an open door. The horrible dissolution of her marriage to Dally permits Susan to make again the choice between domesticity and art, this time with greater deliberation and maturity. When Colonel Hamilton's nephew Archie acknowledges his love for her, Susan cannot envision creating any kind of life with him, despite her long-standing affection for him. She explains to Archie, "My heart is like a harried nest; I have no more part in that side of life" (301). Susan's eschewal of love, marriage, and domesticity – "that side of life" – is not simply the New Woman's rejection of an oppressive social institution. It is also a rejection of worldly concerns in favor of "indestructible joys."

Although *The Rose of Joy* endorses Dally's belief that domesticity and artistry are incompatible for women, it represents these two callings as equally legitimate and worthy options and refrains from judging either form of work as more valuable than the other. Four years elapse between Dally's departure and the novel's final chapter, during which time Susan's drawings have brought her "a certain repute, as well as more material results" (306). Now the owner of the late Miss Mitford's cottage, Susan is sitting in the garden with Carrie Pewlitt, Dally's married sister, who has recently given birth to her first child. When Carrie tentatively asks Susan whether she is happy, Susan points her to the passage in Emerson's essay "Love" about the rose of joy. Carrie responds, "That's beautiful Susan, I suppose . . . but do you think after all . . . that anything would make up for a husband and a baby?" (311). It would be easy to conclude that Carrie's deep contentment with her own husband and child indicate her intellectual or spiritual inferiority to the artistic Susan. But Susan's fate was too nearly Carrie's to justify this conclusion. She has become an artist by chance rather than choice, and cannot claim any moral stature over women who choose marriage and motherhood. After all, it was only the discovery of Dally's bigamy and her consequent status as neither wife nor maid that gave Susan the freedom to develop her artistic talents. Findlater is ultimately uninterested in issuing a moral edict or deciding between the comparative value of domesticity and artistry, even though she herself definitively chose the latter.

It is through her appreciation of beauty rather than her political opinions or defiance of social convention that Susan becomes a New Woman.

Her ability to find something of interest and value even in the most dire or drab circumstances enables her to thrive in rural Scotland in a way that neither Alex Hope nor Hadria Fullerton can. Alex and Hadria might have more fully developed theories about women's systematic oppression than does Susan, but Susan achieves the economic self-sufficiency and moral autonomy that Alex and Hadria long for. Susan's success is in part due to the modesty of her ambitions. Caird leads us to understand that Hadria has the capacity for genius and the talent to become an internationally renowned composer. The thwarting of her abilities is thus a loss to the musical world. By contrast, Findlater celebrates Susan's ability to support herself by selling her paintings. Genius and fame have no place in Susan's worldview; she merely wants the independence to be able to look long and hard at the world without interruptions. While Susan's ambitions are modest, Findlater's claim is correspondingly more radical than Caird's; for, it is not merely the rare woman of genius who deserves the liberty to determine the ending of her own narrative, but even women of modest abilities and means. In representing Susan's satisfaction with her circumstances at the end of *The Rose of Joy*, Mary Findlater celebrates her own, and perhaps also her sister Jane's, literary pursuits. Although much better known in their own day than they are now, even then they were not classed with the geniuses. Yet if it is possible to glimpse aspects of the Findlater sisters in *The Green Graves of Balgowrie*'s Henrietta and Lucie, who sustain each other in their deprivation and isolation, it is also possible to find them in Susan. Like Susan, the Findlaters found beauty in the minutiae of the mundane world and had the talent to share their impressions with readers.

CHAPTER 4

The Colonial Adventure Story and the Return of Romance

Flora Annie Steel and Violet Jacob were among the many Scotswomen who spent some part of their lives in India participating in the running of Britain's empire. Steel spent twenty-two years in the Punjab, where her husband was an engineer with the Indian Civil Service and where she eventually became Inspectress of Schools.[1] She began writing novels only after she returned to Britain, but most of her fiction is set in India. Jacob, by contrast, spent only five years in India, and although she wrote extensively about her time there in her diaries and letters, India played a very small role in her published fiction, which tends to be set either in the northeast of Scotland, where she grew up, or in Wales, where she lived for some time as an adult.[2] Steel and Jacob belong in a chapter together not simply because of their sojourns in India, however, but rather because of their contributions to the late nineteenth-century romance revival, which produced the adventure stories of Robert Louis Stevenson, H. Rider Haggard, and Rudyard Kipling. The late nineteenth-century adventure story, termed by scholars the imperial romance, was inextricably bound up in the New Imperialism.[3]

It is possible that Steel's and Jacob's first-hand experiences of empire-building in India, some of which were quite adventuresome, may have shaped their predilections for a genre that was typically the province of men. During their time in India, both women avoided what Jacob

---

[1] For further biographical details, see Flora Annie Steel, *The Garden of Fidelity* (London: Macmillan, 1930); Daya Patwardhan, *A Star of India, Flora Annie Steel: Her Works and Times* (Bombay: A. V. Griha Prakashan, 1963); and Violet Powell, *Flora Annie Steel: Novelist of India* (London: Heinemann, 1981).

[2] Jacob did not publish the diaries she kept while in India during her lifetime, but they are available as *Diaries and Letters from India, 1895–1900*, ed. Carol Anderson (Edinburgh: Canongate, 1990). For further biographical details, see Carol Anderson's introduction to the diaries.

[3] Laura Chrisman's *Rereading the Imperial Romance: British Imperialism and South African Resistance in Haggard, Schreiner, and Plaatje* (Oxford: Oxford University Press, 2000) provides an overview of the genre.

described as "the watertight little world of the cantonment," where bored women spent their days drinking tea, gossiping, and flirting with soldiers.[4] Steel spent three years in the District of Kasur, where she began to attend to sick women and children after learning that the restrictions of purdah prevented many of them from receiving even the most basic medical care. At the suggestion of Kasur's Chief Native Administrator, Steel also opened a school for girls and women, the first of several schools that she would help to establish before she became Inspectress of Schools for the region between Peshawar and Delhi, "an area of some 141 thousand square miles."[5] Jacob, a talented artist and an enthusiastic botanist, thought nothing of riding out alone into the countryside around Mhow in search of botanical specimens. She traveled widely, sometimes with her husband and sometimes with her female friends, searching out remote locations in which they might find themselves the only Europeans. "I could wander forever about this Indian country," she wrote. "With all its drawbacks it is the most congenial environment to me that I have ever been in."[6] Both Steel and Jacob wanted to understand what Adela Quested, in E. M. Forster's *A Passage to India* (1924), called "the real India" beyond the Anglo-Indian station; but, again like Adela, neither woman was free of the racial prejudices common to Victorian Britons, and their versions of the "real India" were inevitably colored by their preconceptions.[7] Nonetheless, Steel and Jacob brought some nuance to a genre that tended to depict Britain's empire quite literally in black and white terms. Their novels are therefore important to our understanding of the late nineteenth-century adventure story.

The imperial romance flourished between the so-called scramble for Africa in the 1880s and the outbreak of World War I, a period when Britons' anxieties about their country's ability to maintain control over its far-flung possessions were on the rise. While it often celebrated the heroic victories of British men over the indigenous peoples of Africa and India, the genre did not uniformly endorse imperial expansion. Yet even adventure stories that expressed ambivalence about or criticism of Britain's imperial endeavors tended to convey "nostalgia for older forms of

---

[4] Jacob, *Diaries and Letters from India*, 26.   [5] Steel, *Garden of Fidelity*, 164.
[6] Jacob, *Diaries and Letters from India*, 61.
[7] For scathing but undoubtedly merited criticisms of Steel's and Jacob's representations of the "real India," see, respectively, Benita Parry, *Delusions and Discoveries: India and the British Imagination, 1880–1930* (London: Verso, 1998), 103–25; and Brijraj Singh, "Violet Jacob and India: A Question of Stereotypes," *Journal of Commonwealth and Postcolonial Studies* 15.2 (2008): 3–27.

chivalric behavior."[8] For, as Indrani Sen has argued, nineteenth-century adventure stories conceptualized – and justified – British imperialism through the conventions of romance:

> the Victorian imagining of the colonial enterprise itself was underwritten by the chivalric paradigm of a morally righteous adventure, involving hardships, self-sacrifice and fired by the noble cause of "rescuing" the darker races in multifarious ways. Under this self-righteous rubric of knight-errantry, the coloniser's authority in terms of race, class, gender, and religion could be given moral sanction.[9]

The late nineteenth-century adventure story's representation of imperial conquest as a chivalric endeavor can be traced back to Walter Scott's Waverley novels.[10] Scott's questing heroes participate, albeit often obliquely and inadvertently, in adventures that consolidated the power and furthered the values of metropolitan England, the center of the British empire. In *Waverley* (1814) and *Rob Roy* (1817), for instance, Highlanders occupy the position that in the novels of Haggard and Kipling would belong to the indigenous peoples of Africa and India. As Peter Keating points out, the tendency to see so-called primitive peoples as culturally belated, or as so many versions of England's past, "made it increasingly difficult to distinguish in any clear-cut way between an historical and an adventure novel" or "to determine where 'history' ended and 'contemporary' adventure began."[11]

Much as Scott's historical romances were regarded by his contemporaries as rescuing the early nineteenth-century novel from the sickly extravagances of gothic and sentimental fiction, the fin-de-siècle imperial romance was seen as reinvigorating the morbidly introspective tendencies of psychological realism.[12] The late nineteenth-century adventure story generally takes as its protagonist a young man on the cusp of adulthood and dramatizes his loyalties, rivalries, and love affairs, as he undertakes a

---

[8] Susan Jones, "Into the Twentieth Century: Imperial Romance from Haggard to Buchan," in *A Companion to Romance from Classical to Contemporary*, ed. Corinne Saunders (Malden, MA: Blackwell, 2004), 409.

[9] Indrani Sen, *Woman and Empire: Representations in the Writing of British India, 1858–1900* (Hyderabad: Orient Longman, 2002), 6.

[10] On the Waverley novels as the origin of imperial romance, see Robert L. Caserio, "Imperial Romance," in *The Cambridge History of the English Novel*, ed. Robert L. Caserio and Clement Hawes (Cambridge: Cambridge University Press, 2012), 517–32.

[11] Peter Keating, *The Haunted Study: A Social History of the English Novel 1875–1914* (London: Secker & Warburg, 1989), 353.

[12] See, for instance, Andrew Lang's essay "Realism and Romance," which was published in the *Contemporary Review* 52 (Nov. 1887): 683–93.

quest to prove his worthiness to other, often older or more powerful, men. The genre's exotic settings and focus on cultural conflict and conquest were the antithesis of the everyday life that Steel's and Jacob's country-women tended to depict.

However, Steel and Jacob did not simply imitate or borrow wholesale the generic conventions developed by Scott, Kipling, Haggard, and Stevenson, but instead challenged what Anna Vaninskaya describes as "the cult of manliness and patriotism" that the imperial romance tended to promote.[13] Steel mounted this challenge by drawing on the conventions of the New Woman novel to foreground women's participation in the adventures of empire-building. She critiqued the masculine exclusivity of adventure fiction, but not the imperial ideologies it propagated. Jacob's novels take male adventurers as their protagonists but turn the imperial romance's focus on conflict and conquest inward in two senses, from Britain's overseas empire to its Celtic peripheries, and from physical to psychological struggle. Set in Wales and Scotland, Jacob's novels explore the borderlands where metropolitan English policies and practices meet indigenous traditions and where divided cultural allegiances lead to moral conflict.

Feminizing the Imperial Romance

Literary scholars working in postcolonial and gender studies have focused their readings of Steel's novels on the figure of the memsahib, the British woman in India, but have reached little agreement regarding the extent of Steel's complicity with or resistance to British imperial ideology, on the one hand, and her endorsement or condemnation of Victorian feminism, on the other.[14] The scholars who, in the early 1990s, recovered Steel from the obscurity into which she had fallen condemned her as racist and antifeminist. For instance, Nancy Paxton allows that Steel's novels "show more than usual insight and sympathy into the lives of her Indian characters," but declares that her autobiography reveals "a self-importance inflated by the authority she claimed as a *memsahib*" that could only have

---

[13] Anna Vaninskaya, "The Late Victorian Romance Revival: A Generic Excursis," *English Literature in Transition, 1880–1920* 51.1 (2008): 60.

[14] On women's roles in British India, see Antoinette Burton, *Burdens of History: British Feminists, Indian Women, and Imperial Culture, 1865–1915* (Chapel Hill: University of North Carolina Press, 1994); and Margaret McMillan, *Women of the Raj* (London: Thames and Hudson, 1988).

impeded Steel's relationships with Indian women.[15] Benita Parry describes Steel's "assured self-righteousness" in her encounters with Indians as "the insolence of the powerful" but praises her representations of "British Victorian woman's experience in the alien environment of the Indian empire."[16]

Recent scholarship has been more sympathetic to the conflicted position of British women in imperial India – disempowered within a patriarchal system, but powerful in a racialized one. Hsu-Ming Teo explains that Steel and other late nineteenth- and early twentieth-century British women writers who wrote imperial romances modified the genre's focus on masculine adventure by introducing the conventions of the domestic novel – "attraction, courtship, tribulations, suffering and marriage" – into imperial territory.[17] Their hybrid novels tend to promote "a conservative notion of femininity" that distinguished British women from "oriental femininity," imagined as "graceful, sensual, and alluring to British men," and affirmed their importance as wives and mothers in the government of Britain's empire.[18] LeeAnne Richardson suggests that Steel's novels stand out among these female-authored revisions of the imperial romance in that they bring elements of the New Woman novel into the adventure plot. In contrast to female characters in works by other so-called Raj writers, such as Maud Diver, Bithia Mary Croker, Fanny Emily Farr Penny, Alice Perrin, Alice Eustace, and Juliet Armstrong, Steel's heroines become participants in rather than spectators or victims of imperial adventures. Their rejection of the restrictions imposed on them by a rigidly conventional Anglo-Indian society is enabled, Richardson argues persuasively, by their "increasing respect for, understanding of, and participation in, Indian culture."[19]

Steel signals her respect for and understanding of Indian culture in part by refusing to explain it to readers. Her novels throw them into the midst of a mix of languages, religions, and practices that must have been bewildering to readers even at a time when British imperial power in India was at its height and affairs of British India were constantly before

---

[15] Nancy Paxton, "Feminism under the Raj: Complicity and Resistance in the Writings of Flora Annie Steel and Annie Besant," *Women's Studies International Forum* 13.4 (1990): 337.

[16] Parry, *Delusions and Discoveries*, 105, 104, 107.

[17] Hsu-Ming Teo, "Imperial Affairs: The British Empire and the Romantic Novel, 1890–1939," in *New Directions in Popular Fiction: Genre, Distribution, Reproduction*, ed. Ken Gelder (London: Palgrave, 2016), 90.

[18] Teo, "Imperial Affairs," 100.

[19] LeeAnne M. Richardson, *New Woman and Colonial Adventure Fiction in Victorian Britain: Gender, Genre, and Empire* (Gainesville: University Press of Florida, 2006), 100.

the public. Her refusal to translate this heterogeneous world is a rejection of the British imperial gaze, which imposes order on perceived disarray. Just as she eschews the traditional courtship plot through which other women writers of the Raj domesticate imperial romance, Steel avoids the feminized world of the British cantonment. Steel's readers must work to make sense of the diverse mélange of cultures in which they find themselves, as must Belle Stuart, protagonist of *Miss Stuart's Legacy* (1893), when she takes one of her "solitary morning rides ... through the alleys and bazaars" of Faizapore only to find herself caught in the crosshairs of a conflict between Muslims celebrating Muharram and Hindus marking Dusserha. On one side, Belle is met by a "crowd of men flourishing quarterstaves and shouting 'Hussan! Hussain!'" followed by "a swaying, top-heavy *tazzia*, looking every instant as through it must shake to pieces, and behind it more quarterstaves and more *tazzias*, more shouts."[20] The other end of the alley is "blocked by a similar crowd," the look of which "as she neared it was startling, but the cry of '*Jehâd! Jehâd!* Death to the infidel!' seemed too incredible for fear" (233). The passage is notable both for its orientalism and its opacity; for, other than indicating which is Muslim and which Hindu, Steel provides no explanation of what the crowd's chants signify, what the religious holidays marked by the two processions are about, or what a *tazzia* might be. Nor can readers simply dismiss the scene as providing local color, for it leads to a murder about which Belle must testify in court, and on which later plot points hinge. Steel's refusal to slow down and explain the nuances of this scene is in part determined by the conventions of the adventure novel, which demand fast-paced action. But it also has the effect of forcing readers to share in Belle's cultural estrangement, immersing them in a world that they must work hard to understand.

Miss Stuart's Legacy complicates the figure of the memsahib and models this process of cultural interpretation by tracing the development of its Scottish protagonist Belle Stuart into a New Woman. Shortly after her arrival in Faizapore, Belle is manipulated into marriage with a crooked military officer, John Raby, who knows what Belle does not – that she is about to receive a legacy of £30,000 from a distant cousin who had loved her deeply. The boorish Raby squashes Belle's desire to learn more about "what the people we govern think, and say, and do," encouraging her instead to confine her interests to ball gowns and babies (210). As she

[20] Flora Annie Steel, *Miss Stuart's Legacy* (London: Macmillan, 1897), 232. Subsequent references to this edition will be made parenthetically.

gradually comes to detest her husband, Belle struggles against her feelings, reminding herself that "life ... was not a novel; nothing wrong or undignified, nothing extravagant or unseemly should come into it; and it was surely all this not to be in love with one's lawful husband" (221). Belle associates marital discontent with the titillating French novels that Raby reads, and so fears that her inability to love him is shameful and improper. She mistakenly identifies marriage and romantic love as inseparable, initially failing to realize that "what they call Love is the bribe held out by Nature to induce her thoughtless children to undertake a difficult duty" (223). Even when she learns that Raby married her for her inheritance, she continues to feel that she is bound to love her husband, rather than approaching marriage as a pragmatic relationship – a "duty" – to which romantic love is incidental.

Steel suggests that if women understood marriage pragmatically, as a social relationship founded in mutual obligations, rather than idealizing it as an exalted state founded in romantic love, they might not only be happier with their lot, but also find fulfillment in pursuits beyond the home. As she grows more distant from her husband, Belle, who has learned Hindustani, begins to take an interest in "the tragic, poverty-stricken, yet contented lives of the poor around her" (231) and to administer basic medical treatment to women and children in purdah, as did Steel herself. Belle's independence from conventional ideals of British womanhood develops along with her ability to navigate the world outside the cantonment. Her immersion in this world offers her new perspectives on the predicament of her unhappy marriage, contextualizing it in a larger drama of human suffering.

Steel uses the Indian customs with which Belle becomes familiar to critique the Western institution of marriage that many New Woman novels denounced. Although Belle believes that her own marriage ought to be founded in romantic love, she does not apply this standard to Indian marriages, observing around her numerous household arrangements and marital relationships – arranged, polygamous, informal – all of which appear to her equally functional. While the novel uses Indian marriages to defamiliarize British ideals of romantic love, it does not idealize these alternatives as free from conflict. Kirpo, an Indian woman whose baby Belle nurses back to health, provides a counterpoint to the privileged position of the British memsahib. Kirpo's husband cut off her nose and abandoned her after learning that, while he was in prison, she had an affair with another man. Disfigurement and expulsion from her community are the price Kirpo pays for using adultery as a means of obtaining a protector and provider while her husband was imprisoned. Kirpo can tell that Raby is intellectually and morally inferior to Belle, and also that Belle loves the vastly superior army officer Philip Marsden, so she cannot understand why Belle does not simply have an affair with Marsden. She wonders, "Why did the *mem* look so unhappy? The *sahib logue* did not cut off their wives' noses, or put them in prison; so what did it matter?" (350). Kirpo, who is well acquainted with the adultery rife in Anglo-Indian station life, knows that Belle would not be punished inhumanely or even rendered an outcast if she had an affair with Marsden. That Belle does not have an affair demonstrates her adherence to a different ethical code than either Kirpo's or that of some other British women in India. She fulfills her wifely duties to Raby, but for Steel and eventually for Belle, these duties do not include loving her husband.

Steel had originally wanted *Legacy Duty*, rather than *Miss Stuart's Legacy*, as the title of her novel, but was persuaded by her publisher, William Heinneman, to adopt the latter, perhaps in order to appeal to women readers.[21] The original title captures the two senses of duty that operate in the novel: duty as responsibility or obligation and duty as a tax. Belle pays a heavy tax on her £30,000 inheritance insofar as it lands her in marriage with a man whom she cannot love, but to whom she must be dutiful even when she falls in love with Marsden. The "last legacy" of her marriage is a mentally and physically disabled child, whose infirmities we are invited to attribute to Raby's debauchery (443). This child entails a whole new set of duties on Belle, reminding her of the misery of her marriage long after Raby's death in a skirmish with Indian natives frees her from it. Belle uses the remains of her legacy to open a hospital for "incurable" children like her son, rejecting Marsden's proposal of marriage so that she can enjoy moral and economic independence. Belle's exposure to the plight of women and children in India thus bears fruit on her return to England, and her experience of cultural difference assists her transformation into a New Woman.

If *Miss Stuart's Legacy* tends more toward the New Woman novel or domestic fiction than to adventure fiction, Steel's later novels integrated these genres to feminize the masculine genre of the imperial romance. This feminized imperial romance represents British imperialism as a chivalric endeavor in which women, rather than men, play the parts of rescuers and protectors. Steel's understanding of imperialism as a chivalric endeavor is nowhere more apparent than in *The Hosts of the Lord* (1900), whose central

---

[21] Steel, *Garden of Fidelity*, 195.

male characters bear the romantic names of Lance Carlyon and Vincent
Dering. The two men, soldiers stationed in Eshwara, are represented as
latter-day knights in shining armor. Lance's "earnestness," we learn,
"would have suited a knight-errant of old on the quest of the Holy
Grail," and when a fancy-dress ball is held at the palace, he dresses as his
namesake, Lancelot du Lac, in a heavy suit of armor.[22] Vincent Dering,
whose name evokes deeds of derring-do, is known for his gallant ways with
women. He begins a flirtation with Laila Bonaventure, a young Eurasian
woman of mixed Italian and Indian blood who lives in a crumbling palace
under the guardianship of Father Bruce Ninian, a Scotsman and a Catholic
priest. To the sheltered Laila, Vincent "might have been another knight-
errant of old, riding across to the enchanted castle of his beloved" (11).
Laila's isolation has left her unfamiliar with and uninhibited by British
conventions of feminine propriety. She and Vincent play at Romeo and
Juliet, sharing "the love which hides in balconies" (151). Although enrap-
tured by Laila's beauty and flattered by her devotion to him, Vincent
cannot bring himself to think of marrying her because of her mixed blood.
Chivalry toward Eurasian, as opposed to British, women has its limits.

Although Steel invites us to see Vincent and Lance as knights protecting
the British community in Eshwara, it is Erda, a missionary woman, who
ultimately saves the city and the life of her suitor, Lance. If imperialism is
for Steel a chivalric enterprise, a civilizing mission that will rescue the
"natives" from themselves, she allows that Britain's women are as capable
of heroism in this enterprise as its men. *The Hosts of the Lord* revises the
imperial romance by taking a woman as its adventurer. Erda's work takes
her among the native inhabitants of Eshwara, and she has a much deeper
understanding of Hindu and Muslim culture than does Lance, a relatively
new arrival, or the more experienced Vincent. It is through Erda that
readers are immersed in the water-logged underworld of Eshwara, where
the "primitive" and "practically amphibious" (33, 40) Gu-gu and Am-ma
dwell. Erda's cousin and fiancé, a rather rigid clergyman in the Free
Presbyterian Church, dislikes her familiarity with this underworld and
seeks to restrict her missionary work, ordering her out of Eshwara as
thousands of pilgrims descend on the city on their way to the Cradle of
the Gods. Like Belle in *Miss Stuart's Legacy*, Erda's interest in the lives of
Indian natives brings her a kind of knowledge and power denied to British
military officers. From Am-ma, whose wife she assisted in childbirth, Erda

---

[22] Flora Annie Steel, *The Hosts of the Lord* (London: Thomas Nelson, 1907), 10. Subsequent
references to this edition will be made parenthetically.

learns that the followers of a discontented yogi plan to release convicts from the local jail and assume control of the sluices regulating the city's waterways. Fearing for the safety of the British in Eshwara, Erda returns to the city on Am-ma's raft, and despite a rising storm arrives "not dead, like the Lily Maid to Lancelot – but alive" (229) – and finally alive to her love for Lance. When she arrives at the army's quarters, Lance is "filled with a great joy at her courage ... for to most men," Steel explains sardonically, "the possibility of a woman acting as a man might act comes as a wonder" (251). Erda's voyage down a tumultuous river enables the army to prevent widespread chaos among the thousands of pilgrims passing through the city, but perhaps the greater act of courage lies in recognizing her love for Lance and breaking off her engagement to her cousin.

In taking a woman as its adventurer, *The Hosts of the Lord* also revises the imperial romance's ideology of conquest and cultural homogenization, offering in its place a tolerance of and even respect for cultural difference. Erda shares with Father Ninian, whose work similarly takes him among the Indian natives, a recognition of a common humanity belonging to colonizers and colonized. Father Ninian understands the pilgrims' journey toward the Cradle of the Gods as the expression of a universal human impulse rather than simply the ritual of a single faith. The pilgrims have "their faces set to the eternal goal of humanity," he explains, "to the finding of something we have lost" (188). This "something" is perhaps the recognition of the interconnectedness of death and birth as "pivots of the Wheel of Life" (126) and universal human experiences. Erda, who ministers to native women during births and beside deathbeds, already recognizes their interconnectedness. After she assists at the birth of his son, Am-ma delightedly describes the British as "the Light-bringers, the Birth-bringers," but a bystander chimes in, "Ay! And Death-bringers too!" (163). Steel acknowledges the duality of the British imperial mission, which has brought "steam and electricity" to India (133) but has also wantonly destroyed native people and ways of life.

In *The Hosts of the Lord* and other novels, Steel frequently represents British officers as ignorant and culpable, inadvertently causing unrest that they must then quell. But if her feminized imperial romance promotes a more culturally sensitive form of imperialism, one rooted in Erda's values, Steel by no means idealizes women. On the contrary, critics have taken her to task for her seeming misogyny.[23] After the unrest in Eshwara has subsided, it is discovered that Laila, the mixed-race ward of Father

[23] See, for instance, Paxton, "Feminism under the Raj," 337–8; and Sen, *Woman and Empire*, 134–5.

Ninian, has been killed. Mystified by her death, District Commissioner declares that "there never was a row like this in India but there is something in it about a woman, which we've got to hush up" (359). The Commissioner's remark is undoubtedly misogynistic, but it illuminates Steel's larger point: that women are moral agents in British India as much as men. Laila becomes the victim of interracial conflict, but she is also depicted in largely positive terms as a woman unfettered by convention who loves Vincent wholeheartedly, if not wisely. Erda, in acting on her love for Lance, becomes more like Laila, undermining the colonial opposition between the chaste white woman and passionate Eurasian woman. And to some extent the District Commissioner is correct in his attribution of blame, for the yogi who incites unrest among the pilgrims calls "for blood to appease [Kali] – the mother of all – the Eternal Womanhood" (316). Kali is of course not only "the mother of all" but also the great destroyer. In recognizing women as moral agents capable of creation and destruction, Steel accords them a role in Britain's imperial projects and a share in the responsibility for their outcomes.

Imperial Romance in the Celtic Peripheries

In a diary entry written on April 11, 1897, in the city of Dhar, Violet Jacob mentions that she has spent the day lying on her bed reading *On the Face of the Waters*, "a book by Mrs. Steel, which we have heard a lot of. It is enormously interesting."[24] At this time, Jacob was at work on her first novel, *The Sheepstealers* (1902), which is set in the Welsh marches during the 1830s. This setting is not as distant from Steel's India as it might seem, for in the nineteenth century both the Welsh marches and the Punjab were unevenly transformed by the English elite's introduction of new technologies that often altered forever the lives of native artisans and peasants. *The Sheepstealers*, like Jacob's later novel *The History of Aythan Waring* (1908), employs the conventions of adventure fiction to explore the borderlands between England and Wales, which like the outskirts of empire were a site of cultural hybridity. While Wales may have been England's first colony, by Jacob's time it had become "part of an expanded England or Greater Britain."[25] In *The Interloper* (1904) and *Flemington* (1911), she turned to Scotland, another nation that retained some degree of cultural

---

[24] Jacob, *Diaries and Letters from India*, 74.
[25] Chris Williams, "Problematizing Wales: An Exploration in Historiography and Postcoloniality," in *Postcolonial Wales*, ed. Jane Aaron and Chris Williams (Cardiff: University of Wales Press, 2005), 5.

distinctiveness despite its incorporation into a Great Britain dominated by metropolitan England.

With a Welsh mother, a Scottish father, and an Irish husband, Jacob was perhaps particularly sensitive to the challenges of cultural hybridization, whether within the United Kingdom or overseas. Yet she avoids mention in her fiction not only of India but also of Ireland, which, during the Home Rule struggles of the late nineteenth and early twentieth century was something of a "frontier zone ... within the core of empire."[26] By returning to the historic struggles that accompanied Wales's and Scotland's integration into Great Britain, Jacob highlights the centuries-long process of resistance and negotiation that went into the making of Great Britain. While these historical precedents might seem to forecast success over time for British imperial rule of India and Ireland, Jacob's novels focus on the cost of political conflict to those inhabiting cultural and geographic borderlands, who are torn by dual allegiances. As a Scot who spent much of her adult life outside Scotland, Jacob perhaps experienced these conflicted allegiances herself. She, too, occupied a kind of cultural borderland, albeit one that she carried within her.

With the exception of *Flemington*, Jacob's novels have been overlooked by scholars of Scottish literature because they either do not represent Scotland at all or do not represent it in the "correct" way. The final years of Jacob's literary career coincided with the beginnings of the Scottish Renaissance, when writers including Hugh MacDiarmid, Edwin Muir, Neil Gunn, and Lewis Grassic Gibbon sought to cultivate a distinctively Scottish cultural nationalism through their works. Jacob occupied a marginal position in this movement. Her vernacular poetry implicitly staked a claim for the status of Scots as a literary language and won high praise from MacDiarmid, who anthologized it in *Northern Lights*. Yet he complained that Jacob's Scottishness was merely "a quality of her being," and that she was oblivious to "the vital problems confronting Scottish nationality today."[27] In MacDiarmid's opinion, Jacob's novels did not adequately thematize the question of Scottish identity, and if a novel must represent Scotland in order to be Scottish, then Jacob is arguably guilty as charged. Yet her self-divided and doubled characters belong to a tradition of Scottish fiction stretching back at least to James Hogg's *Memoirs and*

---

[26] James Anderson and Liam O'Dowd, "Imperialism and Nationalism: The Home Rule Struggle and Border Creation in Ireland, 1885–1925," *Political Geography* 26 (2007): 934.

[27] Hugh MacDiarmid, "Violet Jacob," in *Contemporary Scottish Studies*, ed. Alan Riach (Manchester: Carcanet, 1995), 34.

Confessions of a Justified Sinner (1824). Moreover, her novels question the linearity of the narratives of historical progress espoused by thinkers of the Scottish Enlightenment. Like Walter Scott's, Jacob's historical novels instead explore the temporal and spatial coexistence of cultures in different states of modernization.

The Sheepstealers and *The History of Aythan Waring* exemplify Jacob's fascination with such cultural hybridity. Both novels are set in the Welsh marches, a site of colonial contest, where the vestiges of Welsh traditions linger in spite of centuries of Anglicization. Here, at "the border-line of two countries," there is a great degree of admixture between Welsh peasantry and English elite, but little assimilation. Welsh-speakers might possess a "smattering" of English, and English-speakers a "few words of Welsh", for "a man whose mother-tongue was English had neighbours a mile away who spoke Welsh alone."[28] Like northeastern Scotland – the setting of *Flemington, The Interloper,* and many of Jacob's short stories – the Welsh borderlands are a region in transition, only partially modernized. The *Sheepstealers* describes the marches as "a kind of intermediate stage" both geographically and temporally, for they belong to "neither yesterday nor today."[29] The "hill people" who live at the foot of the Black Mountains embody "the struggle between nature and civilization" and possess "that strenuousness which all transition must bring with it";[30] yet they are subject to the legal and economic power of metropolitan England, represented most immediately by the town of Hereford, just on the other side of the Black Mountains.

The imposition of English practices and English laws on a politically and economically subordinated people contributes to the social unrest that features in *Aythan Waring* and *The Sheepstealers.* The latter is set during the Rebecca riots (1839–43), a series of protests made by tenant farmers in rural Wales against a Highway Act that increased turnpike tolls. The narrator explains that tollgates

> had, in some cases, been taken by professional toll-renters, men who came from a distance, and who were consequently regarded with suspicion by the intensely conservative population of the rural districts. These people, having higher rents to make up, had refused to give credit to farmers, or to allow them to compound for tolls on easy terms, as had formerly been their custom.[31]

---

[28] Violet Jacob, *The History of Aythan Waring* (New York: Dutton, 1908), 41.
[29] Violet Jacob, *The Sheepstealers* (London: Heinneman, 1902), 3, 4.   [30] Jacob, *Sheepstealers*, 4.
[31] Jacob, *Sheepstealers*, 23.

In response to these newcomers' disregard for local custom, tenant farmers, some dressed as women, attack and destroy the tollgates. They call themselves "Rebecca and her children," in an allusion to "an Old Testament text, which tells how Rebecca, bride of Isaac, on leaving her father's house, was blessed by Laban in these words, 'Let thy seed possess the gate of those that hate them.'"[32] The Rebecca riots spread like "a wave of wrath which had a considerable foundation of justice ... surging over South Wales," leaving not just wrecked gates but also wrecked lives in its wake.[33]

The History of Aythan Waring, also set in the first half of the nineteenth century, brings to bear on its characters an 1827 act levying a £200 fine for "fraudulent concealment of malting" and an 1829 act making attempted strangulation a capital offense. More broadly, the novel shows the Welsh peasantry hemmed in by regulations that prevent them from eking out a living in inhospitable terrain. Wern village comprises "a clustered handful of dwellings which hardly deserved the name of cottages," and its inhabitants survive by carrying on a "semi-illicit trade in 'whiskets' and besoms," or baskets and brooms, "the raw materials for which precedent had made it allowable to cut from the neighbouring scrub."[34] Custom permits the villagers to take dead twigs and branches from the farms around them, but should they take "the forbidden green boughs of the valley," they risk prosecution.[35] Although *Aythan Waring* features no organized rebellion against English legislation of the sort embodied in the Rebecca riots, it shows the Welsh peasantry's repeated efforts to manipulate or evade the laws that circumscribe their livelihoods.

Jacob's interest in states of cultural conflict lent itself to naturalism, and whereas Steel was sometimes dubbed "the female Kipling," Jacob's early readers compared her to Thomas Hardy.[36] Naturalism eschews the progressive liberalism that the realist novel embraces. While the realist novel depicts a world of moral free agents who overcome problems and right wrongs without leaving too many casualties by the wayside, the naturalist novel portrays a world "in which individual effort guarantee[s] neither eternal salvation nor momentary happiness."[37] Instead, characters' fates are to a great extent determined by heredity, environment, and chance. Like Hardy's, Jacob's fiction often depicts rural communities whose existence is

---

[32] Jacob, *Sheepstealers*, 24.   [33] Jacob, *Sheepstealers*, 24.   [34] Jacob, *Aythan Waring*, 47–8.
[35] Jacob, *Aythan Waring*, 49.
[36] Following the publication of *The Sheepstealers*, reviews comparing Jacob to Hardy appeared in *The Spectator*, *The Scotsman*, *The Daily Telegraph*, and *The Morning Post*.
[37] Donna Campbell, "American Literary Naturalism: Critical Perspectives," *Literature Compass* 8 (2011): 499.

under threat, and like Hardy, she was fascinated by chance or contingency – by the seemingly impossible coincidences and the ironic turns of fate so common to romance. Her characters make choices and exercise agency, but because they are also subject to others' choices and historical forces beyond their control, their actions are never entirely their own.

The very possibility of narrative, Jacob suggests, is born out of contingency. Her novella *Irresolute Catherine* (1908) illustrates this point through the narrator's reflections on the fact that Susannah Moorehouse, a very attractive woman and a good housekeeper, is, in her late thirties, still inexplicably unmarried:

> most people scarcely realize as a truth that, to the accomplishment of any end, no matter how obvious or how commonplace, there is required a procession of acquiescent circumstances which would make the observer giddy, could he see it. Any human being who meets a stranger in the road has only to think of the chain of chances – each of which has fulfilled itself – to be forged before that meeting can be brought about, and of the one link whose lack would be the undoing of the whole.[38]

The giddying chain of chances that make up each individual's life has not, in Susannah's case, led to marriage, despite her evident marriageability. The narrator's musings reveal the contingency of the event with which so many Victorian novels conclude; in doing so, they also emphasize the haphazardness underlying the seemingly natural or even inevitable happenings of everyday life on which the domestic realist novel imposes a false sense of order. In this passage, Jacob makes a move that George Levine identifies as characteristic of nineteenth-century realism: to claim the faithfulness to life of their own fiction, novelists "self-contradictorily dismiss previous conventions of representation while, in effect, establishing new ones."[39] Jacob claims that her representation of contingency is more realistic – and less constructed – than the realist novel's conventions. But, of course, her foregrounding of the contingency of her characters' experiences is its own ordering device.

The Sheepstealers dramatizes a series of contingencies produced by the "intermediate stage" of the Welsh marches' development. It explores the conflict between the Anglo-Welsh elite who impose the laws and the Welsh peasantry who resist them through Rhys Walters, a man who belongs to neither group. Rhys's father, a prosperous sheep farmer, has

---

[38] Violet Jacob, *Irresolute Catherine* (London: John Murray, 1908), 122.
[39] George Levine, *The Realistic Imagination: English Fiction from Frankenstein to Lady Chatterley* (Chicago: University of Chicago Press, 1981), 8.

worked hard to send his son to school in Hereford, where Rhys is educated with the children of the English elite and acquires "a veneer of sophistica-tion, which hid from view the fact that he had no more changed his character than a man changes who accustoms himself to the perpetual wear of his Sunday clothes."[40] What seems like sophistication is in fact just a sense of superiority to the less well-to-do Welsh farmers with whom Rhys somewhat reluctantly associates. Rhys's education has taught him to despise his origins, but it has not transformed him into one of the elite English landowners whom he emulates. When he is invited to participate in an attack on a local tollgate, and to play the part of Rebecca, he succumbs to "his love of adventure" even though he is embarrassed "to think what a ridiculous troop he was heading."[41] To the less wealthy farmers, by contrast, the "matter was sober earnest, and ... the burlesque view of it occurred to them not at all."[42] While the smaller farmers are motivated by a real sense of injustice, Rhys is more concerned with the impression he will make on spectators. He is punished for his shallowness when he is called out, unjustly, as the murderer of Vaughan, the tollkeeper, and must go into hiding; and it is on this contingency that the unraveling of his identity turns.

Rhys finds his entire sense of self altered by the crime he has supposedly committed, as he is stripped of the elite affiliations that had sustained his sense of superiority. "All his life he had been accustomed to be somebody," and now he finds himself "a beggar practically, an outlaw."[43] Rhys's superiority is revealed to be entirely performative. Without the trappings that connote Englishness – friends, clothes, possessions – he turns out to be no better than the men he has looked down on. That Rhys's regret is primarily for his former status rather than for the murder he believes himself to have committed shows him to be utterly selfish. His unworthi-ness contrasts with the genteel Harry Fenton, who belongs to the English elite, and the upstanding George Williams, a farmhand who has turned to sheep-stealing to pay off his debts.

The Sheepstealers traces the effects of Rhys's supposed crime on Harry, George, and Rhys himself through a series of events that shows Rhys's flaws to be the product of what Jane Aaron describes as his "border condition": the erratic behavior of someone "born in one culture but

[40] Jacob, *Sheepstealers*, 17.   [41] Jacob, *Sheepstealers*, 29, 42.   [42] Jacob, *Sheepstealers*, 44.
[43] Jacob, *Sheepstealers*, 73.

educated in another and without an abiding loyalty to either."[44] In order to keep his whereabouts hidden, Rhys abandons his pregnant lover, Mary Vaughan, daughter of the dead tollkeeper, thereby opening the way for her eventual marriage to George. George and Mary's humble happiness embodies what Rhys might have enjoyed if he had not considered "a man of his intelligence and standing" above marriage to a woman of Mary's class.[45] As George frees himself from a life of crime, receiving advice, employment, and protection from Rhys's estranged mother, Rhys takes George's place as a sheep-stealer. But whereas George had turned to sheep-stealing reluctantly to repay a debt to his unscrupulous landlord, Rhys finds that thieving from the farmers to whose ranks he had once belonged adds "zest into the constrained life he led," as he hides in George's cottage by day and wanders the countryside at night.[46]

If George Williams represents the peasantry whom Rhys dismisses as beneath him, Harry Fenton, the eldest son of a respected provincial family, represents the elite English society to which he aspires and from which his supposed crime irrevocably excludes him. Rhys's resentment toward Harry begins when the latter, a member of the yeomanry guard that suppresses the tollgate riot, pursues Rhys from the scene of Vaughan's murder almost to the point of death. Harry embodies the force of English law with an unquestioning adherence that Rhys, to his shame, cannot share. Harry also enjoys a secure sense of his identity as an Englishman that is denied to Rhys. When, during his evening wanderings, Rhys encounters Isoline Ridgeway, a pretty young Englishwoman who has injured her foot, he becomes Harry's rival for her affections. Isoline, like sheep-stealing, is a source of diversion and excitement. She belongs to a world that is out of Rhys's reach, and his desire that Harry should not have her blinds Rhys to her shallow and self-interested nature. Unlike George and Mary's marriage, Harry and Isoline's cannot be considered a happy event, nor is it a marriage that bodes well for the Anglo-Welsh elite. Isoline does not love Harry any more than she loves Rhys, but merely wishes to exchange the tedium of her uncle's village manse for the comparative social whirl of Hereford.

Unlikable as he is, Rhys is not entirely to blame for his flaws and mistakes. He resembles Roshan, the soldier in Steel's *Hosts of the Lord*,

---

[44] Jane Aaron, "Taking Sides: Power-Play on the Welsh Border in Early Twentieth-Century Women's Writing," in *Gendering Border Studies*, ed. Jane Aaron, Henrice Altink, and Chris Weedon (Cardiff: University of Wales Press, 2010), 133.
[45] Jacob, *Sheepstealers*, 136.   [46] Jacob, *Sheepstealers*, 145.

who has been Anglicized to the point that he is ashamed of his family and feels an outsider in his native Eshwara, but who is excluded from promotion in the British army because he is Indian. Rhys too has learned to feel ashamed of his origins but does not fully inhabit the position of the Anglo-Welsh elite. Both Rhys and Roshan have learned to identify with the perspective of those in power even while they join forces with those who rebel against that authority. Their divided allegiances condemn them to vacillate between self-loathing, on the one hand, and fierce hatred of those who represent metropolitan English sovereignty, on the other. Roshan dies in a duel with Father Ninian, the very man who instructed him in the European art of swordplay. Rhys plunges to his death from a mist-covered hilltop after learning of Isoline's marriage to Harry. Roshan is a relatively minor character in *The Hosts of the Lord*, which takes white Britons as its central figures. By taking a hybridized character as its center of consciousness, *The Sheepstealers* reveals an ambivalence toward metropolitan English authority that Steel's protagonists do not share. The novel neither valorizes the forces of modernization and Anglicization nor idealizes indigenous traditions. For Jacob, hybridity is not an inherently generative condition, enabling characters to navigate complicated cultural interactions, as Rudyard Kipling's Kim does. Rather, hybridization is a form of loss that leaves inhabitants of borderlands without a cultural home.

Walter Scott of the Punjab?

Steel and Jacob not only revised the imperial romances of their contemporaries – Stevenson, Haggard, and Kipling – but also revisited the forerunners of the imperial romance, Scott's Waverley novels. While both women engaged with the literary trends of their day, their best-known works – Steel's *On the Face of the Waters* (1896) and Jacob's *Flemington* (1911) – are historical novels that return to *Waverley*'s depiction of the 1745 Jacobite rebellion. Peter Keating explains that, of the many varieties of romance that flourished at the end of the nineteenth century, "only historical fiction had to compete with long-established and vital literary traditions. At this time, Scott still provided the virtually automatic standard of comparison for any new historical novel."[47] Steel and Jacob actively invited this comparison. *On the Face of the Waters* and *Flemington* reveal through their allusions to and revisions of *Waverley* the authorial self-consciousness that in the works of other late nineteenth-

---

[47] Keating, *The Haunted Study*, 351.

century Scottish women writers often manifests as metafictional reflection on the value of literary and artistic creation. In returning to *Waverley*, Steel and Jacob write themselves directly into a masculine romance tradition that their female contemporaries claimed, sometimes disingenuously, to reject.

Steel was undoubtedly familiar with Scott's works: in her autobiography she mentions reading the Waverley novels to a group of "country-bred" Anglo-Indian women at a remote station in the Punjab.[48] Her chivalric heroes, who are often rendered helpless at crucial points in their adventures, might number Edward Waverley and Frank Osbaldistone among their literary ancestors. Perhaps more importantly, her understanding of historical change was indebted to the same general principles of Enlightenment historiography that inform Scott's Waverley novels. These principles posit civilization as an inevitable and relentless process, suggesting that all societies progress in stages from primitive origins toward modernity, albeit at different rates. The slower-moving societies are always in danger of being conquered by or otherwise assimilated into more modern ones, and conflicts between so-called primitive and civilized peoples thus generate historical change.[49]

Steel's Mutiny novel, *On the Face of the Waters* (1896), traces the literary lineage from Scott's *Waverley* (1814) to the imperial romance by rewriting the conflict between Highland Jacobites and English troops in 1745 as one between the Muslim Mughal dynasty and British troops in India in 1857. By the time Steel wrote *On the Face of the Waters*, numerous novels had already been written about the series of localized military rebellions against British colonial authority that became known as the Indian Mutiny, all of them representing in lurid terms the dire threat that depraved Muslim rebels supposedly posed to white, Christian womanhood.[50] *On the Face of the Waters* incorporates various forms of official and unofficial history in an admirable but not entirely successful attempt to provide an account of the Mutiny that would represent British *and* Indian perspectives sympathetically. Steel left India in 1889 when her husband retired from the civil service, but she returned alone in 1894 to carry out research for *On the*

---

[48] Steel, *Garden of Fidelity*, 156.
[49] On the stadial theory underpinning Enlightenment historiography, see Christopher J. Berry, *Social Theory of the Scottish Enlightenment* (Edinburgh: Edinburgh University Press, 1997), 91–115; and Silvia Sebastiani, *The Scottish Enlightenment: Race, Gender, and the Limits of Progress*, trans. Jeremy Carden (New York: Palgrave, 2013), 45–58.
[50] Jenny Sharpe discusses these novels in *Allegories of Empire: The Figure of Woman in the Colonial Text* (Minneapolis: University of Minnesota Press, 1993), 57–82.

Face of the Waters. She was given permission to look through "confidential boxes of papers" in government offices in Delhi, which supplied British perspectives, and she also "succeeded in getting oral traditions about most Mutiny incidents" from Indians who had lived through the events or heard stories about them – although these, she remarked in her autobiography, were "very contradictory."[51] LeeAnne Richardson observes that *On the Face of the Waters* departs from the monolithic perspective of most imperial romances because it "orchestrates multiple voices," with Steel playing the role of "the recording camera rather than the partisan analyst."[52] She achieved this dialogic effect by incorporating written and oral sources into a work that was "at once a story and a history," in which "every incident bearing in the remotest degree on the Indian Mutiny, or in the part which real men took in it, is scrupulously exact, even to the date, the hour, the scene, the very weather."[53] The story that weaves together this exactitude of historical detail recalls Scott's *Waverley*.

Steel invites us to recognize her debts to Scott when Jim Douglas compares Bahadur Shah, the last of the Mughal emperors, to Charles Edward Stuart, the Young Pretender, who, as the personable but ineffectual leader of the 1745 Jacobite rebellion, features in *Waverley*. Douglas, a Scot, was ousted from the army and Anglo-Indian society after getting into a fight over another officer's wife. He now works in the household of the recently deposed King of Oude where his observations have convinced him that "a storm was brewing" in which he "might find his chance" for redemption by providing information to British officials (43). These officials are inclined to dismiss the Mughal court in Delhi as "a sham" and its monarch as "a miserable pantaloon of a king, the prey of a designing woman who flatters his dotage" (44). But Douglas differs. Warning of a possible rebellion "comparable to the '15 or the '45," Douglas points out that "Prince Charles Edward was not a very admirable person, nor the record of the Stuarts a very glorious one," and yet he could command a following powerful enough to worry King and Parliament (44). Readers of *Waverley* would recognize, as Douglas does, that the cause of a seemingly wronged ruler carries a seductive charm that might win adherents even to so "miserable" a monarch as Bahadur Shah.

[51] Steel, *Garden of Fidelity*, 213, 218.
[52] Richardson, *New Woman and Colonial Adventure Fiction*, 84.
[53] Flora Annie Steel, *On the Face of the Waters* (London: Arnold-Heinemann, 1985), n.p. Subsequent references to this edition will be made parenthetically in the text.

Douglas is aware of discontents that colonial officials have overlooked and that might incline Indian troops serving in the British army to join forces with the Mughal court because he occupies a liminal position in relation to both Anglo-Indian and native society. As his alias "Greyman" suggests, Douglas is adept at disguise, having practiced this art under traveling tricksters, and can blend into any crowd. Donning a series of disguises, he keeps careful watch on the incendiary Moulvie of Fyzabad, who is stirring up discontent among sepoys about flour contaminated with bone, and cartridges greased with animal fat. The narrator attributes Douglas's penchant for disguise to his "Celtic birth": "He had not been born in the mist-covered mountains of the north for nothing. Their mysticism was part of his nature" (42–3). Imaginative, superstitious, and a devout believer in fate, Douglas exhibits the traits that Matthew Arnold, in *On the Study of Celtic Literature* (1867), attributed to Celts and that in Steel's fiction are also shared by Indians, even those who have been Westernized.

In addition to explaining his talent for disguise and mimicry, Douglas's Highland roots perhaps also account for his ability to perceive analogies between the Jacobite uprising of 1745 and the impending rebellion. He fears the outbreak of resistance to British rule not because he believes that it will succeed, but rather because of the bloodshed that must result. When Major Erlton derides the sepoys as "Disloyal scoundrels! . . . As if they had a chance!," Douglas responds, "They have none. That's the pity of it" (146). And, indeed, Soma, a Rajput soldier who has served Douglas in the past, comes to regret his decision to join the Mughal court, deciding after three months shut inside the city walls that "The Huzoors were the true masters; they had men who could lead men; not princes in Kashmir shawls who couldn't understand a word of what you said" (347). Much as Scott's *Waverley* represents the Jacobite rebellion as destined to fail, Steel never questions that the Mutiny might have succeeded in permanently over-turning colonial authority.

Even while celebrating the retrospectively inevitable triumph of British rule, Steel expresses ambivalence about the so-called progress of civiliza-tion, regretting the loss of culturally distinctive ways of life and rendering history's losers sympathetic to readers. The forward momentum of the plot in *On the Face of the Waters* is retarded by backward glances as Steel attempts to preserve in writing traditions that might otherwise be lost. This nostalgia, which permeated Scott's Waverley novels, is intrinsic to Enlightenment stadial history, as the mores and manners of primitive life must be destroyed or discarded in the process of modernization. For instance, *Waverley* suggests that the inevitable defeat of the courageous but misguided Highlanders who followed Charles Edward into battle hastened the demise of the traditional ways of life that underwrote their feudal loyalties to the Stuart monarchy. In the novel's postscript, Scott remarks, "There is no European nation which, within the course of half a century, or little more, has undergone so complete a change as this kingdom of Scotland," and explains that he wrote the novel "for the purpose of preserving some idea of the ancient manners of which I have witnessed the almost total extinction."[54] The Jacobite rebellion, although not the sole cause of this extinction, was a catalyst, impelling Parliament to bring the Highlands more firmly under centralized rule through legislation proscribing certain aspects of traditional Highland culture including dress, weaponry, and the exercise of heritable jurisdiction.

On the Face of the Waters similarly depicts an India that has already begun modernizing, a process only accelerated by the consolidation of British rule in the wake of the Mutiny. The title of the novel's first chapter, "Going, Going, Gone," refers explicitly to the cry of the auctioneer who is selling off the menagerie previously belonging to the recently deposed King of Oude. But the chapter's title also refers to the disappearance of traditional ways of life. As the crowd of natives listen, it asks,

> What was going? Everything if tales were true; and there were so many tales now-a-days. Of news flashed faster by wires than any, even the Gods themselves, could flash it; of carriages, fire-fed, bringing God knows what grain from God knows where! Could a body eat of it and not be polluted? Could the children read the schoolbooks and not be apostate? Burning questions these, not to be answered lightly. (10)

That India in 1857 was already becoming Westernized is evident in Steel's representations of Indian women. Enlightenment historians posited that the condition of women provided an index to a society's place on the trajectory of development from primitive to civilized society, an idea that continued to inform works such as James Mill's influential *History of British India* (1848).[55] In Delhi, Steel's narrator relates, "even the women-folk on the high roofs knew something of the mysterious woman across the sea, who reigned over the *Huzoors* and made them pitiful to women" (92). Although cloistered by their husbands and allowed limited rights in a strongly patriarchal society, Delhi's women are aware that

---

[54] Walter Scott, *Waverley; or, 'Tis Sixty Years Since*, ed. P. D. Garside (Edinburgh: Edinburgh University Press, 2007), 363.
[55] See Sebastiani, *The Scottish Enlightenment*, 134–41.

Britons are ruled by a woman, Queen Victoria, and believe that this matri-
archal figure accounts for the comparative civility with which Englishmen
treat women. While these women's oppression indicates the backwardness of
Indian society, their very awareness of the possibility of greater equality
between men and women suggests that progress is already underway.

On the Face of the Waters does not question *whether* progress, in the
form of Westernization under British authority, is desirable for India, but
only how quickly it should happen. When Douglas warns British officials
of the general unrest and resentment stirred up by the Moulvie of Fyzabad,
Theophilus Metcalfe, an agent of the Governor General of India, replies
testily, "We simply can't do the work we are doing without making
enemies of those whose vested interests we have to destroy. We may have
gone ahead a little too fast; but that is another question" (125). Steel again
calls into question the pace at which Britain has attempted to Westernize
India when she describes General John Nicholson, the man who planned,
led, and was wounded in the storming of Delhi, as a "symbol of the many
lives lost uselessly in the vain attempt to go forward too fast" (425). Steel's
self-avowed hero-worship of the abrasive Nicholson, the only historical
figure to feature in her cast of military officers, colors her representation of
him as a victim of progress. But she also depicts the detrimental effects of
too-rapid modernization on the many hybridized characters that populate
her novels, such as Tara, the widow who becomes a pariah when Douglas
prevents her from committing suttee by pulling her back from her husband's funeral pyre. Douglas's attempt to "save" Tara from what he
perceives as a barbaric death only leaves her in limbo, rejected by her
own people but unable to assimilate into Anglo-Indian society even
though she secretly dreams of becoming Douglas's wife.[56] Steel elicits
sympathy for characters that the advances of civilization leave behind or
leave out, even though she offers no solution to their plight.

Is *On the Face of the Waters* then a justification of British imperial rule in
India, as Parry and Paxton have argued? If we acknowledge Steel's indebtedness to the Enlightenment historiography brought to life in Scott's
Waverley novels, we must also acknowledge the novel's ambivalence about
the British colonial project. This ambivalence permeates the novel's ending, which finds Douglas convalescing in the Scottish Highlands with Kate
Erlton, the woman who saved his life by disguising herself as an Afghan

---

[56] Tara has attracted a good deal of attention from Steel's critics, including in Jennifer L. Otsuki, "The
Memsahib and the Ends of Empire: Feminine Desire in Flora Annie Steel's *On the Face of the Waters*,"
Victorian Literature and Culture 24 (1996): 1–29, and Nancy Paxton, "Feminism under the Raj."

woman. Helen Bauer reads their retreat to Scotland as a rejection of "the work of imperial government."[57] Yet this reading overlooks the Highlands's central role in British imperialism, both as testing ground for colonial practices in the wake of the 1745 rebellion and as breeding ground for the troops that sustained Britain's imperial projects further afield. It might be more accurate to see Kate and Douglas's enjoyment of the "pleasures of that Scotch home" mentioned so fleetingly in the novel's closing pages as a kind of return to the origins of empire, where Douglas will regain his strength and they will raise up a new generation of soldiers and civil servants (416).

While Steel's account of the Indian Mutiny in *On the Face of the Waters* recalls Scott's recounting of the Jacobite Rebellion in *Waverley*, her subtle exploration of the historic ties between Scotland and India evokes *The Surgeon's Daughter*, the last of the three tales included in Scott's *Chronicles of the Canongate* (1827). The previous stories, "The Highland Widow" and "The Two Drovers," both depict a conflict between traditional Highland manners and mores and those of southern Britain. At the beginning of *The Surgeon's Daughter*, Crystal Croftangry, the fictional compiler of the *Chronicles*, admits that he wants a "topic to supply the place of the Highlands" as "that the theme is becoming a little exhausted."[58] Croftangry's friend Mr. Fairscribe advises him to

> do with your Muse of Fiction, as you call her, as many an honest man does with his own sons in flesh and blood ... Send her to India, to be sure. That is the true place for a Scot to thrive in; and if you carry your story fifty years back, as there is nothing to hinder you, you will find as much shooting and stabbing there as ever was in the wild Highlands.[59]

Scott alludes to the concrete interconnections between Scotland and India – the disproportionate number of Scots who flourished, sometimes through dubious practices in military or civil posts, in India – while also suggesting that the Highlands and India play an analogous role in fiction as exotic imaginary spaces. The terrains of India and the Highlands are mapped by a geography of romance, with each locale offering a complement of lawless rogues, primitive customs, and striking scenery. It does not matter that Croftangry has never been to India, for as Fairscribe tells the

[57] Helen Pike Bauer, "Reconstructing the Colonial Woman: Gender, Race, and the Memsahib in Flora Annie Steel's *On the Face of the Waters*," Nineteenth-Century Feminisms 6 (2002): 84.
[58] Walter Scott, *Chronicles of the Canongate*, ed. Claire Lamont (Edinburgh: Edinburgh University Press, 2000), 154.
[59] Scott, *Chronicles*, 155.

former, the story will be "all the better that you know nothing of what you are saying."[60] India in *The Surgeon's Daughter* is a fictional land of opportunity much as the Highlands in *On the Face of the Waters* is a shadowy space of spiritual regeneration.

From Scott's Wavering Hero to Jacob's True Man

John Buchan, renowned for his adventure novels such as *The Thirty-Nine Steps* (1915) and *Greenmantle* (1916), lauded Jacob's last novel, *Flemington*, as "the best Scots romance since *The Master of Ballantrae*."[61] Given that Robert Louis Stevenson's novel had been published a mere twenty-two years earlier, Buchan's praise might sound rather faint unless we remember that the intervening years had been the heyday of the romance revival and encompassed the publication of works by Stevenson, J. M. Barrie, and Buchan himself. Like *The Master of Ballantrae* (1889), *Flemington* returns to the origins of the imperial romance, Scott's representation of the 1745 Jacobite rebellion in *Waverley*.[62] Yet, in a prefatory note to the novel, Jacob asserted that *Flemington* "has no claim to be considered a historical novel, none of the principle people in it being historic characters."[63] If this declaration was intended to deflect inevitable comparisons between *Flemington* and *Waverley*, it seems somewhat disingenuous; for Scott's historical novels, as is well known, never take historical personages as their main characters.

However, it is true that *Flemington* offers no grand theory of history as revolution, or as linear progress, or as the triumph of civilization over barbarism. History, for Jacob, is made by individuals who cannot be reduced to theories or principles because they are motivated by emotions. For Jacob, the 1745 rebellion offers a context for exploring tensions between political loyalty and personal affection. In *Flemington*, the eponymous protagonist's conflicting allegiances do not reflect his inhabitation of a geographical borderland, as they do in *The Sheepstealers*. Rather, he inhabits a political borderland created by the violent thrust of metropolitan

---

[60] Scott, *Chronicles*, 155.
[61] Letter from John Buchan to Violet Jacob, December 31, 1911, National Library of Scotland, Acc. 6686.
[62] On *The Master of Ballantrae* and *Waverley*, see Jenni Calder, "Figures in a Landscape: Scott, Stevenson and Routes to the Past," in *Robert Louis Stevenson: Writer of Boundaries*, ed. Richard Ambrosini and Richard Drury (Madison: University of Wisconsin Press, 2006), 121–32.
[63] Violet Jacob, *Flemington and Tales from Angus*, ed. Carol Anderson (Edinburgh: Canongate, 1994), 275. Subsequent references will be made parenthetically.

England's authority into the northeast of Scotland. Both *Waverley* and *Flemington* feature as their eponymous protagonist an ordinary man who becomes embroiled in a political conflict and is accused of treason; but while Scott's hero is rescued by friends in high place and emerges "saddened, yet . . . elevated" by his experiences,[64] Jacob's gives "all to disprove the accusation of untruth" (514). As critics from Georg Lukács onward have pointed out, Edward Waverley functions as a lens through which Scott explores the virtues and flaws of both the Jacobite and Whig causes.[65] The rights and wrongs of his personal conduct remain a secondary concern, and we are invited to view his treasonous actions as the result of youthful indiscretion, or perhaps of reading too many romances. Jacob, by contrast, is deeply interested in questions of right and wrong as they pertain to individual conduct, and much less so in the respective merits of the Jacobite and Whig causes. Archibald Flemington is constrained by historical events and by chance, but within these constraints he is a moral agent, and bears responsibility for his actions. Flemington differs from Waverley in his desire to remain loyal, for while Scott's protagonist famously wavers in his allegiances, Jacob's seeks nothing more than to be "a true man" – that is, to maintain a steadfast integrity (514). He is moved by affection and admiration rather than by abstract principles, and his loyalties are ultimately to people rather than to political party.

Flemington is a much more vivid and active character than the passive and rather bland Waverley. Raised by his formidable grandmother in the Northeast of Scotland, he is

> one of those blessed people for whom common sights do not glide by, a mere meaningless procession of alien things. Humanity's smallest actions had an interest for him, for he had that love of seeing effect follow cause, which is at once priceless and childish – priceless because anything that lifts from us the irritating burden of ourselves for so much as a moment is priceless; and childish because it is a survival of the years when the universe was new. (302)

In addition to making him a good artist, Archie's powers of observation make him a useful spy for the Whig government in a part of Scotland that was "Jacobite almost to a man" (315). As an artist, Flemington shares with Jacob herself an ability to find transcendent meaning in the everyday and an interest in causality and contingency. Indeed, Flemington is a feminized

---

[64] Scott, *Waverley*, 315.
[65] Georg Lukács, *The Historical Novel*, trans. Hannah Mitchell and Stanley Mitchell (Boston: Beacon Press, 1963), 35–8.

figure, exhibiting "the refinement of a woman" and a "glamour of manner" (313) that charms more conventionally masculine characters such as the soldier James Logie. Flemington gains entrance to Balnillo, home of the Jacobite Logie family, by posing as a traveling portrait painter – a profession that justifies his fascination with the "smallest actions" of others – and wins Logie's friendship through his unfeigned interest in Logie's personal history.

The very sensitivity that suits Flemington to be a spy also makes it difficult for him to carry out his duty by betraying Logie's confidences. As he and Logie become acquainted, Flemington begins to regret that "he was obliged to shadow a man who pleased him as much as did James Logie" (313), while Logie, for his part, admires Flemington's willingness to struggle "bravely for his bread in an almost menial profession" on account, as Logie believes, of his family's Jacobitism (336). As Logie describes to Flemington how he lost his wife and child through an acquaintance's "endless treachery" (341), Flemington determines that he cannot "raise his hand to strike again at the man who had been stricken so terribly, and with the same weapon of betrayal" (348). But even as he realizes that "friendship with James, had he been free to offer or accept it, would have been a lifelong prize" (347), his grandmother, to whom Flemington has heretofore displayed "the fidelity of a favourite dog" (356), demands that he continue to shadow Logie. Madam Flemington reminds her grandson that "we have to do with principles, not men" (356), but, in fact, her loyalty to the Whig party stems not from abstract principle but rather from a personal grievance – the betrayal of her friendship by insiders at the Jacobite court of St. Germain.

Flemington turns on the conflict not between Jacobites and Whigs but between its protagonist's love for James Logie, a Jacobite, on one hand, and for his grandmother, a Whig, on the other. It is impossible to resolve these two characters into mere representatives of opposing parties or political ideologies because they are so similar. Madam Flemington and James Logie both have been betrayed in the past, and Flemington feels that he must choose which of them to betray again. Both are forceful and unsentimental, placing political allegiance above personal affection. Accordingly, neither can understand Flemington's anguish at the prospect of betraying one of them because neither would ever allow sympathy to come in the way of carrying out their duty. Yet Flemington is faithful to the value of fidelity, even though the conflict between Jacobite and Whig, and his affections for his grandmother and Logie, make loyalty impossible in practice. After the defeat of the Jacobites at Culloden, Flemington and

Captain Callandar are ordered to capture Logie, who is now aware that Flemington is in the employment of the Whig government. When Flemington breaks away to warn one of Logie's men of the search, he knows that he will be caught by the dutiful Callandar and condemned to death for treason. He is not unwilling to die, for he has felt for some time that he had "no chance of being true to anybody, and ... that, in these circumstances, life was scarcely endurable" (392). And yet, until he delivers the message to Logie's servant, he has not betrayed anyone. He has simply compromised, obeying his grandmother's demand that he continue working for the Whigs, but refusing to track Logie's movements any further.

Flemington's decision to communicate to Logie information that will help him escape recalls the novel's prologue, which relates an incident from Archie's childhood. When Mr. Duthie, the Presbyterian minister, complains to Madam Flemington that Archie has painted a caricature of the Pope on the fence outside the manse, she beats her grandson even though she dislikes Mr. Duthie and finds Archie's painting amusing. Archie learns from this experience that "he must pay for his pleasures, and that sometimes they were worth the expense" (285). He later chooses the pleasure of enabling Logie's escape, and willingly pays for it with his life.

The friendship that develops between Captain Callandar and Flemington in the days leading up to the latter's execution is a version of the friendship that Archie had longed to cultivate with Logie, and replays with a different outcome the conflict between duty and sympathy, or the political and the personal.[66] Watching over Flemington, Callandar comes to admire and pity him as Flemington had admired and pitied Logie. However, Callandar never considers allowing Flemington to escape, even though "the duty he must carry out ... was making his heart sink within him" (510). Callandar, we must assume, would have continued to spy on Logie if he had been in Flemington's place, as he cannot understand why Flemington was "undone" by a sentimental "scruple" (510). Yet Callandar is nonetheless capable of regretting that "so gallant, so brilliant a creature was to be cut off from the life of the world, to go down into the darkness, leaving so many of its inhabitants half-hearted, half-spirited, half alive, to crawl on in an existence which only interested them inasmuch as it supplied their common needs" (509). It is precisely Flemington's ability to live wholeheartedly that makes it so difficult for him to hurt anyone he loves, even when it is his duty to do so. Callandar's friendship and respect

---

[66] On the homoeroticism of these friendships between men, see Caroline Bingham, Review of *Flemington*, *Times Literary Supplement* 4784 (Dec. 9, 1994): 22.

are important to Flemington in the last days of his life because he considers Callandar a "true man" – one who always does his duty. Just before he leads Flemington to the wall where he will be shot, Callandar assures him, "You said once that you were not a true man. You lied" (514). This paradox – that Flemington lied about being a true man – encapsulates the difficulty, and perhaps impossibility, of being "true" or loyal to his party *and* Logie, to abstract principles *and* personal feelings.

Flemington examines self-division through a much more likable character than *The Sheepstealer*'s Rhys Walters, but Flemington is nonetheless allied with the Whigs, the representatives of Anglicization and modernization. Although he dies, his party wins. And although Jacob represents both Whigs and Jacobites as flawed, the former are perhaps particularly so. They are led by the Duke of Cumberland, a man who is "sick of Scotland" (503) and who considers women "only in one light," a sexual one (505). His dismissal of Madam Flemington with the remark, "I hate old women! They should have their tongues cut out" (507), is a sign of his unworthiness. Through Cumberland's rudeness, Jacob implies a subtle critique of the Whig government and of the unsympathetic discipline it would impose on the Highlands. It might be possible to read Flemington's attraction to the more generous and dashing James Logie as a manifestation of the seductiveness of the Jacobite cause, similar to Edward Waverley's attraction to Fergus MacIvor and Prince Charles Edward. But Jacob's insistent personalization of Flemington's internal conflict resists a reading that would dissolve characters into mere representatives of their political parties. *Flemington* ultimately valorizes neither Whig nor Jacobite, but rather finds its hero in Skirling Wattie's yellow dog, who is wounded trying to save his master's life and is subsequently rescued and nursed back to health by James Logie. The dog accompanies James in his escape to Holland, and in his new home sleeps with Wattie's "old Kilmarnock bonnet" by his bed (516). "Trust was in his eyes and affection" as he looks at Logie, but although he loves his new master, he remains faithful to the memory of the old one (516). Loyalty, which is such a conflicted concept for the human characters in the novel, is simple for the dog.

While Jacob and Steel were deeply influenced by Walter Scott, they differ from the other women discussed in this book in that they did not eschew the grandiose terms of his narratives in favor of the smaller scale of everyday life. The masculinized genre of the adventure novel, a direct descendant of the Waverley novels, demanded action and event and realized its characters' psyches through the use of symbols and of foils or contrasts, rather than through long discursive passages or extensive use of free indirect discourse. *Flemington* is something of an outlier in the attention it gives to its protagonist's thoughts and feelings, which perhaps explains why some readers have found it to be a novel with a "very female vision," despite its exploration of friendships between men.[67] In revisiting the hallowed literary historical ground of *Waverley*, Jacob and Steel wrote themselves into a masculine literary tradition in which no excuses were necessary for writing to provide readers with ready entertainment, and no self-reflective meditations on aesthetic worth or moral value were required.

---

[67] Joy Hendry, "Twentieth-Century Women's Writing: The Nest of Singing Birds," in *The History of Scottish Literature*, vol. 4, ed. Cairns Craig (Aberdeen: Aberdeen University Press, 1987), 294. See also Carol Anderson, "Tales of Her Own Countries: Violet Jacob," in *A History of Scottish Women's Writing*, ed. Douglas Gifford and Dorothy McMillan (Edinburgh: Edinburgh University Press, 1997), 356.

CHAPTER 5

Scottish Modernism and Middlebrow Aesthetics

Anna Buchan, author of twelve novels, was one of the publishing house Hodder and Stoughton's top-selling writers between the First and Second World Wars.[1] Yet Buchan's name is all but absent from major surveys of Scottish literary history, and not simply because she published her novels under the pseudonym O. Douglas to conceal her kinship to her more famous brother John, author of *The Thirty-Nine Steps* (1915) and *Greenmantle* (1916), among other adventure stories.[2] Early editions of Douglas's novels still linger in secondhand bookshops, but only two – *Pink Sugar* (1924) and *The Day of Small Things* (1930) – have been reprinted recently, and these by the self-described "very niche" Greyladies Press, whose slogan is "Well-Mannered Books by Ladies Long Gone."[3] By contrast, Douglas's contemporary Catherine Carswell is celebrated for her "substantial contribution to literary modernism in Scotland."[4] Her novels *Open the Door!* (1920) and *The Camomile* (1922) have been reprinted by the Virago Press and by Canongate, suggesting that she holds a place in both a British canon of women's writing and in Scottish literary tradition. This chapter will suggest that Douglas's and

---

[1] Wendy Forrester, *Anna Buchan and O. Douglas* (London: Maitland Press, 1995), 60. In keeping with her own practices, I refer to Anna Buchan as "Douglas" when discussing her novels and "Buchan" when referring to the historical personage.

[2] In her autobiography, *Unforgettable, Unforgotten* (London: Hodder and Stoughton 1945), Buchan explains that she chose to use this pseudonym – borrowed from the protagonist and narrator of her first novel *Olivia in India* (1912) – because her eldest brother John "had given lustre to the name of Buchan which any efforts of mine would not be likely to add to" (138). Douglas does receive a few sentences in Robert Crawford's *Scotland's Books: A History of Scottish Literature* (Oxford: Oxford University Press, 2009), 528–9; and several rather scathing pages in Beth Dickson, "Annie S. Swan and O. Douglas: Legacies of the Kailyard," in *A History of Scottish Women's Writing*, ed. Douglas Gifford and Dorothy McMillan (Edinburgh: Edinburgh University Press, 1997), 341–45.

[3] www.greyladiesbooks.co.uk/pages/articles.html.

[4] Margery Palmer McCulloch, "Testing the Boundaries in Life and Literature: Catherine Carswell and Rebecca West," in *Scottish and International Modernisms: Relationships and Reconfigurations*, ed. Emma Dymock and Margery Palmer McCulloch (Glasgow: Association for Scottish Literary Studies, 2011), 159.

Carswell's novels are not in fact as different as their disparate reception by scholars might lead us to expect.

Although Douglas's earliest novels were published at the height of British modernism, they are not concerned with making it new, exploring the workings of the unconscious mind, or challenging readers with their complexity. They are neither metropolitan nor avant-garde in their orientation, and even the expanded understanding of Scottish modernism advocated by Margery Palmer McCulloch and Carla Sassi will not stretch to encompass them.[5] Yet neither do they share the concerns of the strongly nationalist and male-dominated Scottish Renaissance: the revival of Scots vernacular as a literary language, and a focus on the local and traditional. They fit more comfortably into the category of what Nicola Humble has termed the "feminine middlebrow," a type of fiction that emerged between the First and Second World Wars along with an "expanded suburban middle class, more affluent, [and] newly leisured."[6] In many respects, early twentieth-century middlebrow novels differ little from the Victorian realist novel, sharing with their predecessors "a particular concentration on feminine aspects of life, a fascination with domestic space, a concern with courtship and marriage, a preoccupation with aspects of class and manners."[7] It is not surprising then, that Douglas's fiction reveals the influence of Jane Austen and Margaret Oliphant, two novelists that Buchan admired deeply, in its focus on the mundane happenings of domestic life. Priorsford, the fictional border town based on Peebles where several of her novels are set, is another version of Carlingford, Highbury, or Meryton, and the scale of events in Douglas's novels, comprised as it is of walks in the country, teatime visiting, and gossip in the local shop, makes *Miss Marjoribanks* seem almost action-packed by comparison. Douglas's fiction, like so many middlebrow novels of the interwar period, seems, in Alison Light's words, "resistant to analysis" in its "apparent artlessness and insistence on its own ordinariness."[8] Yet Douglas's novels suggest that the ordinary is never entirely "resistant to analysis." Instead, they develop an aesthetics of the ordinary, asserting the ethical value of

[5] Margery Palmer McCulloch, *Scottish Modernism and Its Contexts, 1918–1959: Literature, National Identity and Cultural Exchange* (Edinburgh: Edinburgh University Press, 2009); and Carla Sassi, "Prismatic Modernities: Towards a Recontextualization of Scottish Modernism," in Dymock and McCulloch, *Scottish and International Modernisms*, 184–97.

[6] Nicola Humble, *The Feminine Middlebrow Novel, 1920s to 1950s: Class, Domesticity, and Bohemianism* (Oxford: Oxford University Press, 2002), 10.

[7] Humble, *Feminine Middlebrow*, 11.

[8] Alison Light, *Forever England: Femininity, Literature, and Conservatism between the Wars* (London: Routledge, 1991), 11.

mundane forms of beauty – a colorful arrangement of flowers, a well-cut piece of clothing, a tastefully decorated room, or even just an apt metaphor.

Catherine Carswell is one of a handful of women to be included in studies of Scottish modernism. Indeed, McCulloch and Sassi use Carswell's works to argue for a Scottish modernism that is related to but not synonymous with the Scottish Renaissance, and Carswell's two bildungsromane often are regarded as opening the door to Scotswomen's inclusion in high literary culture.[9] Although *Open the Door!* offers a variation of the Victorian courtship and marriage plot, it employs what McCulloch aptly describes as a "fluid impressionist writing style," providing a density of sensory detail that is almost overwhelming.[10] *The Camomile*, which ultimately rejects the courtship and marriage plot, is written as a series of letters that turns into a journal, providing seemingly unmediated access into its protagonist's mind. Both novels' frank and nonjudgmental depiction of female sexuality outside the confines of marriage is perhaps entirely new in the history of Scottish literature. Carswell's stylistic experiments and exploration of female sexuality certainly merit her a place in Scottish and British modernism, but they need not prevent us from overlooking the commonalities between her novels and Douglas's.

While recognizing that *Open the Door!* was to some extent a new departure and the origin point of an efflorescence of twentieth-century Scottish women's writing, this chapter explores its affiliations with the realist tradition that this book has traced. In Carswell's novels, the appreciation of everyday beauty becomes the modernist epiphany, a moment in which the everyday is transformed, providing the protagonist with new insights that might lead to self-transformation. When Douglas's characters learn to appreciate and to create instances of everyday beauty, they become reconciled to the ordinariness of middle-class, evangelical Scottish society, which they realize is not so ordinary after all. Their aesthetic refinement also prepares them to bring beauty into the lives of others less fortunate in their tastes and means. For Carswell's protagonists, by contrast, epiphany inspires them with a desire to escape the confines of middle-class, evangelical Scottish society entirely.

Douglas's and Carswell's literary celebration of everyday beauty responded to the Free Presbyterian Church's ambivalence toward art by

---

[9] Sassi, "Prismatic Modernities," 194–5; McCulloch, "Testing the Boundaries" and *Scottish Modernism and Its Contexts*, 68–90.
[10] McCulloch, "Testing the Boundaries," 159.

advocating the moral value of aesthetic pleasure. Both authors were born into Scotland's evangelical middle class and spent much of their childhoods in Glasgow, and both describe this world in their fiction, at once valorizing and spurning it. Although Buchan's father was a clergyman in the United Free Church, he does not seem to have censored his children's literary pursuits, but in fact encouraged them. In her autobiography, Buchan describes a father who introduced his children to border ballads and the novels of his hero Walter Scott, and who encouraged them to enjoy the Bible "not . . . because it was the Word of Life, but because it was full of such grand stories."[11] She recalls attending with her father a masque held in Peebles in which various characters from the Waverley novels trooped out: "my father worshipped Sir Walter hardly on this side of idolatry, & nothing pleased him more than to make his children familiar with the writings he loved *so well*. From our earliest years we were brought up on Scott. Our infant tongues lisped not only the psalms of David, but also the lyrics of Sir Walter."[12] Scott's presence infuses Douglas's fiction. At the opening of *Penny Plain* (1920), for instance, the narrator informs us that Priorsford was historically the site of dramatic battles and chivalric romance, "but where once ladies on palfreys hung with bells hunted with their cavaliers, there now stood the neat little dwellings of prosperous, decent folk; and where the good King James wrote his rhymes, and listened to the singing of Mass from the Virgin's Chapel, the Parish Kirk reared a sternly Presbyterian steeple."[13] The landscape is a literary palimpsest, and beneath Douglas's sedate and respectable Priorsford lies the colorful world of Scott's *Lay of the Last Minstrel*.

Despite a childhood that was full of books and beauty, O. Douglas's novels reveal that their author was well aware of Presbyterian suspicions of the pleasures to be found in art and literature. *Eliza for Common* (1928) depicts a family closely based on Buchan's own: Mr. Laidlaw is a minister in the Free Church, but it is Mrs. Laidlaw who is genuinely troubled when their eldest son Jim decides to become a novelist rather than following his father into the ministry.[14] Mrs. Laidlaw belongs to a generation of women brought up "never to read in the daytime" because reading wastes time that could be spent working, and she continually chides her daughter Eliza: "Your head, my dear, is too full of poetry and plays to have room for the

---

[11] Buchan, *Unforgettable, Unforgotten*, 23   [12] NLS Acc. 11627 #117, "Sir Walter Scott."
[13] O. Douglas, *Penny Plain* (London: Hodder and Stoughton, 1920), 1.
[14] O. Douglas, *Eliza for Common* (London: Thomas Nelson, 1930), 65.

things that really matter."[15] As Eliza completes her daily tasks, she often muses "grimly on the great gulf that seemed to be fixed between life in books and life as it was lived at Blinkbonny," the Laidlaws' home in the Glasgow suburbs.[16] Perhaps Eliza's reading has given her unrealistic expectations of how life *could* be lived, but there is certainly some truth in her perception of Blinkbonny as "ugly and drab."[17] Presumably named after John Strathesk's very popular *Bits from Blinkbonny, or Bell o' the Manse* (1885), the Glaswegian Blinkbonny makes an ironic contrast with the quaint village manse of the original. By naming Eliza's home after this book, Douglas acknowledges her indebtedness to and difference from the Kailyard writing of Strathesk and his contemporaries.[18]

Jean Jardine, the protagonist of *Penny Plain* (1920), is more pious and less prone to questioning religious doctrine than Eliza. She has been raised by a great-aunt who had "come out at the Disruption" and who was "frightfully religious – a strict Calvinist – and taught Jean to regard everything from the point of view of her own death-bed."[19] Jean's ways of thinking are challenged and eventually transformed by Pamela Reston, an aristocrat from London who is visiting the small border town of Priorsford. Great-Aunt Alison would have regarded Pamela, with her talk of "clothes, cities, theatres, pictures" as "the personification of the World, the Flesh, and the Devil," but Jean acknowledges that Pamela has "brought colour into all our lives."[20] Through the tasteful touches with which she decorates her rooms and her person, Pamela shows Jean that there is no inherent virtue in choosing the plain over the ornamental, or the colorless over color.

Carswell too grew up in the shadow of Free Church Presbyterianism, in a household where "none of the arts were much regarded."[21] It was not so much that her parents distrusted or condemned artistic pursuits, but simply that they were "poorly read outside the Bible and a few major classics."[22] Living in a kind of artistic deprivation, in a house where there

---

[15] Douglas, *Eliza for Common*, 76, 65.   [16] Douglas, *Eliza for Common*, 65.
[17] Douglas, *Eliza for Common*, 81.
[18] On Strathesk's *Blinkbonny*, see Andrew Nash, *Kailyard and Scottish Literature* (New York: Brill, 2007), 19. On Douglas as a belated Kailyard writer, see Dickson, "Annie S. Swan and O. Douglas," 341–5; and Samantha Walton, "Scottish Modernism, Kailyard Fiction, and the Woman at Home," in *Transitions in Middlebrow Writing, 1880–1930*, ed. Kate Macdonald and Christopher Singer (Houndsmill, Basingstoke: Palgrave Macmillan, 2015), 147–50.
[19] Douglas, *Penny Plain*, 39.   [20] Douglas, *Penny Plain*, 90, 139, 61.
[21] Catherine Carswell, *Lying Awake: An Unfinished Autobiography and Other Posthumous Papers*, ed. John Carswell (Edinburgh: Canongate, 1997), 31.
[22] Carswell, *Lying Awake* 17.

were "except for Scott's no novels," prepared Carswell for "the revelation of discovering the existence of the arts."[23] Carswell's protagonists experience similar artistic awakenings, which distance them from their "simple and Philistine" family members and friends.[24] The Bannerman family in *Open the Door!* is proud of its Free Church heritage, alluding frequently to the grandfathers who had "'come out' at the Disruption of 1843."[25] Juley Bannerman, the protagonist's mother, had received "the call to a religious vocation" at a young age, and although marriage put an end to her dream of dedicating her life to the church, she "was swift in leading the talk to eternal verities ... which was a severe trial to her daughters in their sensitive teens."[26] Valuing the "dignity and tact" that their mother lacks, the two eldest daughters, Georgie and Joanna, "turn for help to the fine arts."[27] The Glasgow School of Art opens a new world to Joanna, but she is "spurred on her way far more steadily by the discouragement at home than by all the easily elicited praise outside," and "the true stimulant behind her efforts lay in the handicap her mother was to her."[28] Joanna's mother Juley is a more complex and sympathetic version of Eliza's exasperated mother, Mrs. Laidlaw. As McCulloch observes, Juley is "a tragic figure, a woman with strong religious feelings to whom the Scottish Presbyterian Church cannot offer any public role where she might feel fulfilled."[29] Joanna fears that she too will waste her life in search of self-fulfillment, and seeks in art and romance, or in beauty and love, the sense of wholeness that has eluded her mother.

While Juley is too caught up in her ecclesiastical yearnings to pay much attention to what Joanna does, Ellen Carstairs, protagonist of *The Camomile*, finds her reading and writing policed by her devout but well-meaning aunt, whose attitude toward books is again similar to Mrs. Laidlaw's. Ellen begins going to Glasgow's Mitchell Library because, as she explains to her friend Ruby, "I must have books, and have them without the feeling that Aunt Harry is reading them over my shoulder or burrowing among my underclothes for them when I'm out."[30] An aspiring writer, Ellen vacillates between attempting to cultivate and to repress her "literary tendency," regarding it as rather shameful and decidedly unfeminine.[31] To escape Aunt Harry's vigilance, she rents a room where she can satisfy her "craving to write things down" (50), and although it is a

---

[23] Carswell, *Lying Awake*, 31–2.   [24] Carswell, *Lying Awake*, 31.
[25] Catherine Carswell, *Open the Door!* (London: Virago, 1986), 19.
[26] Carswell, *Open the Door!*, 7.   [27] Carswell, *Open the Door!*, 47.
[28] Carswell, *Open the Door!*, 149–50.   [29] McCulloch, *Scottish Modernism and Its Contexts*, 78.
[30] Catherine Carswell, *The Camomile* (London: Virago, 1987), 77.   [31] Carswell, *Camomile*, 34.

"frowsty and poor" place, Ellen relates, "I fly there as I imagine a lover might fly to his mistress, or anyhow as I should like my lover, if I had one, to fly to me."[32] The comparison is apt, for Ellen's writing is as dangerously illicit in her aunt's eyes as a lover would be, and writing offers Ellen the escape that Joanna Bannerman finds in romance and that Douglas's Eliza Laidlaw and Jean Jardine find in books and beauty.

It is notable in light of Willa Muir's essay *Mrs. Grundy in Scotland* (1936), that in both Douglas's and Carswell's novels, women voice the church's disapproval of literary or artistic pursuits. The Free Church's propensity to thwart or distort the pleasures of imaginative creativity is nowhere more evident than in the protagonists' mothers or foster-mothers, a MacGrundified generation of women against which the protagonists react. This generation regards artistic and literary pursuits as unsuitable for women, because, as Mrs. Laidlaw warns Eliza, they interfere with their duties as daughters, sisters, wives, and mothers in ensuring the smooth running of the household. In *The Camomile*, Ellen's brother Ronald is left with a limp because their mother neglected his illness in order to write, for she too had a "literary tendency." But this neglect "would not have mattered," in Ellen's opinion, if only her mother's "writings were good, or useful, or amusing."[33] Ellen's willingness to excuse her mother reveals her difference from the women in her social circle, who enforce the very social norms that keep them from cultivating aesthetic sensibilities. For Ellen, by contrast, anything that brings beauty or joy into the world is inherently valuable, even if its creation defies gendered social conventions.

Women's double roles as censors of aesthetic pleasure and creators of everyday beauty in Douglas's and Carswell's novels speaks to the changes wrought by the Great War, which had irrevocably transformed Britain's class structure and, with it, women's position within and without the home.[34] As Alison Light and Nicola Humble have shown, English middlebrow novels of the 1920s and 1930s participated in forging a new middle-class identity that included former members of the declining gentry and the rising working class, and in establishing women's place within this newly expanded middle class. Douglas's fiction is similarly invested in shaping the manners and mores of a formative Scottish middle class. Her novels repeatedly suggest that it is the responsibility of the declining

---

[32] Carswell, *Camomile*, 32.   [33] Carswell, *Camomile*, 49.
[34] On the emergence of an expanded middle class, see John Stevenson, *British Society, 1914–1945* (Harmondsworth: Penguin, 1990), 331–35. On women's roles in interwar Britain, see Deirdre Beddoe, *Back to Home and Duty: Women between the Wars, 1914–1939* (London: Pandora, 1989).

gentry, those whose birth is no longer substantiated by wealth, to bring small beauties into the lives of others – particularly those who have only recently worked their way into the middle class – and to teach them how to experience such aesthetic pleasure. By embodying middle-class standards of taste and propriety, Douglas's novels aimed to participate in the educative process that they depict.

Carswell, by contrast, eschews Douglas's gentle didacticism, and with it the middle-class proprieties that Douglas embraces. In Carswell's novels, the ability to appreciate small beauties marks the artist, a woman who rejects the bourgeois social norms that would prohibit her self-realization through creative endeavors. Carswell's heroines impetuously declare their right to live according to their own values but struggle with limited success to escape the constricting social proprieties that the evangelical Scottish middle class imposes on them. The Promethean desires of Carswell's protagonists reflect her own aspirations to create high art, Literature with a capital L. Douglas's protagonists less ambitiously seek to lessen the grip of those proprieties by introducing small instances of beauty into the lives of those who are constrained by them. Much like Annie S. Swan, Douglas sought to provide solace to her readers by adding a little loveliness into their lives.

Douglas's Aesthetics of the Ordinary

Joseph McAleer has documented a substantial increase in working- and lower middle-class readers between the beginning of the First World War and the end of the Second.[35] Reading constituted a relatively inexpensive and harmless source of comfort during a difficult time. In the trade publication *The Bookseller*, publisher Herbert Jenkins remarked, "What a boon new novels are to the man at the Front, the wounded, the bereaved. I have received many very touching testimonies of the gratitude of those who want to forget things occasionally for an hour or so."[36] Although the Great War's resonance in Douglas's fiction is pervasive, she aimed to facilitate such forgetting. With their emphasis on routine social interactions, and their depiction of domestic scenes in which violence is utterly unimaginable, Douglas's novels are intended as a balm for grief. In an instance of the authorial self-representation that Victoria Stewart finds

---

[35] Joseph McAleer, *Popular Reading and Publishing 1914–50* (Oxford: Oxford University Press, 1992), 56.

[36] Qtd. in McAleer, *Popular Reading and Publishing*, 72.

characteristic of middlebrow fiction, *Pink Sugar* (1924) features a novelist called Merren Strang who writes under the pen name Jean Hill.[37] Merren explains to the novel's protagonist Kirsty Gilmour that she began to write during the Great War out of a sense of duty:

> I did what work I could, but I had some spare time when one simply did not dare to have spare time – and the thought came to me to write a book, something simple that would make pleasant reading – you see, there's nothing of Art for Art's sake about me. I thought of all the sad people, and the tired and anxious people, and the sick people. Have you ever had any one lie very ill in a nursing home while you haunted lending libraries and bookshops for something that would help through sleepless nights for him? If you have, you will know how difficult it is to get the right kind of books. Merely clever books are of no use, for a very sick person has done with cleverness. You need a book very much less and very much more than that.[38]

This passage not only explains Douglas's aims as a writer; it also asserts a positive identity and purpose for the middlebrow novel. Virginia Woolf famously defined the middlebrow in negative terms, as "betwixt and between," "neither art itself nor life itself."[39] Whereas Woolf derided the safeness of the middlebrow, its avoidance of anything improper, Douglas asserts the inadequacy of the highbrow or the "merely clever" to comfort or amuse those who are suffering, whether physically or psychologically. And while recent critics have suggested that the middlebrow might be more closely allied to modernism than Woolf would allow, Douglas staunchly rejects any affiliation.[40]

Merren's aims as an author recall Buchan's remark in her unpublished work that she could imagine "no higher recompense" as a writer than "to be told [her] books have cheered and helped people."[41] Novels, for Douglas as for Merren Strang, should distract us from the inevitable dreariness or downright unhappiness of daily existence by focusing instead on its pleasures – its "pink sugar." To provide an absorbing distraction

---

[37] See Victoria Stewart, "The Woman Writer in Mid-Twentieth Century Middlebrow Fiction: Conceptualizing Creativity," *Journal of Modern Literature* 35 (2011): 21–36.

[38] O. Douglas, *Pink Sugar* (London: Thomas Nelson, 1926), 98. Subsequent references to this text will be made parenthetically.

[39] Virginia Woolf, "Middlebrow," in *The Death of the Moth and Other Essays* (New York: Harcourt Brace, 1942), 180.

[40] On the proximity of modernism and the middlebrow, see Melissa Sullivan and Sophie Blanch, "Introduction: The Middlebrow – Within or Without Modernism," *Modernist Cultures* 6.1 (2011): 1–17.

[41] National Library of Scotland Acc. 11627. The quotation is taken from one of Buchan's unpublished lectures called "Writers and Readers."

from suffering in fact requires great skill, Douglas suggests, albeit not of the sort recognized by the Bloomsbury group. In contrast to the "merely clever books" that seek to instruct or dazzle readers with their complexity, Douglas's novels aim to "touch the heart" or to make readers feel better, in part by reminding them of life's mundane pleasures and ordinary beauties (98).

Pink Sugar situates Merren's and by implication Douglas's novels between sensationalist "lowbrow" fiction, on one hand, and avant-garde modernism, on the other. Kirsty and her aunt Fanny are great admirers of Merren Strang's novels, and perhaps represent Douglas's ideal reader, one who turns to fiction for psychological comfort and tasteful entertainment. Aunt Fanny "cannot endure those modern books which launch the reader into unknown seas without chart or compass" and dislikes novels that touch on "any unsavoury subject" (50). Not for Aunt Fanny the narrative complexities of James Joyce's or Virginia Woolf's novels, on one hand, or the "unsavoury" allusions of Ethel M. Dell's racy romances or Michael Arlen's exotic thrillers, on the other. Kirsty, more widely read and more catholic in her tastes than her elderly aunt, is particularly fond of Mary and Jane Findlater's *Crossriggs* (1908), which she and Merren both know "almost by heart" (99). *Crossriggs*, discussed in Chapter 3, is in many ways a precursor to Douglas's own novels, recounting the attachments and frustrations of the inhabitants of a small Scottish village, and their attempts to dignify a state of genteel poverty. Through this allusion, Douglas writes herself into a tradition of Scottish women's fiction that celebrates the romance of everyday life. Merren and Kirsty's familiarity with the novel, based on repeated rereadings, illustrates an understanding of literature as "an object soliciting its audience's . . . affection and fidelity" that, according to Deidre Shauna Lynch, emerged in the nineteenth century.[42] This concept of the literary work as a dear friend informed the practice of "therapeutic" reading – returning repeatedly to favorite texts as a kind of steadying influence. The middlebrow novel, for Douglas, is the literary equivalent of "comfort food" – sustaining and nurturing, without any pretensions to be haute cuisine.

Douglas was aware the readers who wanted "clever" literature would not be interested in her novels. She realized, though, that neither would the growing audience of working- and lower-middle-class readers described by McAleer and accustomed to sensationalist lowbrow fiction. This

---

[42] Deidre Shauna Lynch, *Loving Literature: A Cultural History* (Chicago: University of Chicago Press, 2015), 7.

readership needed to be taught how to enjoy novels in which nothing notable happens – in which pages are devoted to the description of a woman's redecoration of her "grim" rented rooms ("papered in a trying shade of terra-cotta and ... embellished by large photographs of the Bathgate family ... a round table with a red-and-green cloth ... and two armchairs and six small chairs stood about stiffly like sentinels) or of her disappointing supper ("stewed steak, with turnip and carrots, and a large dish of potatoes, followed by a rice pudding made without eggs and a glass dish of prunes").[43] Franco Moretti has argued that the early nineteenth-century novel replaced the rapid turning-points of earlier sentimental fiction with what he rather disparagingly calls "filler" – details about everyday life. The triumph of descriptive detail over dramatic event participated in the regularization of bourgeois life.[44] Douglas's novels aim to introduce a new class of readers to the pleasures of such regularity. They do not simply seek to define good taste; they aim to actively cultivate it.

The purveyors of good taste in Douglas's fiction – the characters who model it for readers – belong almost exclusively to the gentry or former gentry, those who are well-born and well-bred even if they no longer possess the means to keep up an estate. It is the particular duty of these women to bring small beauties into the lives of those of similarly limited means who lack birth and breeding, and those who have newly come into money without having learned to use it tastefully, and to teach them to appreciate the aesthetic pleasures of everyday life. Before exploring the implications of this educative process, I want to illustrate the significant socioeconomic changes that Douglas observed in Scotland following the end of World War I, taking *The Proper Place* (1926) and its sequel *The Day of Small Things* (1930) as examples. It is perhaps worth noting first that even in her own time Douglas's sense of social hierarchy might have been considered snobbish. As a reviewer for the *Times Literary Supplement* observed dryly in 1920, Douglas does not write novels "that the Marxian kind of person would like. Nor does the author like the Marxian kind of person."[45] Douglas has little interest in the working classes except, fleetingly, as the recipients of well-meant charity. She is concerned entirely with distinguishing among various elements of Britain's newly expanded middle class, and with teaching the newly wealthy to understand the moral

[43] Douglas, *Penny Plain*, 31–2.
[44] Franco Moretti, "Serious Century," in *The Novel*, ed. Franco Moretti, vol. 1 (Princeton, NJ: Princeton University Press, 2006), 376–97.
[45] Qtd. in Forrester, *Anna Buchan*, 59.

and aesthetic codes of the declining gentry so that they might spend their money wisely.

Through the interconnected stories of the Rutherfurd women and the Jackson family, *The Proper Place* and *The Day of Small Things* trace the decline of the "County" people or gentry in rural Scotland and the increasing socioeconomic power of the mercantile middle class. Following her brothers' and father's deaths during the war, Nicole Rutherfurd and her mother Lady Jane can no longer afford to maintain the family estate in Peeblesshire and move to the small seaside town of Kirkmeikle in Fife. The Rutherfurd estate is purchased by Mr. and Mrs. Jackson, who have made their money in manufacturing, but who began their married life in a "semi-detached villa" called Abbotsford on the outskirts of Glasgow.[46] In naming a house consisting of "just six rooms and a kitchen" after Walter Scott's estate, the Jacksons reveal their long-standing aspirations to become "County" folk, a desire for upward mobility that Scott had shared.[47] Yet purchasing Rutherfurd does not automatically win them acceptance among the landed families of Peeblesshire. The endearingly gauche Mrs. Jackson is only too well aware of her social shortcomings among the gentry, explaining, "I can never be natural: I've to watch myself all the time, for the things I say, just ordinary things, seem to surprise the people here."[48] But her husband understands that upward mobility is a multigenerational process: his "own father rose from being a workman to a master" in the factory that Mr. Jackson now owns,[49] and he determines that his son Andrew will learn to "play the part of the young laird and play it well."[50] When Andrew marries, Mrs. Jackson is delighted to leave the new couple at Rutherfurd and abscond with her husband to the suburb of Pollokshields, having acquired "a certain amount of aplomb" and "the status of a county lady" through her short residence in Peeblesshire.[51] While Mr. and Mrs. Jackson acquire the outward trappings of gentility, they remain in their manners and habits solidly middle class.

Nicole and Lady Jane, for their part, bring their gentility with them from Rutherfurd to Harbour House in Kirkmeikle, which they transform into a bastion of feminized gentility. Nicole accepts her family's declining circumstances philosophically and even takes pleasure in their new situation. Now that the Rutherfurds have "come down in the world," she wants

<hr>

[46] O. Douglas, *The Proper Place* (London: Hodder and Stoughton, 1926), 60.
[47] Douglas, *The Proper Place*, 60.   [48] Douglas, *The Proper Place*, 243.
[49] O. Douglas, *The Day of Small Things* (London: Thomas Nelson, 1933), 181.
[50] Douglas, *The Proper Place*, 53.   [51] Douglas, *Day of Small Things*, 120.

"to know everybody there is to know, butcher and baker and candlestick-maker. Yes even the people who live in the smart villas."[52] Her appreciative interest in the inhabitants of Kirkmeikle soon wins her a heterogeneous circle of friends ranging from the drab and "profoundly pious" spinster Janet Symington to Mrs. Curle, a joiner's widow.[53] Mrs. Heggie, owner of one the "smart villas," remarks that before Nicole and her mother arrived in Kirkmeikle, "we were a dull, detached little community, and the Rutherfurds seemed to link us all together in some strange new way. They showed us to each other in a new light, so that we all became better friends. And they do things, take on responsibilities that no one else would dream of."[54] The Rutherfurd women's sense of responsibility, which leads them to adopt Miss Symington's orphaned nephew Alastair and to ensure that the dying Mrs. Curle's wishes are fulfilled, derives from their former social status. Although Nicole and her mother no longer have much money, they continue to see themselves as benefactors and to take a proprietary interest in their neighbors' well-being. Lady Jane suggests that gentility is not dependent on wealth when she expresses her fear that the "new people," as she calls mercantile families like the Jacksons, might fail "to establish relations with the people who serve them" because "they look at everything from a business point of view, which means that they want their money's worth and have no use for sentiment."[55] By bringing their capacity for sentiment to Kirkmeikle, the Rutherfurd women, as Mrs. Heggie observes, infuse the little community with a new appreciation for courtesy, generosity, and good taste – the markers of gentility.

The Proper Place, whose title alludes to a fairy tale by Hans Christian Anderson, questions whether "place," or social status, is determined by money or behavior. The fairy tale tells of a magic flute that, when played, sends everyone to their proper place including the unwitting flautist, a baron who ends up in the herdsman's cottage, which fits his boorish behavior. While Mr. and Mrs. Jackson take their comic vulgarity back to its supposedly proper place in Glasgow's suburbs, the Rutherfurds do not regain their former estate in Peeblesshire, which is now occupied by Andrew and his status-conscious wife Barbara. Instead, in the sequel, *The Day of Small Things*, we see Nicole and Lady Jane embrace the "small things" that fill their seemingly circumscribed existence with contentment: "A new bit of work, old books to read," and their attention to the many

[52] Douglas, *The Proper Place*, 75.   [53] Douglas, *The Proper Place*, 63.
[54] Douglas, *Day of Small Things*, 19.   [55] Douglas, *Day of Small Things*, 164.

"women in the world who need comforting."[56] Through their ministrations, Nicole and Lady Jane hope to bring the same consolation and enjoyment to these women that Merren Strang in *Pink Sugar* hopes to bring to the readers of her novels and that O. Douglas aimed to give to her own readership.

The sort of pleasure that Douglas sought to impart to readers requires an appreciation of ordinary beauty. While genteel women like the Rutherfurds seem to possess this aesthetic appreciation almost innately, those like Miss Symington, who have recently ascended into the middle class, must learn to acquire it, and some, like Mrs. Jackson, may never succeed. Miss Symington inhabits one of Kirkmeikle's "smart villas," dwellings that display their owners' affluence and lack of taste. The only daughter of a factory owner, Miss Symington is financially independent, with money to spare. Yet, after visiting her "smart villa," Lady Jane remarks, "It's odd that a woman can live in a house like that and make no effort to make it habitable. I wonder if it has ever occurred to her how ugly everything is."[57] Evidently, this has not occurred to Miss Symington. Only after she calls on the Rutherfurd women is she struck by the dreariness of her own villa: "When she opened her own front door and went into the hall she stared round her as if she were seeing it for the first time. After the Harbour House how bare it looked, how bleak."[58] She begins to wonder if "many people considered it worth while to do everything in their power to make themselves and their surroundings attractive, but in this fleeting world was it not a waste of time?"[59] Miss Symington, like Jean Jardine in *Penny Plain*, has been taught to consider all her expenditures of time, money, and ability within a religious framework, and to account for their relative worth in the eyes of God. When Nicole gives her a "fragile gilt bowl" as a Christmas present, Miss Symington notices how out of place "the frivolous, pretty thing" looks in her drab bedroom and is inspired to redecorate her house.[60] She comes to see that nurturing small instances of beauty is neither "a waste of time" nor an end in itself, but rather a means of bringing happiness into the world and thus a spiritual act or even a kind of religious observance. For, as Nicole asks, "Would God have troubled to make this world so beautiful if He had wanted us to go about all sad-hued and dreary?"[61] While tasteful interior decoration may not save souls on the Day of Judgment, it can

---

[56] Douglas, *Day of Small Things*, 280, 279.   [57] Douglas, *The Proper Place*, 87.
[58] Douglas, *The Proper Place*, 115.   [59] Douglas, *The Proper Place*, 153.
[60] Douglas, *The Proper Place*, 151.   [61] Douglas, *The Proper Place*, 198.

bring pleasure to others in the meantime. For Douglas, the creation of beauty that might bring happiness to others is neither a frivolous nor an unimportant endeavor. On the contrary, it is the moral obligation of those who have the means to do so. Miss Symington's new willingness to spend money on tasteful decoration demonstrates her improved understanding of these obligations and increases her standing in the community. By training readers to recognize and appreciate beauty in ordinary, everyday things, Douglas's fiction sought to impart to them a genteel sensibility regardless of their income and social standing.

All of Douglas's novels embody an aesthetics of the ordinary and assert the moral value of mundane forms of beauty. But some are more successful than others at justifying or concealing the socioeconomic disparities underlying a seemingly egalitarian aesthetic and moral philosophy. The most successful are perhaps those like *Penny Plain* and *Eliza for Common*, in which it is the protagonist who discovers the contentment that mundane forms of beauty can provide. Douglas's defense of everyday beauty is less successful in novels that take as their protagonist not a woman who learns to appreciate the moral and aesthetic value of tasteful decoration, but one who attempts to teach others its worth. This is most clearly the case in *Pink Sugar*, a novel that exposes the class conflicts that Douglas's aesthetics of the ordinary attempt to resolve, or at least to conceal. Kirsty Gilmour, the well-to-do protagonist of *Pink Sugar*, embraces a "pink sugar view of life," savoring small pleasures and finding joy in everyday beauty – "summer sun and foxgloves," a "rose-trimmed hat," or the "pink sugar hearts" she coveted as a child (155–6). Such sources of pleasure require little money to enjoy; they are dependent only on the faculty of sensory perception and are almost always available in some form, even in times of great sadness. Kirsty's friends accuse her of "wrapping up ugly facts in pink chiffon," but Douglas makes it clear that Kirsty is not blind to her neighbors' problems, nor is she without any of her own (15). Indeed, Kirsty acknowledges that precisely because the world is such an imperfect place, full of "ugly facts," "we want every crumb of pink sugar that we can get" (156). Aware that she has more money and leisure than many people, Kirsty aims "to make just as many people happy as [she] possibly can" by scattering some figurative crumbs of pink sugar their way (16).

Kirsty's sunny disposition contrasts with the dour practicality of Rebecca Brand, the minister of Muirburn's sister, and the self-pity of Colonel Home, the "morose bachelor" and war veteran on whose land Kirsty's house is situated (40). Rebecca is a "solid, dumpy little person, with her practical ways, her sledge-hammer common sense, her gift for peeling the gilt from the gingerbread" (29). She seems determined to inflict her disavowal of all forms of pleasure on her brother Robert – for instance, by urging him to subscribe to the didactic periodical *Sunday at Home* rather than the *Times Literary Supplement*, which he would far rather read. On her own bookshelf, the writings of Marcus Aurelius reside beside the Bible and Louisa May Alcott's *Little Women*, a collection consonant with Rebecca's stoic reconciliation to things as they are. While Marcus Aurelius and the Bible preach the endurance of suffering, *Little Women* describes the efforts of Jo March and her sisters to "make do" during the depriva-tions imposed by the American Civil War, as well as Jo's attempts to conceal her unrequited love for the handsome and wealthy Laurie.[62] Like Jo, Rebecca has a secret love. The "one touch of romance" in her existence is her adoration of "the young laird," Colonel Home, who "seemed to her all the heroes of legend and fairy tale come to life" (137). Rebecca's dream of marrying the Colonel, a man her superior in rank and wealth, suggests that even she, despite her seeming acceptance of the dreariness of existence, is susceptible to romance. Kirsty, for her part, is far from regarding Colonel Home as a knight in shining armor, initially describing him as "the very angriest man I ever came across" (51). His anger is a legacy of the Great War, which has left him disillusioned and slightly disabled, with a permanent limp.

Whereas Rebecca actively excises the smallest of aesthetic pleasures from daily life, Colonel Home is only guilty of failing to appreciate everyday beauty. When the Colonel speaks in a "bitter and hopeless" tone of the limp caused by his war wounds, Kirsty, in a moment of uncharacteristic anger, chides him for failing to be "grateful enough for the good things God had given him," for failing to appreciate "the beauty of the glen, the sound of the water, the crying of birds, and the sweet-scented air" (107). She cries,

> How can you! I don't say the dead weren't the lucky ones – they made a great finish – but think, won't you, about all the poor men still lying in hospital, the blinded men, the men who lost their reason – and others trying to earn their bread and failing to find work. They were all willing to give their lives, but they were asked to do a much harder thing in these

---

[62] Humble observes that Louisa May Alcott's *Little Women* "is among the most popular of novels with the characters of the feminine middlebrow" (*The Feminine Middlebrow Novel*, 173). Shirley Foster and Judy Simon argue that the novel was dear to generations of female readers because it provides models of both conservative and radical womanhood – of "female domesticity" and "creative independence." See *What Katy Read: Feminist Re-readings of "Classic" Stories for Girls* (Ames: University of Iowa Press, 1995), 87.

> days – to live.... Oh, you should be down on your knees thanking
> Heaven fasting. (108)

The argument that the war had left others much worse off than Colonel
Home might seem naïve and even ungracious on Kirsty's part if she did
not acknowledge that living through the war might be more difficult than
dying in it. After all, Colonel Home is not only surrounded by natural
beauty and in possession of his senses; he is the owner of a prosperous
estate and enjoys all the benefits that come with rank and wealth. When
Kirsty points out his "grousing" to him, the Colonel begins to notice these
fairly considerable sources of pleasure. Not least among them is Kirsty
herself, whom the Colonel finds as charming as if she was "the Queen of
Elfland" (155).

However, Rebecca is less susceptible to these charms than Colonel
Home, and her biting criticisms of Kirsty's "pink sugar" philosophy expose
the socioeconomic privilege it depends on. If, in *The Proper Place*, Janet
Symington is receptive to Nicole's efforts to introduce the beauty of
ornamentation into her drab existence, it is perhaps because Janet has
more money than Nicole and can easily afford to implement the improve-
ments Nicole suggests. By contrast, Rebecca resents, and on several occasions rejects, Kirsty's similar attempts to bring "colour" into her life. She
asks Kirsty bluntly,

> did you ever think how irritating unwanted kindness can be to the recip-
> ient? Did you ever think how much more grace it requires to be a receiver
> than a giver? From the first I could feel you saying to yourself, "Oh, the
> poor plain good little thing! I must be kind to her and try to brighten life for
> her a little." (233)

Rebecca's resentment of Kirsty's kindness perhaps stems from her comparative poverty. While Kirsty spends her days playing house at the aptly
named Little Phantasy, Rebecca runs the manse singlehandedly because
she and her brother cannot afford to keep a servant, and sometimes feels
that her life is "one long preparing of meals and clearing them away" (234).
Rebecca implies that she would have been happier without Kirsty's over-
tures of friendship, which have served only to make her aware of what she
lacks. "You had everything I hadn't," Rebecca explains; "I never knew how
plain I was till I saw you" (234). For her part, Kirsty has never given much
thought to the fact that her comparative affluence underlies many of the
simple pleasures that she enjoys, including the pleasure of sharing her joys
with others. Before her awkward conversation with Rebecca, "Kirsty had
taken it more or less for granted that every one lay in bed till morning tea

was brought to them, and then went into a well-warmed bathroom smelling of the best kinds of bath salts, and bathed and dressed at leisure" (250). Despite her desire to "brighten life" for Rebecca, Kirsty has never really understood *why* the minister's sister's clothes are so plain and the manse so drab until Rebecca describes what "doing with as little as possible" is like (234).

Although *Pink Sugar* acknowledges the potential for condescension in Kirsty's desire to help others find crumbs of beauty, and by implication in Douglas's own efforts to instill in her readers proper aesthetic tastes, it is unable to satisfactorily resolve the socioeconomic conflict informing Rebecca's criticisms. Whereas Rebecca sees Kirsty's generosity as "a form of selfishness" – a way of making "everyone pleased and happy around you so that you may feel pleased and happy" (233) – Kirsty views the fortune she has inherited as a liability, and hopes that if she continues "collecting people and providing for them at the rate she was doing, the fortune her father had left her would soon cease to be a burden" (251). Kirsty's understanding of other people as objects to be collected and as so many means of ridding herself of her burdensome fortune suggests that there is truth in Rebecca's claim that Kirsty's kindness is a form of selfishness, or at least self-gratification. Although Kirsty does not renounce her mission to bring "colour" into Rebecca's life, she does come to realize that generosity can look like condescension, and so finds a way to conceal her aim. She pays for Rebecca to accompany the novelist Merren Strang to Italy, even though Merren would rather travel alone. She complains to Kirsty, "Your living for others, my dear, makes life very difficult for your friends. There's nothing I enjoy so much as going about alone, following my own free will, and Rebecca, I know, will gloom disapprovingly at the pictures" (237). Although voiced much more gently, Merren's complaint is not very different from Rebecca's: both perceive Kirsty's desire to be generous as selfish in that it causes inconvenience or embarrassment to others. Undeterred, Kirsty argues that the trip will bring more pleasure to Rebecca than suffering to Merren, who acknowledges that "there is a tremendous satisfaction in doing what you feel to be your duty, and a great deal of happiness got that way" (177).

Douglas seems unable to rescue Kirsty from the charges of condescension and selfishness leveled at her by Rebecca and, to a lesser extent, by Merren. However, by changing the narrative focus in the final chapter so that we are given Rebecca's rather than Kirsty's perspective, she salvages Kirsty's "pink sugar" philosophy. If Kirsty learns that the appreciation of mundane beauty is made easier by money, Rebecca, for her part, eventually comes to believe in the spiritual value of tasteful ornamentation. When Rebecca hears of Kirsty's engagement to Colonel Home, whom she has long adored from a distance, she imagines with shame "how amused every one would be if they knew that she, Rebecca Brand, the little, plain, ill-dressed, unattractive sister of the minister, had been dreaming dreams about the laird of Phantasy" (285). Interestingly, Rebecca does not imagine that her poverty might render her an unfit wife for Colonel Home; instead, it is her dowdiness that she fixates on – her failure to make herself more attractive to behold. Rebecca imagines herself to be "utilitarian, like a vegetable garden," whereas Kirsty is "like a flower garden, something fair and pleasant to delight all comers – something fragrant to be remembered" (286–7). Flowers, Rebecca realizes, are not merely frivolous indulgences; they have a use, too: to bring enjoyment to those who behold them. Rebecca is shocked to realize that "self-complacency" has led her to confuse the rejection of aesthetic pleasures, or pink sugar, with virtue (287). The novel ends not with Kirsty, its ostensible protagonist, but with Rebecca heading downstairs to make a pudding: "not a plain rice pudding as she had at first intended, but a bread pudding with jam on top, and switched white of egg to make an ornamentation" (288). Even something as ordinary as a pudding can be made more pleasurable with a little effort, for, as Rebecca acknowledges, "if you are clever about that sort of thing, beauty costs no more than ugliness" (287). Rebecca learns that to neglect opportunities to adorn or embellish what is plain or undistinguished is to neglect opportunities to bring happiness to others – and to oneself.

Yet, in terms of the novel's structure, Rebecca perhaps learns this lesson too late. In most of Douglas's novels, women who learn to appreciate the significance of small beauties are rewarded with marriage. Eliza in *Eliza for Common* and Jean in *Penny Plain* make marriages that raise them into a higher social class, one that their new understanding of the aesthetics of the ordinary has prepared them to occupy. Even brusque Janet Symington in *The Proper Place* elicits a successful proposal from a widower clergyman after she begins to adorn her home and her person. In *Pink Sugar*, however, it is Kirsty who makes the good marriage while Rebecca must make do with an all-expenses-paid trip to Italy. Debbie Sly has argued persuasively that "although most of Douglas's novels do end in marriage, their emotional heart is elsewhere,"[63] and *Pink Sugar* offers numerous examples of unmarried women living happy and fulfilling lives. It would

---

[63] Debbie Sly, "Pink Sugary Pleasures: Reading the Novels of O. Douglas," *The Journal of Popular Culture* 35.1 (2001): 15.

be a mistake to see Douglas as condemning Rebecca to miserable spinsterhood as punishment for her aesthetic insensibility, but Colonel Home's fascination with Kirsty's charms does emphasize by contrast Rebecca's belated awareness of her own failure to please.

Rebecca Brand is the most problematic instance of a figure that appears frequently in Douglas's fiction – the woman who has learned under the auspices of the Free Church "to think it wrong to spend much time or money on [her] appearance" or surroundings and who must be taught the spiritual and aesthetic value of tasteful decoration.[64] Although Douglas counters the Free Church's disavowal, and indeed disapproval, of embellishment – whether sartorial, artistic, or literary – her novels by no means reject the Church's influence entirely. After all, their religious training is what enables Rebecca, Janet, Eliza, Jean, and other Free Church women to understand beautification as a moral duty of sorts, a way of bringing happiness not only to oneself but to others. And once they have learned this lesson, their Calvinist sensibilities prevent these characters from taking the decoration of their persons and surroundings to distasteful extremes. Douglas's aesthetics of the ordinary offers a middle way between deprivation and excess, austerity and frivolity. Following the lead of Edwin Muir, literary critics have tended to see the legacies of Calvinism as repressing or negating an authentic Scottish identity.[65] Yet Douglas's fiction lends support to Cairns Craig's suggestion that we might see it instead as a generative element of such an identity.[66] Douglas's aesthetics of the ordinary finds in Scotland's Calvinist heritage the potential for a distinctively Protestant form of beauty – unostentatious but striking in its simplicity, inspiring critical appreciation, and providing contentment without complacency. Her aesthetics of the ordinary also claims a place for women in the Scottish history of the novel, eschewing the "Big Bow-wow strain" of Walter Scott and Robert Louis Stevenson to offer instead a tastefully embellished version of everyday domestic and social life between the wars.[67]

[64] Douglas, *The Proper Place*, 120.

[65] Muir blames Calvinism for Scotland's failure to develop a national literature. See *Scott and Scotland: The Predicament of the Scottish Writer*, introduction by Allan Massie (Edinburgh: Polygon, 1982), esp. 44–51.

[66] Cairns Craig, *The Modern Scottish Novel: Narrative and National Imagination* (Edinburgh: Edinburgh University Press, 1999), 35.

[67] Scott used this phrase to distinguish his own style from Jane Austen's "exquisite touch, which renders ordinary commonplace things and characters interesting." See *The Journal of Sir Walter Scott*, ed. W. E. K. Anderson (Oxford: Clarendon, 1972), March 14, 1826, 114.

Carswell's Epiphanic Escapes from the Ordinary

O. Douglas's female protagonists cultivate an appreciation of beauty, learning to ornament themselves and their surroundings tastefully, but they do not aspire to become professional artists or to earn a living through their skills. *Open the Door!* and *The Camomile*, by contrast, take female artists as their protagonists: Joanna Bannerman, who studies at the Glasgow School of Art, designs fashion plates and sketches theater costumes to support herself, and Ellen Carstairs, who, like Carswell, studied music in Frankfurt, teaches music for a living, although she hopes to be a writer. In both novels, then, the arts offer middle-class Scotswomen a respectable way to make a living, even though neither Joanna nor Ellen is especially talented in their chosen art form. Joanna is "neat fingered ... and at school she generally carried off a second prize for drawing" – hardly a sign of exceptional promise.[68] Ellen came to recognize during her years in Frankfurt just "how trifling" her "musical powers" are, but on her return to Glasgow believes she has found her true métier in writing.[69] In taking artists as their protagonists, Carswell's novels immediately pose a greater challenge to evangelical middle-class propriety than do Douglas's heroines, who merely evince artistic sensibilities. Douglas's protagonists teach others that good taste or refined aesthetic judgment is not incompatible with piety and that the creation of small beauties can be a way of honoring the divine. Carswell's heroines, by contrast, shock the sensibilities of Mrs. MacGrundy, Willa Muir's name for those who equate morality with conventionality, as their artistic pursuits seem incompatible with women's traditional role as homemakers. While Douglas's protagonists shape middle-class tastes and aspirations, Carswell's try unsuccessfully to reject those tastes and aspirations entirely.

Like a long line of Scottish heroines before them – from Ellen Percy in Brunton's *Discipline* to the eponymous protagonist of Oliphant's *Kirsteen* and Susan Crawford in Mary Findlater's *Rose of Joy* – Joanna and Ellen use their artistic skills to support themselves, making no claim to genius, talent, or anything more than exceptional competency. Yet their appreciation of beauty distinguishes them from the evangelical, middle-class Glaswegian society in which they move. This society values the arts only as entertainment, and then only in their most conventional form. Aunt Harry, the embodiment of evangelical mores, disapproves of Ellen merely attending a performance of Richard Brinsley Sheridan's *The Rivals*, and is

---

[68] Carswell, *Open the Door!*, 50   [69] Carswell, *Camomile*, 87.

quite devastated when Ellen plays Kate Hardcastle in a school performance of Oliver Goldsmith's *She Stoops to Conquer*. Yet even less religiously devout Glaswegians are "crassly provincial and ignorant," Ellen finds.[70] She is mortified by the reception given to her friend Dobbin, "a pianist of the first rank, but young and unknown, a heaven-sent genius with fire and honey in her finger-tips," when, because Dobbin "cuts her hair short and wears a black velvet jacket like a boy's" her playing is drowned out by the "titters of Hillhead."[71] The concert-goers are motivated by "the need for distraction" rather than by an informed appreciation of musical talent, and Dobbin's haircut meets this need more easily than her playing.[72] Ellen's musical training in Frankfurt has inculcated in her an appreciation for great art that her childhood friends, who remained in Glasgow, cannot share. Joanna, much to her mother's chagrin, socializes with a superficially artistic set that is given more to gossip than to art appreciation, evincing the provincial "need for distraction" that Ellen deplores. Yet there is true artistry in Phemie Pringle, a shop-owner's daughter whom Joanna initially judges to be a "silly, common little person . . . with a villainous South Side accent, and . . . a runaway chin," but whose voice as she sings is "like a fine-drawn thread of gold."[73] From childhood onward, Joanna is alive to beauty, whether she finds it in the "haunted pool, with its girdle of beech trees" at Duntarvie, or in Phemie's singing. Joanna's and Ellen's ability to appreciate great artistry, even if they are not themselves great artists, marks their difference from their social circles.

Aware of this difference, Joanna and Ellen feel confined by the conventions and expectations of middle-class, evangelical society. For Joanna, escape comes through the discovery of her sexuality and through a series of relationships with men. As Cheryl Maxwell observes, Joanna's "epiphanies are mostly erotic," although they are often couched in religious language;[74] for she has been "swaddled from before birth in religious emotionalism, in romance and spiritual exaltation."[75] Joanna seeks to transcend her mundane material circumstances through romance much as her mother Juley seeks transcendence in religious devotion. Kissing her childhood friend Bob Rankin offers Joanna her first experience of "forfeiting [her] identity."[76] She is disappointed to find that Bob is not "bolder, rougher, and

---

[70] Carswell, *Camomile*, 231.   [71] Carswell, *Camomile*, 232.   [72] Carswell, *Camomile*, 232.
[73] Carswell, *Open the Door!*, 167.
[74] Cheryl Maxwell, "'I'd rather be a girl . . . because I like boys best': Building the Sexual Self in *Open the Door!*," in *Opening the Doors: The Achievement of Catherine Carswell*, ed. Carol Anderson (Edinburgh: Ramsay Head Press, 2001), 111.
[75] Carswell, *Open the Door!*, 211.   [76] Carswell, *Open the Door!*, 61.

more demanding," for she believes that love requires suffering and is "gluttonous for sacrifice."[77] Mario Rasponi's almost violent jealousy during their brief marriage brings the suffering Joanna desires, but even as she begins "to feel herself a prisoner," she also finds in sex with Mario "such release, such harmony with the golden world and the violet heavens."[78] Her affair with the middle-aged, married artist Louis Pender offers Joanna a multitude of opportunities to prove herself "great in love," as she believes that Louis "could be wholly won only by the giving of herself in faith."[79] But Louis, it turns out, could never be "wholly won," and his hypocritical condemnations of the polite society he in fact venerates suggests that he is not really worth winning. Joanna's sexual experiences bring her epiphanies that are denied to the heroines of most Scottish middlebrow novels, and certainly to O. Douglas's. Yet Carswell's comparative frankness in writing about female sexuality was not unique among early twentieth-century writers of middlebrow fiction, which, as Nicola Humble explains, "indulged in a curious flirtation with bohemianism."[80] Rose Macaulay in *Told by an Idiot* (1923), Margaret Kennedy in *The Constant Nymph* (1924), and Sylvia Townsend Warner in *Lolly Willowes* (1926), among others, used the safe vehicle of the eccentric family circle to explore "gender and sexual identities which were otherwise perceived as dangerously disruptive of social values."[81]

The demise of Joanna's affair with Louis Pender follows swiftly on Juley's death, a particularly devasting experience for Joanna because she is forced to confront her mother's failure to achieve the self-fulfillment that Joanna in her own way is seeking. Juley, Joanna feels, "had gone without once attaining the stature of her soul, without once uttering clearly the word it should have been hers to utter."[82] Having failed to heed "the call to a religious vocation" that might have brought her a sense of purpose, Juley has sought it instead through her children, hoping that they might in turn feel "the call to be missionaries."[83] The "word" Juley has not uttered, then, is her spiritual calling, and in reflecting on her mother's failure, Joanna decides that "one must utter one's own word of truth in one's own lifetime," that she must heed her calling, whatever it might be.[84] The figuration of a calling or inner truth as a "word" has biblical resonances that become stronger when Joanna, lying awake and afraid in the

[77] Carswell, *Open the Door!*, 63.   [78] Carswell, *Open the Door!*, 118, 109.
[79] Carswell, *Open the Door!*, 219.   [80] Humble, *Feminine Middlebrow*, 5.
[81] Humble, *Feminine Middlebrow*, 5.   [82] Carswell, *Open the Door!*, 333.
[83] Carswell, *Open the Door!*, 13, 50.   [84] Carswell, *Open the Door!*, 362.

temperance hotel in Edinburgh after Louis's departure, wonders, "Had it not been said 'My word shall not return unto Me Void?' What was oneself, if not a word?"[85] Envisioning herself as God's word made flesh, Joanna summons faith to believe that she shall not be "Void," but rather will manifest the truth she has been brought into the world to utter, or achieve the purpose for which she is intended. The passage that Joanna recalls here, Isaiah 55:11, evokes John 1:1, in which "the word" is the generative origin of the world. In both passages, the word is a creative force. In addition to biblical resonances, the figuration of one's calling or inner truth as a "word" has literary implications. For although Joanna is not a writer, she is Carswell's created "word," the embodiment of her creator's calling. The extensive exploration of "the word" as a creative origin or force in *Open the Door!* is thus perhaps a metafictional commentary on the novel's status as the result of Carswell's own search for literary self-fulfillment.[86]

Metafictional reflection on its own status as art is not the only convention that *Open the Door!* shares with other early twentieth-century middlebrow fiction by women. The novel's ending, with Joanna's recognition of her enduring love for Lawrence Urquhart, is another. The rhapsodic conclusion, which takes place on the moors near Duntarvie, brings Joanna full circle and intimates her rebirth after the spiritual death wrought by the end of her affair with Louis Pender. During childhood visits to Duntarvie, the young Joanna had "entered deeply into Nature's heart" and learned "that she might make of her rapture a place of retreat for future days."[87] The ecstasy that she feels in communing with nature is both spiritual and sexual, as, lying face down by the side of a spring, she lavishes "embraces . . . on the earth."[88] The spring with which Joanna communed as a child is both a literal source of regeneration as it waters the nearby land and a symbol of spiritual regeneration. When she returns alone to Duntarvie as an adult after her separation from Louis and the death of her mother, Joanna finds again the "living, undespoilable spring that had been set here to spill and spill for ever from its far hidden source in the earth." "Here surely was the new birth," Joanna feels, although it has "come by such a widely circling and deathly route."[89] And her sense of

---

[85] Carswell, *Open the Door!*, 386.
[86] Autobiographical readings of *Open the Door!*, which understand Joanna as a version of Carswell, offer further support for reading the novel as its author's "word." See, for instance, Glenda Norquay, "Catherine Carswell: *Open the Door!*," in *A History of Scottish Women's Writing*, ed. Douglas Gifford and Dorothy McMillan (Edinburgh: Edinburgh University Press, 1997), 389–99.
[87] Carswell, *Open the Door!*, 32.   [88] Carswell, *Open the Door!*, 31.
[89] Carswell, *Open the Door!*, 389.

rebirth is affirmed when she spies Lawrence, the "Adam to her Eve," walking on the moors ahead of her.[90]

Even critics who are sympathetic to Carswell's representations of female sexuality in *Open the Door!* have found the novel's conclusion disappointing, as it seems to suggest that Joanna's happiness, in Maxwell's words "depends on her ability to find the 'perfect' mate."[91] Despite Joanna's series of unfulfilling relationships, *Open the Door!* insists that heterosexual love offers the ultimate happiness for its heroine. As Maxwell convincingly argues, Joanna's reunion with Lawrence, who has dogged her steps since before she met Mario Rasponi, is carefully marked by Carswell as different from Joanna's previous encounters with men in that it occurs on the moors, beyond the strictures of society. But although Lawrence has been highlighted throughout the novel as the "right" man for Joanna, their reunion at the end remains embryonic and inconclusive. On the one hand, if Joanna and Lawrence are Eve and Adam, the novel ends before they have a chance to be expelled from Paradise. But on the other hand, if, as Sarah M. Dunnigan has suggested, Juley's "emotional investment in religion is partly a consequence of her failure to find fulfilment in the orthodox late-nineteenth-century secular vocation of marriage," then Joanna's reunion with Lawrence may bring success where her mother failed.[92]

Whereas Joanna's relationship to middle-class, evangelical Glaswegian society remains ambivalent, Ellen, in *The Camomile*, makes a more decisive break with the world in which she was brought up. *The Camomile*, generally considered the less successful of Carswell's novels, is arguably more original and formally interesting than *Open the Door!* It rejects the plot of female development that ends in marriage but retains affiliations with a tradition of Scottish women's middlebrow writing, particularly in its celebration of everyday beauty. The novel, in Glenda Norquay's words, contains "little in the way of dramatic action or extravagant emotion."[93] Like Douglas's fiction, *The Camomile* instead invests the familiar with quiet emotional significance, as Ellen aims to "keep my eyes fixed on life itself, most of all on the life that is going on immediately around me."[94]

---

[90] Carswell, *Open the Door!*, 397.
[91] Maxwell, "'I'd rather be a girl,'" 120. See also Alison Smith, "And God Created Woman: Carswell, Shepherd and Muir, and the Self-Made Woman," in *Gendering the Nation: Studies in Modern Scottish Literature*, ed. Christopher Whyte (Edinburgh: Edinburgh University Press, 1995), 29.
[92] Sarah M. Dunnigan, "The Hawk and the Dove: Religion, Desire and Aesthetics in *Open the Door!*," in Anderson, ed., *Opening the Doors*, 101.
[93] Glenda Norquay, "Flourishing through Oppression: *The Camomile*," in Anderson, ed., *Opening the Doors*, 129.
[94] Carswell, *Camomile*, 34.

Told through the letters and journals that Ellen writes for her friend Ruby, the novel's form lends itself to this exploration of everyday life. It also, as Norquay observes, interpellates a sympathetic woman reader.[95] While Joanna learns to see herself through and adorn herself for a male gaze, Ellen writes for a female friend. It is significant, too, that this friend is an aspiring artist. Ruby, whom Ellen met in Frankfurt and who lives in London, is trained to teach music but hopes to earn a living drawing caricatures. Ellen is something of a verbal caricaturist, and her writing tends to exaggerate for comic effect – as, for instance, when she describes her Aunt Harry's horror on discovering that Ellen has left her underwear drying in the parlor during a meeting of the Tea-and-Prayer society. As a Londoner, Ruby is distanced from the middle-class, evangelical Glaswegian society that Ellen inhabits, while as an aspiring artist she sympathizes with Ellen's ambitions and sensibilities.

In Ellen's social circle, these sensibilities mark her as decidedly odd. Ruby's "very modern" mother allows her to do as she pleases, but Ellen must contend with a constant barrage of religious moralizing from her Aunt Harry and with her friends' expectations that she shares their desire for marriage and motherhood above all else.[96] Only in her rented room and in her conversations with Don John, a scholar she meets at the Mitchell Library, does Ellen manage to evade others' consternation and criticism. These momentary escapes are hard won, leading Ellen to question whether there is not

> something radically wrong with a civilization, society, theory of life – call it what you like – in which a hard-working, serious young woman like myself cannot obtain, without enormous difficulty, expense or infliction of pain on others, a quiet, clean, pleasant room in which she can work, dream her dreams, write out her thoughts, and keep her few treasures in peace?[97]

The "theory of life" that seeks to deny Ellen this refuge also posits that she ought to find fulfillment in marriage and motherhood, as her friends do. To eschew these normative desires is, as far as Ellen's friends are concerned, to criticize their choices and to offer them "a personal affront."[98]

Ellen's longing for her friends' approval leads her to accept a proposal of marriage from her friend Madge's brother, Duncan Bruce, whom she does quite genuinely love. But she realizes in retrospect that her engagement to Duncan was motivated by "the desire to do what is held to be the right

---

[95] Norquay, "Flourishing," 134.   [96] Carswell, *Camomile*, 47.   [97] Carswell, *Camomile*, 41.
[98] Carswell, *Camomile*, 21.

thing, and so to become a part with the great world which till then had always seemed to thrust me out from its common experience."[99] Marriage promises to bring Ellen within the pale of convention, but she soon realizes that the transformation will be external only, and that marriage will not resolve but rather intensify her sense of self-division or of standing apart from "common experience." For Duncan instructs Ellen that "I must not speak of anything abstract or 'superior' or of 'high-brow works of art,' unless I am content to be regarded as a bore and a blue-stocking. I am to keep all my real thoughts for him."[100] His concern with appearances and proprieties wears on Ellen until she asks herself, "Is this indeed a part of love – this strain and effort to be what the loved one wants, or at any rate not to appear different from his ideal?"[101] Duncan takes Aunt Harry's place as the social super-ego that Ellen strives to please. And while her love for Duncan makes her try harder to conform than she ever did for her aunt, the preciseness of his demands – that she be sexually desirable but not too sexually available, clever but not noticeably so – makes it impossible for her to win his approval.

Don John, a former Catholic priest, shows Ellen that honesty to her personal ideals even at the price of ostracism is preferable to the approval of others if it requires her to betray her talents. Like Ruby, Don John stands outside Ellen's middle-class, evangelical community and offers her an outsider's perspective on her own position within it. Don John knows the price of defying social norms: his decision to leave the church has left him impoverished and he substitutes alcohol for the "narcotic" that religious faith once provided.[102] But Don John finds solace in books – albeit not the kind of solace that O. Douglas offers. Ellen describes him as a person "for whom books really live and matter" rather than serving as "a kind of general adornment to life," and she admires that "his knowledge of books and history and things has never at any point got detached from his everyday, human knowledge."[103] For Don John, literature neither replaces life (as it did for Ellen's mother) nor merely ornaments it (as it does for her friends), but is a dynamic part of it. In her autobiography, Carswell describes her own relationship with literature in similar terms, writing that books "never cease to reply to us, correct us, remain with us when most of what they say verbally is forgotten. They probe our weak spots, hurt our consciences, stimulate our efforts, correct our mistakes. But they do it without alienating us or permitting us to annoy them to our own

---

[99] Carswell, *Camomile*, 278.   [100] Carswell, *Camomile*, 236.   [101] Carswell, *Camomile*, 252–3.
[102] Carswell, *Camomile*, 180.   [103] Carswell, *Camomile*, 90, 112.

confusion and humiliation."[104] Like Douglas, Carswell personifies literature, representing it as a kind of friend. But rather than a nurturing and quasi-maternal presence, books are for Carswell and Don John searingly honest and sometimes critical companions. Carswell weds an understanding of therapeutic reading with an appreciation of artistic complexity, a union that reveals her dual allegiances to the middlebrow novel and high modernism.

Don John represents for Ellen a kind of humanistic integrity, demonstrating that a life of the mind need not mean a rejection of the concerns and pleasures of everyday existence. He acquires immense symbolic value for Ellen because he refuses to live a lie, giving up his priesthood when he lost his faith rather than continuing to pretend, as it would have been so easy to do, that he thought and felt as he had once done and as everyone around him did. As Ellen observes, "he had nothing to gain, everything to lose by choosing to be honest. Yet he chose honesty and never once complained" of the ostracism, poverty, and self-doubt that ensued.[105] His example gives her the courage to begin cultivating her talents and to give in to her "craving to write things down."[106] Moreover, Don John's unexpected death is the catalyst for Ellen's decision to break off her engagement. It cuts Ellen's life "in two ... as if by lightning" and "crystallised what before was confused and obscure."[107] Through his death, Don John's "plain and unpretentious truthfulness appeared like a star," revealing to Ellen her "own falsehood" in pretending to herself that she would be happy as Duncan's wife.[108] By breaking off her engagement, Ellen chooses honesty, and like Don John, finds herself "thrust definitely and for ever outside the pale" of all that is familiar to her.[109]

This place outside the pale is where Ellen belongs as a writer, for, she concludes, "one can never write till one stands outside."[110] Although she may not belong to "Duncan's world" – the insular, complacent middle-class Glaswegian world of social and religious proprieties – she now as an outsider has "the whole of Duncan's world to write about."[111] Throughout the novel, Ellen has occasionally and fleetingly inhabited this outsider's perspective. Before the performance of *She Stoops to Conquer*, for instance, she "peep[s] at the audience through a hole in the curtain" and finds "all of a sudden that I was outside," seeing her friends in the audience as if for the

---

[104] Carswell, *Lying Awake*, 122.   [105] Carswell, *Camomile*, 295.   [106] Carswell, *Camomile*, 50.
[107] Carswell, *Camomile*, 292, 293.   [108] Carswell, *Camomile*, 295, 296.
[109] Carswell, *Camomile*, 303.   [110] Carswell, *Camomile*, 305.   [111] Carswell, *Camomile*, 305.

first time.[112] For Carswell, the outsider's perspective is a useful one for a writer, creating the possibility for epiphanic moments of insight. Estrangement allows Ellen to see the everyday and the familiar in a new light, as she does following her illness:

> I am overwhelmed by the majesty and mystery of everything . . . the walls of my being are almost shattered by whatever first meets my sight. It may be something admittedly beautiful, like budding trees, or grass, or the blue sky and sunshine. But it may just as well be a dull sky and grimy back garden wall; the marvel of life strikes no less powerfully at me.[113]

This momentary estrangement, then, is similar in its effects to the aesthetics of the ordinary that Douglas's heroines embrace as a mindset or philosophical attitude. But whereas Douglas's protagonists integrate their love of beauty into everyday life, in *The Camomile* and *Open the Door!* these epiphanies or moments of estrangement mark the heroine's extraordinariness – her artistic potential and her difference from those around her who might see only a dirty wall, or perhaps not see anything at all.

Ellen's struggle for self-realization as a writer is initially hindered, but ultimately assisted, by the opposition she encounters from her friends and relations; for, as Don John observes, her desire to write "is like the camomile – the more it is trodden on the faster it grows."[114] Aunt Harry's religiosity and her friends' expectation that she will find a "nice, sensible fellow" to marry do not succeed in suppressing Ellen's urge to write, but in fact become the stuff of her writing, in both her letters to Ruby and her first published story, which is about her recently married friend Laura.[115] *The Camomile* formally embodies Ellen's transformation into a writer, displaying the metafictional awareness of its own narrative status characteristic of Scottish women's fiction. *The Camomile*'s subtitle, *An Invention*, is ambiguously both musical and literary, reflecting Ellen's search for an art through which to express herself. With the exception of the last, each section of the novel bears a musical title. "Glee for Female Voices" introduces us through Ellen's musings to the many "female voices" that have influenced her development – her mother's, aunt's, and friends'. The title of the next section, "Studies and Inventions," names musical forms used to perfect specific points of technique, but could also refer to the practices that, with Don John's encouragement, enable Ellen's growth as a writer. And finally, "Fantasia on an Old Theme" recounts Ellen's

---

[112] Carswell, *Camomile*, 65.   [113] Carswell, *Camomile*, 262.   [114] Carswell, *Camomile*, 101.
[115] Carswell, *Camomile*, 130.

engagement and its demise – her unique improvisation on the "old theme" of courtship.

The brief, final section of *The Camomile* abandons musical metaphors. Titled "Also, Vorwärts!" a favorite phrase of one of Ruby and Ellen's music teachers in Frankfurt, this section marks Ellen's movement toward a literary life. Ellen declares herself "done with music as a profession" and ready to embrace writing as "wage-earning work" when she joins Ruby in London.[116] Although less densely detailed and rich in symbolism than *Open the Door!*, *The Camomile* is formally more experimental, reflecting Carswell's own growth as a writer. It is also a more hopeful novel than its predecessor insofar as it ends with Ellen's escape from middle-class Glasgow and her embrace of moral and economic independence.

Carswell occupied the literary historical crossroads of the middlebrow and modernism, the Victorian era and the postwar world. If, as Margery Palmer McCulloch has shown, Carswell's relationship to the Scottish Renaissance was oblique, her relationships to the middlebrow novel, and to the nineteenth-century tradition of Scottish women's writing, were no less so. Her protagonists, perhaps like Carswell herself, sought to escape the strictures of the middle-class, evangelical Scottish society that Douglas's heroines aimed to beautify and uplift. But, at the same time, Carswell's eccentric families, artistic heroines, and interest in everyday forms of beauty are taken directly from a middlebrow playbook. That this is so should not be surprising, for Carswell was Annie S. Swan's and O. Douglas's contemporary as well as Hugh McDiarmid's and Virginia Woolf's. While *The Camomile* was formally innovative and *Open the Door!* boldly explored female sexuality, these novels' exceptionalism compared with the long nineteenth-century tradition of Scottish women's writing has been overstated. Reading Carswell's novels against the literary tradition developed by Scottish women writers between the middle of the nineteenth and the beginning of the twentieth century suggests that it is perhaps more useful to conceive of the middlebrow and modernism, or popular literature and high art, as a continuum than as an opposition. Carswell opened the door for the Scotswomen who came after her – Willa Muir, Muriel Spark, and Nan Shepherd, among others – to explore the breadth of this continuum in ways that they had not done before.

[116] Carswell, *Camomile*, 304.

Conclusion
The Ethics and Politics of Transfiguring the Commonplace

What I have described in this book as the romance of everyday life did not disappear with the advent of the First World War, or even the Second. Explicit allusions to and rewritings of Scott's romances did diminish in Scottish women's writing over the course of the twentieth century. But a fascination with "The Transfiguration of the Commonplace" – the title that Sandy Stranger gives to her "treatise on the nature of moral perception" in *The Prime of Miss Jean Brodie* (1961) – continued to characterize the works of a new and increasingly diverse body of postwar literature by Scotswomen.[1] The religious connotations of "transfiguration" are befitting Sandy's conversion to Catholicism and subsequent metamorphosis into Sister Helena. But "transfiguration" also describes the effects of Miss Brodie's practice of living primarily in an aesthetic rather than an ethical register. In the pursuit of beauty, Miss Brodie substitutes fiction for reality. The practice of looking for or creating small instances of beauty embraced in the novels of O. Douglas, Mary and Jane Findlater, and Catherine Carswell becomes in *The Prime of Miss Jean Brodie* what Cairns Craig describes as a "commitment to the aesthetic" unchecked by ethics, religion, or real life.[2]

Spark is far from the only instance of Scottish women writers' continued interest in the romance of everyday life, although she perhaps is the best-known. The exploration of the significance of the mundane illuminates a wide range of mid-century Scottish women's writing, from the "light romantic" fiction of D. E. Stevenson to the "sma' perfect" novels of Jessie Kesson.[3] A concern with the aesthetics of the ordinary establishes a commonality among writers whose works otherwise occupy different ends

---

[1] Muriel Spark, *The Prime of Miss Jean Brodie* (New York: Plume, 1984), 53.
[2] Cairns Craig, *Muriel Spark, Existentialism and the Art of Death* (Edinburgh: Edinburgh University Press, 2019), 83.
[3] www.historicenvironment.scot/about-us/news/commemorative-plaque-due-to-be-mounted-on-stan-laurel-s-glasgow-home/.

of the spectrum between popular fiction and high art discussed in Chapter 5. Stevenson, for instance, follows Oliphant and Douglas in using taste or aesthetic sensibility as a marker of social class. When Julia Harburn, the genteel protagonist of *The Blue Sapphire* (1963), is forced to support herself by working in a hat shop, she is surprised to find that although she is "completely untrained," she "can do this job rather well" and that "there's quite a lot in it."[4] Indeed, her innate good taste and refined manners make her a good saleswoman, and she immediately outstrips the other assistants. As even these short quotations illustrate, clever dialogue is not Stevenson's strength, but her romances unite Douglas's detailed descriptions of clothing and interior decoration with Swan's wish-fulfilling marriage and inheritance plots. Having proven that she can take care of herself, Julia is nonetheless rewarded with marriage to a man who treats her as an equal, even teaching her how to invest her money. Kesson's novels resembles the Findlaters' and Violet Jacob's in their lyrical prose and their exploration of out-of-the-way places and "ootlin," or marginalized, people, such as the women and children who inhabit the sordid squalor of the Lane in *The White Bird Passes* (1958). Even the Lane is not utterly devoid of beauty, though, nor are its inhabitants unable to see it. Young Janie recalls how the tendrils of her mother's hair curl and shine in the rain, and Liza, although often inattentive to Janie's physical and emotional needs, can name the birds and flowers and bring the history of Elgin Cathedral alive through her power as a storyteller. Stevenson and Kesson are more different from each other, and from Muriel Spark, than they are similar, but they share in common an ability to transfigure the commonplace.

The persistence of Scottish women writers' interest in the romance of everyday life has been met with a similarly persistent devaluation of their work on the grounds of its supposed triviality. Even Spark, arguably the best Scottish novelist of the twentieth century, is "not thought serious enough" by some critics to merit the title.[5] In an assessment that could have been written of Margaret Oliphant as easily as Muriel Spark, Leo Robson described the flaws of the latter's fiction:

> She was incapable of picturing real heartbreak or malice; she preferred types to characters, and telling to showing; she was excessively fond of formulae and gimmicks; she offered little in the way of verbal reward; she was manipulative and coercive; she alerted the reader to how little was at stake

---

[4] D. E. Stevenson, *The Blue Sapphire* (New York: Holt, Rinehart and Winston, 1963), 103, 89.
[5] Craig, *Muriel Spark*, 2.

in reading a novel rather than encouraging what Coleridge called "the willing suspension of disbelief."[6]

The same faults have been pointed out of virtually every one of the women featured this book and, with the exception of the gendered charges of manipulation and coercion, of Walter Scott before them: lack of psychological depth, flat characters, formulaic plots, unsophisticated prose, and the consistent rending apart of the seams of their own fiction, whether through the narrator's intrusions or metafictional commentary. These judgments take as their implicit point of reference the standards of high art that consolidated over the course of the nineteenth century, found their full expression in the modernist literature of the early twentieth century, and were enshrined by literary scholars as touchstones of value – depth, originality, and complexity.

The writers I have discussed in this book were not unaware of these aesthetic standards; rather, they consciously eschewed them. They embraced a more democratic or popular understanding of literary value. For these writers, literature should enable a kind of spiritual renewal – a temporary escape from the petty trials of everyday life that prepares readers to reengage with those trials, newly restored, possibly even fortified. The aim of literature, in short, was to provide comfort, refreshment, and pleasure, affective qualities that scholars have largely forgotten about. Robson is correct to conclude that "for Spark, the novel was a frivolous, earthbound endeavor," but he is incorrect to imply that she accordingly considered it of little value.[7] The women I have discussed in this book were occasionally self-deprecating about their work, pointing out its lack of seriousness or magnitude in order to preempt their critics. But they were nonetheless quiet advocates for the importance of the trivial, the nonserious, and possibly even the frivolous. Life, and particularly life pervaded by the ethos of Scottish Presbyterianism, was a momentous enough affair in itself without requiring art and literature to be serious. It is not a coincidence that Spark's Sandy Stranger used to "go and stand outside St. Giles' Cathedral or the Tolbooth, and contemplate these emblems of a dark and terrible salvation which made the fires of the damned seem very merry to the imagination by contrast, and much preferable."[8] It was perhaps the darker aspects of Presbyterianism that drove Spark and her protagonist to Catholicism and compelled Spark's nineteenth-century predecessors to

---

[6] Leo Robson, "Cold Mistress," *New Statesman* 138 (Aug. 10, 2009): 40.
[7] Robson, "Cold Mistress," 40.   [8] Spark, *Jean Brodie*, 158.

seek the romance in everyday life, to appreciate small instances of beauty where they could be found. As one of the characters in the Findlaters' *Penny Monypenny* (1911) says scornfully when Pen, who believes her heart has been broken, complains of unhappiness: "*Happy* – I've always considered that was a word for children to use, not for men and women."[9] And so Pen determines to find new purpose in making others happy, and to "begin by doing the very smallest things as well as [she] can."[10] In the works of Scottish women writers, the small, trivial, and frivolous are never to be dismissed simply because they are small, trivial, and frivolous. They are quite possibly all we have.

Judged by the standards they rejected, nineteenth-century Scottish women writers will inevitably be found wanting. To judge them instead by the values they advocated, as I have tried to do in this book, is not to renounce all distinctions of quality. Some of Oliphant's ninety-odd novels or of Swan's almost two hundred serial stories are bound to be more engrossing and emotionally satisfying than others, just as some are bound to be more original or formally complex. As George Levine has observed of Oliphant's novels, there are passages in most of them equal in style and thought-provoking ingenuity to anything to be found in the novels of Eliot, Dickens, or Trollope.[11] But it is also possible – and I would suggest important – to try to assess Oliphant's and Swan's respective outputs as a whole, and to do the same for the impressively large bodies of fiction produced by Sarah Tytler (Henrietta Keddie; 103 novels) Lucy Walford (45 novels), Flora Annie Steel (30 novels), and Isabella Fyvie Mayo (28 novels). Their fecundity, I suggest, is crucial to these authors' understanding of reading as a therapeutic practice. As Deidre Shauna Lynch explains, nineteenth-century theories and practices of therapeutic reading were informed by the idea that "every reading should represent a resumption of an earlier, interrupted reading."[12] Therapeutic reading, or reading to heal the frazzled soul, often entailed returning to a single favorite novel or set of novels. The practice of writing to a pattern – repeatedly drawing on a limited repertoire of plot devices and character types – allowed Oliphant, Swan, Tytler, and, to a lesser extent, Walford, Steel, and Mayo to offer readers the comforting familiarity they sought while also producing a "new" novel. Serialization, which regularized readers'

[9] Jane Findlater and Mary Findlater, *Penny Monypenny* (London: Thomas Nelson, 1918), 326.
[10] Findlater and Findlater, *Penny Monypenny*, 337.
[11] George Levine, "Reading Margaret Oliphant," *Journal of Victorian Culture* 19.2 (2014): 232–46.
[12] Deidre Shauna Lynch, *Loving Literature: A Cultural History* (Chicago: University of Chicago Press, 2015), 181.

consumption of their novels in weekly or monthly intervals, only wove their fiction more tightly into the routines of everyday life.

A second generation of Scottish women writers – Mary and Jane Findlater, Violet Jacob, O. Douglas, Sarah MacNaughtan, and Catherine Carswell, among others – absorbed the concept of therapeutic reading into a broader philosophy of aesthetic appreciation, suggesting that spiritual solace might be found not only in books but in small instances of beauty, whether naturally existing or artificially created. Their novels embody this aesthetics of the ordinary in a variety of ways. Douglas writes novels in which nothing happens. Characters read books, go for walks, have conversations with each other over cups of tea, and occasionally redecorate a room, but the momentous event defining their lives – the Great War – is always excluded from representation. The Findlaters more subtly transform everyday items – a broken glass, an out-of-tune piano, a beetle, or a bird – into indices of their protagonists' psychological states and artistic sensibilities. Their descriptions are vivid, concrete, and richly textured. In Douglas's and MacNaughtan's novels, small details – from hat trimmings to table decorations – carry great weight, signifying socioeconomic status and aesthetic sensibilities that are sometimes misleadingly misaligned. In MacNaughtan's *The Expensive Miss Du Cane* (1900), the protagonist's excellent taste in borrowed clothes hides her dispiriting poverty, as she visits one great house after another in the hope of finding a wealthy and tolerably interesting husband. And in the same author's hilarious *Fortune of Christina M'Nab* (1901), the newly wealthy protagonist's ignorance of refined manners and tastes make her the laughingstock of the English elite whose country homes she visits, until she returns home, disabused of her social ambitions, to marry the man who loved her before she became rich. In Carswell's novels, well-developed aesthetic sensibilities give way to the modernist epiphany, marking her protagonists as artists rather than mere tastemakers.

Through their use of details as signifiers of socioeconomic status, taste, or moral worth, the women in this second generation of novelists encourage readers to cultivate the aesthetic sensibilities exhibited by their protagonists and to become attuned to the possibilities of beauty in everyday objects and experiences. Both generations of Scotswomen, then, implicitly or explicitly conceived of writing as what we would now call affective labor. They aimed to bring cheer and comfort to the overworked, the bereaved, the displaced, the sick, and perhaps most of all to the vast majority of people whose lives would never be anything but ordinary.

A much more recent Scottish writer, Kathleen Jamie, suggests a newly urgent reason for returning to the works of earlier Scotswomen when, in her essay "Lissen Everything Back," she advocates attentiveness or "serious noticing" as a form of "resistance and renewal," if not to the grandiose political posturing that currently dominates the news, at least to capitalist consumerism. Serious noticing entails the kind of receptiveness to detail exhibited by Susan in *The Rose of Joy*, who can "make a meal off the colour of the sea," or by Archie in *Flemington*, for whom "humanity's smallest actions had an interest."[13] When we "step outdoors, smell Autumn in the wind, *seriously notice*," Jamie writes, "we're not little cogs, little consumers, in someone else's machine. We are not doing what the forces of destruction and inattention want us to do."[14] In itself, serious noticing will not settle divisive political debates or resolve the climate crisis any more than a century ago it relieved the burdens placed on working-class women or restored to life those who had died on the battlefield. Yet attentiveness *is* an assertion of personal agency. The choice to attune the senses to the here and now reveals the aesthetic richness of the ordinary. If it is not precisely a political act, it is at least an ethical one. As Jamie recognizes, it provides a momentary escape from the constant "noise" – visual, aural, tactile, olfactory – that impinges on us all the time but that we do not pause to process.

Although Jamie here writes nonfiction prose rather than a novel, she does not stand outside the tradition of Scottish women's writing I have discussed in this book. She is part of it, and her admittedly tentative and playful thesis in "Lissen Everything Back" is subject to some of the criticisms levied at O. Douglas, the Findlaters, and Catherine Carswell. For instance, Jamie's suggestion that the habit of noticing is "democratic" because it "employs the faculties we all have in common, honed over millions of years of evolutionary history," is debatable. We may all share the ability to notice, but we do not all have equal opportunities to cultivate it. While there is no correlation between wealth and attentive ability, money buys time to practice the art of noticing, as *Crossriggs*'s Alex Hope and *Pink Sugar*'s Rebecca Brand knew to their cost. There is, moreover, a kind of quietism inherent in the suggestion that noticing is an act of resistance to the forces of late capitalist modernity. I do not mean to suggest that it is a worthless endeavor, but merely that if real world change is the goal, then serious noticing is only the first step. Jamie

[13] Mary Findlater, *The Rose of Joy* (London: Methuen, 1903), 96; Violet Jacob, *Flemington and Tales from Angus*, ed. Carol Anderson (Edinburgh: Canongate, 1998), 302.
[14] This and all subsequent quotations from Kathleen Jamie, "Lissen Everything Back," *The Clearing*, Sept. 4, 2019, www.littletoller.co.uk/the-clearing/lissen-by-kathleen-jamie/.

186 Scottish Women's Writing in the Long Nineteenth Century

acknowledges as much when she observes that "what we subsequently do with that noticing, whether we transform it into poetry, art, science or activism comes a little later." Ultimately, though, Jamie suggests that noticing is an important skill to cultivate precisely because it is not an instrumental or goal-oriented practice: the experience is its own end. Perhaps, she muses, "only through our attending can the universe reflect upon and celebrate itself." Attentiveness, the act of becoming absorbed in the everyday world around us, lifts us out of the self and restores us to a momentary unity with that world. For a brief while, we are part of the romance of everyday life.

Bibliography

Aaron, Jane. "Taking Sides: Power-Play on the Welsh Border in Early Twentieth-Century Women's Writing." In *Gendering Border Studies*. Ed. Jane Aaron, Henrice Altink, and Chris Weedon. Cardiff: University of Wales Press, 2010. 127–41.

Alker, Sharon. "The Business of Romance: Mary Brunton and the Virtue of Commerce." *European Romantic Review* 13 (2002): 199–205.

Anderson, Benedict. *Imagined Communities: Reflections on the Origins and Spread of Nationalism.* Revised ed. London: Verso, 1991.

Anderson, Carol. "Tales of Her Own Countries: Violet Jacob." In *A History of Scottish Women's Writing*. Ed. Douglas Gifford and Dorothy McMillan. Edinburgh: Edinburgh University Press, 1997. 347–59.

Anderson, James, and Liam O'Dowd. "Imperialism and Nationalism: The Home Rule Struggle and Border Creation in Ireland, 1885–1925." *Political Geography* 26 (2007): 934–50.

Anon. "A Little Chat about Mrs. Oliphant," *Blackwood's Edinburgh Magazine* 133.807 (Jan. 1883): 73–91.

"Mrs. Oliphant." Obituary. *The Athenaeum* 3636 (July 3, 1897): 35–6.

"Mrs. Oliphant." Obituary. *Blackwood's Edinburgh Magazine* 162 (July 1897): 161–64.

Ardis, Anne. *New Woman, New Novels: Feminism and Early Modernism.* New Brunswick, NJ: Rutgers University Press, 1990.

Armstrong, Nancy. *Desire and Domestic Fiction: A Political History of the Novel.* New York: Oxford University Press, 1987.

Arnold, Matthew. *On the Study of Celtic Literature and on Translating Homer.* New York: Macmillan, 1906.

Auyoung, Elaine. *When Fiction Feels Real: Representation and the Reading Mind.* New York: Oxford University Press, 2018.

Bagehot, Walter. "The Waverley Novels." *National Review* 6 (April 1858): 444–72.

Barringer, Tim. *Reading the Pre-Raphaelites*. Revised ed. New Haven, CT: Yale University Press, 2012.

Bauer, Helen Pike. "Reconstructing the Colonial Woman: Gender, Race, and the Memsahib in Flora Annie Steel's *On the Face of the Waters.*" *Nineteenth-Century Feminisms* 6 (2002): 74–86.

Beddoe, Deirdre. *Back to Home and Duty: Women between the Wars, 1914–1939.* London: Pandora, 1989.

Beetham, Margaret. *A Magazine of Her Own? Domesticity and Desire in the Woman's Magazine, 1800–1914.* London: Routledge, 1996.

Berry, Christopher J. *Social Theory of the Scottish Enlightenment.* Edinburgh: Edinburgh University Press, 1997.

Bingham, Caroline. Review of *Flemington. Times Literary Supplement* 4784 (Dec. 9, 1994): 22.

Blair, Emily. *Virginia Woolf and the Nineteenth-Century Domestic Novel.* Albany: State University of New York Press, 2007.

Blair, Kirstie. *Working Verse in Victorian Scotland: Poetry, Press, Community.* Oxford: Oxford University Press, 2019.

Bourdieu, Pierre. *The Field of Cultural Production: Essays on Art and Literature.* Ed. Randal Johnson. New York: Columbia University Press, 1993.

Bowden, Martha F. *Descendants of Waverley: Romancing History in Contemporary Historical Fiction.* Lewisburg, PA: Bucknell University Press, 2016.

Brake, Laurel. *Print in Transition, 1850–1910: Studies in Media and Book History.* Houndsmills, Basingstoke: Palgrave, 2001.

Brown, Callum G. *Religion and Society in Scotland since 1707.* Edinburgh: Edinburgh University Press, 1997.

Brown, Callum G., and J. D. Stephenson. "Sprouting Wings? Women and Religion in Scotland, c. 1890–1950." In *Out of Bounds: Women in Scotland in the Nineteenth and Twentieth Centuries.* Ed. E. Breitenbach and E. Gordon. Edinburgh: Edinburgh University Press, 1992. 95–120.

Brunton, Mary. *Discipline.* London: Pandora, 1986.

Emmeline, with some other pieces by Mary Brunton, to which is prefixed a memoir of her life including some extracts from her correspondence. Edinburgh: Manners and Miller, 1819.

Buchan, Anna. *Unforgettable, Unforgotten.* London: Hodder and Stoughton, 1945.

Burton, Antoinette. *Burdens of History: British Feminists, Indian Women, and Imperial Culture, 1865–1915.* Chapel Hill: University of North Carolina Press, 1994.

Caird, Mona. *The Daughters of Danaus.* New York: Feminist Press, 1989.

"Marriage." *The Westminster Review* 130.1 (1888): 186–201.

Calder, Jenni. "Figures in a Landscape: Scott, Stevenson and Routes to the Past." In *Robert Louis Stevenson: Writer of Boundaries.* Ed. Richard Ambrosini and Richard Drury. Madison: University of Wisconsin Press, 2006. 121–32.

Campbell, Donna. "American Literary Naturalism: Critical Perspectives." *Literature Compass* 8 (2011): 499–513.

Campbell, Ian. *Kailyard.* Edinburgh: Ramsay Head 1981.

Carlyle, Thomas. "Biography." *Fraser's Magazine.* 27.5 (April 1832): 253–60.

"Memoirs of the Life of Scott." *Westminster Review.* 6.2 (Jan. 1838): 293–345.

Sartor Resartus. Ed. Kerry McSweeney and Peter Sabor. Oxford: Oxford University Press, 2008.

Carruthers, Gerard, David Goldie, and Alastair Renfrew. "Introduction." In *Scotland and the 19th-Century World*. Ed. Gerard Carruthers, David Goldie, and Alastair Renfrew. Amsterdam: Rodopi, 2012. 15–20.

Carswell, Catherine. *The Camomile*. London: Virago, 1987.

Lying Awake: An Unfinished Autobiography and Other Posthumous Papers. Ed. John Carswell. Edinburgh: Canongate, 1997.

Open the Door! London: Virago, 1986.

Caserio, Robert L. "Imperial Romance." In *The Cambridge History of the English Novel*. Ed. Robert L. Caserio and Clement Hawes. Cambridge: Cambridge University Press, 2012. 517–32.

Çelikkol, Ayşe. *Romances of Free Trade: British Literature, Laissez-Faire, and the Global Nineteenth Century*. Oxford: Oxford University Press, 2011.

Chrisman, Laura. *Rereading the Imperial Romance: British Imperialism and South African Resistance in Haggard, Schreiner, and Plaatje*. Oxford: Oxford University Press, 2000.

Coghill, Mrs. Harry, ed. *Autobiography and Letters of Mrs. Margaret Oliphant*. Introduction by Q. D. Leavis. Leicester: Leicester University Press, 1974.

Cohen, Monica. "Maximizing Oliphant: Begging the Question and the Politics of Satire." In *Victorian Women Writers and the Woman Question*. Ed. Nicola Diane Thompson. New York: Cambridge University Press, 1999. 99–115.

Professional Domesticity in the Victorian Novel: Women, Work, and Home. Cambridge: Cambridge University Press, 1998.

Colby, Vinetta, and Robert A. Colby. *The Equivocal Virtue: Mrs. Oliphant and the Victorian Literary Marketplace*. Hamden, CT: Archon Books, 1966.

"Mrs. Oliphant's Scotland: The Romance of Reality." In *Nineteenth-Century Scottish Fiction*. Ed. Ian Campbell. New York: Barnes & Noble, 1979. 89–104.

Craig, Cairns. *The Modern Scottish Novel: Narrative and the National Imagination*. Edinburgh: Edinburgh University Press, 1999.

Muriel Spark, Existentialism and the Art of Death. Edinburgh: Edinburgh University Press, 2019.

Crawford, Robert. *Scotland's Books: A History of Scottish Literature*. Oxford: Oxford University Press, 2009.

D'Albertis, Deirdre. "The Domestic Drone: Margaret Oliphant and a Political History of the Novel." *SEL* 37 (1997): 805–29.

Darlow, T. H. *William Robertson Nicoll: Life and Letters*. London: Hodder and Stoughton, 1925.

Dickson, Beth. "Annie S. Swan and O. Douglas: Legacies of the Kailyard." In *A History of Scottish Women's Writing*. Ed. Douglas Gifford and Dorothy McMillan. Edinburgh: Edinburgh University Press, 1997. 329–46.

Donaldson, William. *Popular Literature in Victorian Scotland: Language, Fiction and the Press*. Aberdeen: Aberdeen University Press, 1986.

Douglas, O. [Anna Buchan] *The Day of Small Things*. London: Thomas Nelson, 1933.

[Anna Buchan] *Eliza for Common*. London: Thomas Nelson, 1930.

[Anna Buchan] *Penny Plain*. London: Hodder and Stoughton, 1920.

[Anna Buchan] *Pink Sugar*. London: Thomas Nelson, 1926.

[Anna Buchan] *The Proper Place*. London: Hodder and Stoughton, 1926.

Duncan, Ian. *Modern Romance and Transformations of the Novel: The Gothic, Scott, Dickens*. Cambridge: Cambridge University Press, 1992.

Scott's Shadow: The Novel in Romantic Edinburgh. Princeton, NJ: Princeton University Press, 2007.

Dunnigan, Sarah M. "The Hawk and the Dove: Religion, Desire and Aesthetics in *Open the Door!*" In *Opening the Doors: The Achievement of Catherine Carswell*. Ed. Carol Anderson. Edinburgh: Ramsay Head Press, 2001. 93–108.

Easley, Alexis. *First Person Anonymous: Women Writers and Victorian Print Media*. Aldershot: Ashgate, 2004.

Elliott, Dorice. *The Angel Out of the House: Philanthropy and Gender in Nineteenth-Century England*. Charlottesville: University of Virginia Press, 2002.

Emerson, Ralph Waldo. *Essays*. London: Fraser, 1841.

Ferris, Ina. *The Achievement of Literary Authority: Gender, History, and the Waverley Novels*. Ithaca, NY: Cornell University Press, 1992.

Findlater, Jane. *The Green Graves of Balgowrie*. London: Methuen, 1896.

Findlater, Jane, and Mary Findlater. *Crossriggs*. London: Virago, 1986.

Penny Monypenny. London: Thomas Nelson, 1918.

Findlater, Mary. *The Rose of Joy*. London: Methuen, 1903.

Forrester, Wendy. *Anna Buchan and O. Douglas*. London: Maitland Press, 1995.

Foster, Shirley, and Judy Simon. *What Katy Read: Feminist Re-readings of "Classic" Stories for Girls*. Ames: University of Iowa Press, 1995.

Fraser, Hilary, Stephanie Green, and Judith Johnston. *Gender and the Victorian Periodical*. Cambridge: Cambridge University Press, 2003.

Galperin, William. *The History of Missed Opportunities: British Romanticism and the Emergence of the Everyday*. Stanford, CA: Stanford University Press, 2017.

Gifford, Douglas. "Introduction." In *The History of Scottish Literature*, vol. 3: *The Nineteenth Century*. Ed. Douglas Gifford. Aberdeen: Aberdeen University Press, 1988. 1–12.

"Preparing for the Renaissance: Revaluing Nineteenth-Century Scottish Literature." *Scotland and the 19th-Century World*. Ed. Gerard Carruthers, David Goldie, and Alastair Renfrew. Amsterdam: Rodopi, 2012. 21–35.

Gilbert, Sandra, and Susan Gubar. *The Madwoman in the Attic: The Woman Writer and the Nineteenth-Century Literary Imagination*. New ed. New Haven, CT: Yale University Press, 2000.

Greiner, Rae. *Sympathetic Realism in Nineteenth-Century British Fiction*. Baltimore, MD: Johns Hopkins University Press, 2012.

Harris, Beth. "Introduction." In *Famine and Fashion: Needlewomen in the Nineteenth Century*. Ed. Beth Harris. Burlington, VT: Ashgate, 2005. 1–10.

Harsh, Constance D. "Gissing's The Unclassed and the Perils of Naturalism." *ELH* 59.4 (1992): 911–38.

Harvie, Christopher. "Industry, Religion and the State of Scotland." In *The History of Scottish Literature*, vol. 3: *The Nineteenth Century*. Ed. Douglas Gifford. Aberdeen: Aberdeen University Press, 1988. 23–41.

Hayden, John O. "Introduction." In *Scott: The Critical Heritage*. Ed. John O. Hayden. London: Routledge & Kegan Paul, 1970. 1–23.

Heilmann, Ann. *New Woman Strategies: Sarah Grand, Olive Schreiner, Mona Caird.* Manchester: Manchester University Press, 2004.

Hendry, Joy. "Twentieth-Century Women's Writing: The Nest of Singing Birds." In *The History of Scottish Literature*. Vol. 4. Ed. Cairns Craig. Aberdeen: Aberdeen University Press, 1987. 291–308.

Homans, Margaret. *Royal Representations: Queen Victoria and British Culture, 1837–1866.* Chicago: University of Chicago Press, 1998.

Hughes, Linda K., and Michael Lund. *The Victorian Serial.* Charlottesville: University of Virginia Press, 1991.

Humble, Nicola. *The Feminine Middlebrow Novel, 1920s to 1950s: Class, Domesticity, and Bohemianism.* Oxford: Oxford University Press, 2002.

Jacob, Violet. *Diaries and Letters from India, 1895–1900.* Ed. Carol Anderson. Edinburgh: Canongate, 1990.

The History of Aythan Waring. New York: Dutton, 1908.

Irresolute Catherine. London: John Murray, 1908.

The Sheepstealers. London: Heinneman, 1902.

James, Henry. Review of *Essays on Fiction*, by Nassau Senior. *North American Review* 99 (Oct. 1864): 580–8.

Jameson, Fredric. *The Antinomies of Realism.* London: Verso, 2013.

Jamie, Kathleen. "Lissen Back Everything." *The Clearing.* Sept. 4, 2019. www.littletoller.co.uk/the-clearing/lissen-by-kathleen-jamie/.

Jay, Elisabeth, ed. *The Autobiography of Margaret Oliphant.* Peterborough, Ont.: Broadview, 2002.

Jay, Elisabeth. *Mrs Oliphant: "A Fiction to Herself." A Literary Life.* Oxford: Clarendon, 1995.

Jeffrey, Francis. Review of *Tales of My Landlord. Edinburgh Review* 28.55 (Mar. 1817): 193–260.

Jones, Susan. "Into the Twentieth Century: Imperial Romance from Haggard to Buchan." In *A Companion to Romance from Classical to Contemporary.* Ed. Corinne Saunders. Malden, MA: Blackwell, 2004.

Keating, Peter. *The Haunted Study: A Social History of the English Novel 1875–1914.* London: Secker & Warburg, 1989.

Keddie, Henrietta. *Three Generations: The Story of a Middle-Class Scottish Family.* London: John Murray, 1911.

Kelly, Stuart. *Scott-land: The Man who Invented a Nation.* Edinburgh: Polygon, 2010.

Kerrigan, John. *Archipelagic English: Literature, History, and Politics 1603–1707.* Oxford: Oxford University Press, 2008.

Knowles, Thomas D. *Ideology, Art and Commerce: Aspects of Literary Sociology in the Late Victorian Scottish Kailyard.* Göteborg: Göteborg University, 1983.

Kouidis, Virginia M. "Emersonian True Romance and the Woman Novelist." *North Dakota Quarterly* 60.4 (1992): 84–104.

Krueger, Kate. "*The Woman at Home* in the World: Annie Swan's Lady Doctor and the Problem of the Fin de Siècle Working Woman." *Victorian Periodicals Review* 50.3 (2017): 517–33.

Lang, Andrew. "Realism and Romance." *Contemporary Review* 52 (Nov. 1887): 683–93.

Langbauer, Laurie. *Novels of Everyday Life: The Series in English Fiction, 1850–1930.* Ithaca, NY: Cornell University Press, 1999.

Langland, Elizabeth. *Nobody's Angels: Middle-Class Women and Domestic Ideology in Victorian Culture.* Ithaca, NY: Cornell University Press, 1995.

Law, Graham. *Serializing Fiction in the Victorian Press.* Houndsmills: Palgrave Macmillan, 2000.

Ledger, Sally. *The New Woman: Fiction and Feminism at the Fin de Siècle.* Manchester: Manchester University Press, 1997.

Lefebvre, Henri. *Everyday Life in the Modern World.* Trans. Sacha Rabinovitch. Introduction by Philip Wander. New Brunswick, NJ: Transaction Publishers, 1990.

Levine, George. "Reading Margaret Oliphant." *Journal of Victorian Culture* 19.2 (2014): 232–46.

Realism, Ethics and Secularism: Essays on Victorian Literature and Science. Cambridge: Cambridge University Press, 2008.

Light, Alison. *Forever England: Femininity, Literature, and Conservatism between the Wars.* London: Routledge, 1991.

Lockhart, John Gibson. *The Life of Sir Walter Scott.* London: J. M. Dent, 1912.

Losano, Antonia. *The Woman Painter in Victorian Literature.* Columbus: Ohio State University Press, 2008.

Lukács, Georg. *The Historical Novel.* Trans. Hannah and Stanley Mitchell. Boston: Beacon Press, 1963.

Lyall, David [Annie S. Swan]. *David Lyall's Love Story.* London: Hodder and Stoughton, 1897.

[Annie S. Swan]. *Flowers o' the Forest.* London: Hodder and Stoughton, 1900.

Lynch, Deidre Shauna. *Loving Literature: A Cultural History.* Chicago: University of Chicago Press, 2015.

MacDiarmid, Hugh. "The Scott Centenary." In *Modernism and Nationalism: Literature and Society in Scotland 1918–1939.* Ed. Margery Palmer McCulloch. Glasgow: Association for Scottish Literary Studies, 2004. 125–6.

"Violet Jacob." In *Contemporary Scottish Studies.* Ed. Alan Riach. Manchester: Carcanet, 1995. 27–34.

MacDonald, Leslie Orr. *A Unique and Glorious Mission: Women and Presbyterianism in Scotland, 1830–1930.* Edinburgh: John McDonald, 2000.

Mackenzie, Eileen. *The Findlater Sisters: Literature and Friendship.* London: John Murray, 1964.

Marshall, Rosalind K. *Virgins and Viragos: A History of Women in Scotland from 1080 to 1980.* London: Collins, 1983.

Maxwell, Cheryl. "'I'd rather be a girl . . . because I like boys best': Building the Sexual Self in *Open the Door!*" In *Opening the Doors: The Achievement of Catherine Carswell.* Ed. Carol Anderson. Edinburgh: Ramsay Head Press, 2001. 109–23.

McAleavey, Maia. *The Bigamy Plot: Sensation and Convention in the Victorian Novel.* Cambridge: Cambridge University Press, 2015.

McAleer, Joseph. *Popular Reading and Publishing 1914–50.* Oxford: Oxford University Press, 1992.

McCulloch, Margery Palmer. *Scottish Modernism and Its Contexts, 1918–1959: Literature, National Identity and Cultural Exchange.* Edinburgh: Edinburgh University Press, 2009.

"Testing the Boundaries in Life and Literature: Catherine Carswell and Rebecca West." In *Scottish and International Modernisms: Relationships and Reconfigurations.* Ed. Emma Dymock and Margery Palmer McCulloch. Glasgow: Association for Scottish Literary Studies, 2011. 148–60.

McMillan, Margaret. *Women of the Raj.* London: Thames and Hudson, 1988.

Mitchell, Jerome. *Scott, Chaucer, and Medieval Romance: A Study in Sir Walter Scott's Indebtedness to the Middle Ages.* Lexington: University Press of Kentucky, 1987.

Michie, Elsie B. "History after Waterloo: Margaret Oliphant Reads Walter Scott." *ELH* 80.3 (2013): 897–916.

The Vulgar Question of Money: Heiresses, Materialism, and the Novel of Manners from Jane Austen to Henry James. Baltimore, MD: Johns Hopkins University Press, 2011.

Muir, Edwin. *Scott and Scotland: The Predicament of the Scottish Writer.* Introduction by Allan Massie. Edinburgh: Polygon, 1982.

Muir, Willa. "Mrs. Grundy in Scotland." In *Imagined Selves.* Ed. Kirsty Allen. Edinburgh: Canongate, 1996.

Murphy, Patricia. *Time Is of the Essence: Temporality, Gender, and the New Woman.* Albany: State University of New York Press, 2001.

Nash, Andrew. *Kailyard and Scottish Literature.* New York: Brill, 2007.

Nicoll, Mildred Robertson, ed. *The Letters of Annie S. Swan.* London: Hodder and Stoughton, 1945.

Norquay, Glenda. "Catherine Carswell: *Open the Door!*" In *A History of Scottish Women's Writing.* Ed. Douglas Gifford and Dorothy McMillan. Edinburgh: Edinburgh University Press, 1997. 389–99.

"Flourishing through Oppression: *The Camomile.*" In *Opening the Doors: The Achievement of Catherine Carswell.* Ed. Carol Anderson. Edinburgh: Ramsay Head Press, 2001. 124–36.

Oberhelman, David. "Waverley, Genealogy, History: Scott's Romance of Fathers and Sons." *Nineteenth-Century Contexts* 15.1 (1991): 29–47.

Oliphant, Margaret. "A Century of Great Poets, from 1750 Downwards. No. II – Walter Scott." *Blackwood's Edinburgh Magazine* 110.670 (August 1871): 229–256.

Harry Muir; A Story of Scottish Life. New York: Appleton, 1853.

Kirsteen; The Story of a Scotch Family Seventy Years Ago. Ed. Anne M. Scriven. Glasgow: Association for Scottish Literary Studies, 2010.

"The Old Saloon." *Blackwood's Edinburgh Magazine* 146.856 (Aug. 1889): 244–75.

The Quiet Heart. Edinburgh: Blackwood, 1854.

Review of *The Letters of Walter Scott. Blackwood's Edinburgh Magazine* 155.939 (Jan. 1894): 15–26.

Royal Edinburgh: Her Saints, Kings, Prophets and Poets. London: Macmillan, 1890.

The Selected Works of Margaret Oliphant, vol. 17: *Miss Marjoribanks.* Ed. Joseph Bristow. London: Routledge, 2014.

Olson, Leisl. *Modernism and the Ordinary.* Oxford: Oxford University Press, 2009.

O'Mealy, Joseph H. "Mrs Oliphant, Miss Marjoribanks, and the Victorian Canon." *Victorian Newsletter* 82 (1992): 44–9.

Onslow, Barbara. "'Humble comments for the ignorant': Margaret Oliphant's Criticism of Art and Society." *Victorian Periodicals Review* 31.1 (1998): 55–74.

Otsuki, Jennifer L. "The Memsahib and the Ends of Empire: Feminine Desire in Flora Annie Steel's *On the Face of the Waters.*" *Victorian Literature and Culture* 24 (1996): 1–29.

Parker, Rozsika. *The Subversive Stitch: Embroidery and the Making of the Feminine.* London: Women's Press, 1984.

Parry, Benita. *Delusions and Discoveries: India and the British Imagination, 1880–1930.* London: Verso, 1998.

Patwardhan, Daya. *A Star of India, Flora Annie Steel: Her Works and Times.* Bombay: A. V. Griha Prakashan, 1963.

Paxton, Nancy. "Feminism under the Raj: Complicity and Resistance in the Writings of Flora Annie Steel and Annie Besant." *Women's Studies International Forum* 13.4 (1990): 333–46.

Perkins, Pamela. "'We who have been bred upon Sir Walter': Margaret Oliphant, Sir Walter Scott, and Women's Literary History," *English Studies in Canada* 30.2 (2004): 90–104.

Peterson, Linda. "The Female *Bildungsroman*: Tradition and Subversion in Oliphant's Fiction." In *Margaret Oliphant: Critical Essays on a Gentle Subversive.* Ed. D. J. Trela. Selinsgrove, PA: Susquehanna University Press, 1995. 66–79.

Pittock, Murray G. H. *Celtic Identity and the British Image.* Manchester: Manchester University Press, 1999.

Poovey, Mary. *Uneven Developments: The Ideological Work of Gender in Mid-Victorian Britain.* London: Virago, 1989.

Powell, Violet. *Flora Annie Steel: Novelist of India.* London: Heinemann, 1981.

Prochaska, Frank. *Women and Philanthropy in Nineteenth-Century England.* Oxford: Clarendon Press, 1980.

Pykett, Lyn. "Portraits of the Artist as a Young Woman: Representations of the Female Artist in the New Woman Fiction of the 1890s." In *Victorian Women Writers and the Woman Question*. Ed. Nicola Diane Thompson. Cambridge: Cambridge University Press, 1999. 135–50.

Quayle, Eric. *The Ruin of Sir Walter Scott*. London: Rupert Hart-Davis, 1968.

Radway, Janice. *Reading the Romance: Women, Patriarchy, and Popular Literature*. Revised ed. Chapel Hill: University of North Carolina Press, 2009.

Richardson, LeeAnne M. *New Woman and Colonial Adventure Fiction in Victorian Britain: Gender, Genre, and Empire*. Gainesville: University Press of Florida, 2006.

Robertson, Fiona. "Romance and the Romantic Novel: Sir Walter Scott." In *A Companion to Romance: From Classical to Contemporary*. Ed. Corinne Saunders. Malden, MA: Blackwell, 2004. 287–304.

Robinson, Amy. "Margaret Oliphant's Miss Marjoribanks: A Victorian Emma." *Persuasions* 30 (2008): 67–76.

Robson, Leo. "Cold Mistress." *New Statesman* 138 (Aug. 10, 2009): 40–2.

Rosenthal, Jesse. *Good Form: The Ethical Experience of the Victorian Novel*. Princeton, NJ: Princeton University Press, 2017.

Roye, Susmita, ed. *Flora Annie Steel: A Critical Study of an Unconventional Memsahib*. Edmonton: University of Alberta Press, 2017.

Sassi, Carla. "Prismatic Modernities: Towards a Recontextualization of Scottish Modernism." In *Scottish and International Modernisms: Relationships and Reconfigurations*. Ed. Emma Dymock and Margery Palmer McCulloch. Glasgow: Association for Scottish Literary Studies, 2011. 184–97.

Schaffer, Talia. *The Forgotten Female Aesthetes: Literary Culture in Late-Victorian England*. Charlottesville: University of Virginia Press, 2000.

Novel Craft: Victorian Domestic Handicraft and Nineteenth-Century Fiction. New York: Oxford University Press, 2011.

Schaub, Melissa. "Middlebrow Feminism and the Politics of Sentiment: From the *Moonstone* to Dorothy L. Sayers." *Modern Language Studies* 43.1 (2013): 10–27.

"Queen of the Air or Constitutional Monarch?: Idealism, Irony, and Narrative Power in Miss Marjoribanks." *Nineteenth-Century Literature* 55.2 (2000): 195–225.

Schor, Naomi. *Reading in Detail: Aesthetics and the Feminine*. 2nd ed. London: Routledge, 2007.

Scott, Paul H. "The Last Purely Scotch Age." In *The History of Scottish Literature*, vol. 3: *The Nineteenth Century*. Ed. Douglas Gifford. Aberdeen: Aberdeen University Press, 1988. 13–21.

Scott, Walter. *Chronicles of the Canongate*. Ed. Claire Lamont. Edinburgh: Edinburgh University Press, 2000.

"Essay on Romance." In *The Miscellaneous Prose Works of Sir Walter Scott, Bart*. Vol. 6. Edinburgh: Cadell, 1827. 153–256.

The Journal of Sir Walter Scott. Ed. W. E. K. Anderson. Oxford: Clarendon, 1972.

Waverley; or, 'Tis Sixty Years Since. Ed. P. D. Garside. Edinburgh: Edinburgh University Press, 2007.

Sebastiani, Silvia. *The Scottish Enlightenment: Race, Gender, and the Limits of Progress*. Trans. Jeremy Carden. New York: Palgrave, 2013.

Sen, Indrani. *Woman and Empire: Representations in the Writing of British India, 1858–1900*. Hyderabad: Orient Longman, 2002.

Sharpe, Jenny. *Allegories of Empire: The Figure of Woman in the Colonial Text*. Minneapolis: University of Minnesota Press, 1993.

Shaw, Harry E. *Narrating Reality: Austen, Scott, Eliot*. Ithaca, NY: Cornell University Press, 1999.

Shepherd, Gillian. "The Kailyard." In *The History of Scottish Literature*, vol. 3: *The Nineteenth Century*. Ed. Douglas Gifford. Aberdeen: Aberdeen University Press, 1988. 309–20.

"Should Married Women Engage in Public Work?" In *Woman at Home*. Vol. 4. London: Hodder and Stoughton, 1895. 111–14.

Siegel, Daniel. *Charity and Condescension: Victorian Literature and the Dilemmas of Philanthropy*. Athens: Ohio University Press, 2012.

Singh, Brijraj. "Violet Jacob and India: A Question of Stereotypes." *Journal of Commonwealth and Postcolonial Studies* 15.2 (2008): 3–27.

Sly, Debbie. "Pink Sugary Pleasures: Reading the Novels of O. Douglas." *The Journal of Popular Culture* 35.1 (2001): 5–19.

Smith, Alison. "And God Created Woman: Carswell, Shepherd and Muir, and the Self-Made Woman." In *Gendering the Nation: Studies in Modern Scottish Literature*. Ed. Christopher Whyte. Edinburgh: Edinburgh University Press, 1995.

Spark, Muriel. *The Prime of Miss Jean Brodie*. New York: Plume, 1984.

Spivak, Gayatri. "The Making of Americans." *New Literary History* 21 (1990): 781–98.

St. Clair, William. *The Reading Nation in the Romantic Period*. Cambridge: Cambridge University Press, 2004.

Steel, Flora Annie. *The Garden of Fidelity*. London: Macmillan, 1930.

The Hosts of the Lord. London: Thomas Nelson, 1907.

Miss Stuart's Legacy. London: Macmillan, 1897.

On the Face of the Waters. London: Arnold-Heinemann, 1985.

Stetz, Margaret D. "Internationalizing Authorship: Beyond *New Grub Street* to *The Bookman* in 1891," *Victorian Periodicals Review* 48.1 (2015): 1–14.

Stevenson, D. E. [Dorothy Emily Peploe]. *The Blue Sapphire*. New York: Holt, Rinehart and Winston, 1963.

Stevenson, John. *British Society, 1914–1945*. Harmondsworth: Penguin, 1990.

[Stewart, Andrew.] "Annie S. Swan." *The People's Friend* 1306 (Jan. 1895): 3–4.

Stewart, Victoria. "The Woman Writer in Mid-Twentieth Century Middlebrow Fiction: Conceptualizing Creativity." *Journal of Modern Literature* 35 (2011): 21–36.

Sturrock, June. "Emma in the 1860s: Austen, Yonge, Oliphant, Eliot." *Women's Writing* 17.2 (2010): 324–42.

Swan, Annie S. *Elizabeth Glen, M.B., the Experiences of a Lady Doctor*. London: Hutchinson & Co., 1895.

The Gates of Eden. London: Oliphant & Ferrier, 1949.

The Guinea Stamp: A Tale of Modern Glasgow. London: Oliphant, Anderson & Ferrier, 1892.

Mary Garth: A Clydeside Romance. London: Hodder and Stoughton, 1904.

Memories of Margaret Granger, Schoolmistress. London: Hutchinson & Co, 1896.

My Life: An Autobiography. London: Ivor Nicholson, 1934.

Tange, Andrea Kaston. "Redesigning Femininity: Miss Marjoribanks' Drawing Room of Opportunity." *Victorian Literature and Culture* 36 (2008): 163–86.

Teo, Hsu-Ming. "Imperial Affairs: The British Empire and the Romantic Novel, 1890–1939." In *New Directions in Popular Fiction: Genre, Distribution, Reproduction*. Ed. Ken Gelder London: Palgrave, 2016. 87–110.

Townsend, Meredith. "Mrs. Oliphant." *The Cornhill Magazine* 79 (June 1899): 773–79.

Trumpener, Katie. *Bardic Nationalism: The Romantic Novel and the British Empire*. Princeton, NJ: Princeton University Press, 1997.

Tytler, Sarah [Henrietta Keddie]. *Saint Mungo's City: A Novel*. 3 vols. London: Chatto and Windus, 1884.

Vaninskaya, Anna. "The Late Victorian Romance Revival: A Generic Excursis." *English Literature in Transition, 1880–1920* 51.1 (2008): 57–79.

Waller, Philip. *Writers, Readers, and Reputations: Literary Life in Britain, 1870–1918*. New York: Oxford University Press, 2006.

Walton, Samantha. "Scottish Modernism, Kailyard Fiction, and the Woman at Home." In *Transitions in Middlebrow Writing, 1880–1930*. Ed. K. MacDonald et al. Houndsmills, Basingstoke: Palgrave Macmillan, 2015. 141–59.

Webster, Augusta. *A Housewife's Opinions*. London: Macmillan, 1879.

Weliver, Phyllis. *Women Musicians in Victorian Fiction, 1860–1900: Representations of Music, Science and Gender in the Leisured Home*. Aldershot: Ashgate, 2000.

Welsh, Alexander. *The Hero of the Waverley Novels*. Revised ed. Princeton, NJ: Princeton University Press, 2014.

Williams, Chris. "Problematizing Wales: An Exploration in Historiography and Postcoloniality." In *Postcolonial Wales*. Ed. Jane Aaron and Chris Williams. Cardiff: University of Wales Press, 2005. 3–22.

Williams, Merryn. *Margaret Oliphant: A Critical Biography*. London: Macmillan, 1986.

Wilson, Carol Shiner. "Lost Needles, Tangled Thread: Stitchery, Domesticity, and the Artistic Enterprise in Barbauld, Edgeworth, Taylor, and Lamb." In *Revisioning Romanticism: British Women Writers, 1776–1837*. Ed. Carol Shiner Wilson. Philadelphia: University of Pennsylvania Press, 1994. 167–90.

Woolf, Virginia. *The Death of the Moth and Other Essays.* New York: Harcourt
    Brace, 1942.
Yeazell, Ruth Bernard. *Art of the Everyday: Dutch Painting and the Realist Novel.*
    Princeton, NJ: Princeton University Press, 2008.
Young, Arlene. "Workers' Compensation: (Needle)Work and Ideals of
    Femininity in Margaret Oliphant's *Kirsteen.*" In *Famine and Fashion:
    Needlewomen in the Nineteenth Century.* Ed. Beth Harris. Burlington, VT:
    Ashgate, 2005. 41–51.
Zakreski, Patricia. *Representing Female Artistic Labour, 1848–1890: Refining Work
    for the Middle-Class Woman.* Aldershot: Ashgate, 2006.
Zlotnick, Susan. "Passing for Real: Class and Mimicry in Miss Marjoribanks."
    Victorian Review 38.1 (2012): 173–92.

Index

Aaron, Jane, 135
adventure story. *See* imperial romance
aesthetic value, 17–19, 75
  relationship to economic value, 34, 37–39,
    41–42, 54–55
aestheticism, 21, 29–30, 95
aesthetics of the ordinary, 16, 29, 31–32, 50, 52,
    151, 164, 168–69, 178, 180, 184
Alcott, Louisa May
  Little Women, 100, 165
Alker, Sharon, 17
Allan, Dot, 26, 31
Anderson, Benedict, 1
Angus, Marion, 26
Armstrong, Juliet, 124
Arnold, Matthew
  On the Study of Celtic Literature, 108, 140
artist-figures, 28, 41–42, 95–96, 105, 114–16,
    145–46
attentiveness, 185–86
Austen, Jane, 6, 10–11, 52
  Emma, 47
  and the everyday, 12–13
  Pride and Prejudice, 11
authorship
  celebrity, 67
  as a skilled trade, 39–40

Bagehot, Walter, 4
Barrie, James, 5, 10, 73, 89, 144
  Auld Licht Idylls, 89
  A Window in Thrums, 25, 47, 89, 97
Barringer, Tim, 96
Bauer, Helen, 143
Blackwood's Edinburgh Magazine, 1, 25, 28,
    33–35, 37, 43, 46
Bourdieu, Pierre, 34
Braddon, Mary Elizabeth, 33
The British Weekly, 73, 91
  and Kailyard fiction, 89
Brontë, Charlotte, 11

Brown, Callum, 19
Brown, George Douglas
  House with the Green Shutters, 97
Brunton, Mary, 3, 17
  Discipline, 17–19, 170
  Self-Control, 17
Buchan, Anna, 14, 26, 52, 150, *See also* Douglas,
    O.
  and Margaret Oliphant, 21
  and Walter Scott, 153
Buchan, John, 5, 144
  Greenmantle, 144, 150
  The Thirty-Nine Steps, 144, 150
Burnett Smith, Mrs. *See* Swan, Annie S.
Burns, Robert, 27, 36, 77

Caird, Mona, 6, 31, 94–96
  artist-figures in the works of, 95–96, 109
  Daughters of Danaus, 96, 104, 106–11
  and Matthew Arnold, 108
  music in, 108–9
  and Ralph Waldo Emerson, 107, 109
  and realism, 110
  Scotland in, 108–9
  Marriage, 105
  writing as G. Noel Hatton, 106
Carlyle, Thomas, 35, 39–41
  Sartor Resartus, 42–43, 64
Carswell, Catherine, 6, 31, 150–52, 184–85
  artist-figures in the works of, 171
  The Camomile, 31, 150, 155, 174–79
  conformity in, 175–78
  formal attributes of, 175, 178–79
  epiphany in the works of, 152, 171, 177–78
  everyday beauty in the works of, 152–53, 156
  female sexuality in the works of, 152, 171–72,
    174
  as a middlebrow writer, 170, 179
  and modernism, 152, 179
  Lying Awake, 176
  Open the Door!, 31, 150, 155

CAMBRIDGE STUDIES IN NINETEENTH-CENTURY LITERATURE AND CULTURE

General Editors
KATE FLINT, *University of Southern California*
CLARE PETTITT, *King's College London*

Titles published

For EU product safety concerns, contact us at Calle de José Abascal, 56–1°, 28003 Madrid, Spain or eugpsr@cambridge.org.

www.ingramcontent.com/pod-product-compliance
Ingram Content Group UK Ltd.
Pitfield, Milton Keynes, MK11 3LW, UK
UKHW020352140625
459647UK00020B/2421

* 9 7 8 1 1 0 8 9 9 9 8 1 6 *